Would you like to...

- Protect...
  yourself
  your assets and
  your business
  from the IRS?

- Solve your tax troubles...
  for less than you ever
  thought possible?

- Avoid future IRS hassles?

If you answer "*YES*" read...

How to
settle with the
IRS
...for pennies
on the dollar

How to settle with the
IRS
...for pennies on the dollar

Arnold S. Goldstein, J.D., LL.M., Ph.D.

Published By:

GARRETT PUBLISHING, INC.
384 S. Military Trail • Deerfield Beach, Florida 33442

How to Settle with the IRS For Pennies on the Dollar

By Arnold S. Goldstein, J.D., LL.M., Ph.D.
Copyright ©1994 by Garrett Publishing, Inc.

Published by
Garrett Publishing, Inc.
384 South Military Trail
Deerfield Beach, FL 33442
Tel. 305-480-8543
Fax 305-698-0057

This publication is designed to provide accurate and authoritative information in regard to the subject matter covered. It is sold with the understanding that neither the publisher nor the author is engaged in rendering legal, accounting, or other professional service. If legal advice or other expert assistance is required, the services of a competent professional should be sought. *From a Declaration of Principles jointly adopted by a Committee of the American Bar Association and a Committee of Publishers.*

Library of Congress Cataloging-in-Publication Data

Goldstein, Arnold S.
    How to settle with the IRS for pennies on the dollar/Arnold S. Goldstein, Ph.D.
       p. cm.
    Includes bibliographic references.
    ISBN 1-880539-13-6 : $19.95
       1. United States. Internal Revenue Service. 2. Tax Protests and appeals -- United States. 3. Tax remission -- United States.
4. Compromise (Law) -- United States.   I. Title.
KF6301. G65 1994
343. 7305'2 -- dc20
[347.30352]   93-43810
                                                   CIP

Printed in the United States of America
10 9 8 7 6 5 4 3 2

★ ABOUT THE AUTHOR

Dr. Arnold S. Goldstein is a veteran attorney with nearly thirty years' experience representing taxpayers with serious tax problems.

He is now a senior partner in the Florida and Massachusetts law firm of Goldstein & Randall that offers tax representation, asset protection and debt restructuring to individuals and businesses nationwide.

He has written over 50 books on law, business and finance. His titles include: *Asset Protection Secrets; The Business Doctor; How to Save Your Business from Bankruptcy; Commercial Transactions Deskbook;* and *The Small Business Legal Advisor.* Major media reviewers cite these and his other publications as complete, practical and enjoyable.

Dr. Goldstein and his financial and legal strategies have also been featured in over 350 magazines, journals and newspapers. A popular speaker on taxes, the IRS, asset protection and related subjects, Dr. Goldstein presents nationwide workshops and guest lectures on these topics. With a distinguished academic career as professor emeritus at Boston's Northeastern University, he also taught law, finance and management at several other colleges and universities and has appeared on numerous radio and television talk shows.

Dr. Goldstein is a graduate of Northeastern University (B.S., 1961) and Suffolk University (MBA, 1966, and LL.M., 1975), received his law degree from the New England School of Law (J.D., 1964) and a doctorate from Northeastern University (Ph.D. in business and economic policy, 1990). He is a member of the Massachusetts and Federal Bars and various professional, academic and civic organizations

TABLE OF CONTENTS

INTRODUCTION
What this book will do for you!

DO YOU OWE THE IRS?

HOW TO PROTECT YOUR ASSETS FORM THE IRS

FOUR ALTERNATIVES TO THE OFFER IN COMPROMISE

3

THE OFFER IN COMPROMISE PROGRAM IN A NUTSHELL

4

PLANNING YOUR OFFER

5

HOW TO PREPARE AND SUBMIT YOUR OFFER TO THE IRS

6

IF THE IRS REJECTS YOUR OIC

7

WHEN THE IRS ACCEPTS YOUR OFFER

8

HOW TO GET THE PROFESSIONAL HELP YOU NEED

9

50 ANSWERS TO COMMON QUESTIONS

10

GLOSSARY OF IRS TERMS

INDEX

APPENDIX A

- IRS OFFER IN COMPROMISE PROGRAM
- IRS COLLECTION MANUAL
- YOUR RIGHTS AS A TAXPAYER

APPENDIX B

- IRS FORMS

★ WHAT THIS BOOK WILL DO FOR YOU

Few problems cause people such fear and worry as owing the IRS. These fears are justified. Countless stories abound of individuals, families and businesses who have been financially wiped out by the IRS. Nor are tax problems unusual. About ten million Americans are known tax delinquents and another seven to ten million Americans haven't filed tax returns for years. Many are naturally reluctant to start now and risk detection and a crushing tax liability.

The fact that millions of Americans are in deep trouble with the IRS should hardly be surprising. There are simply too many opportunities to run afoul of the tax laws. As the tax laws become increasingly complex and taxes escalate, more and more Americans will end up with big bills due the IRS.

But there is one item of good news: It is now *easier* than ever before to resolve matters with the IRS. The IRS's "Offer In Compromise" (OIC) program now encourages delinquent taxpayers to settle their back taxes... often for pennies on the dollar!

Tens of thousands of Americans have discovered they can legally and easily solve their tax problems with an OIC. And many of these tax claims will be forgiven for as little as five or ten cents on the dollar, or even less.

Who are these people? Taxpayers with too little earnings and too few assets to fully pay their taxes. Some will be executors of tax-burdened estates, or a business owner hoping to compromise withholding taxes due from the business. The taxpayer may be going through a costly divorce, have health problems or for one of 101 other reasons simply have tax obligations he or she can't fully pay. Yes, the OIC program can also help you solve *your* tax problems whether you are unemployed, a wage earner, a business owner or a professional. It can work for you whether you are poor, enjoy modest wealth or are even a millionaire!

Moreover, you can compromise virtually any type of tax liability. It doesn't matter if it's ordinary income taxes, corporate income taxes, payroll taxes or estate taxes. With few exceptions you can rid yourself of any tax liability due Uncle Sam. You can compromise a tax for $1,000 or less... or a whopping liability measured in the millions. Nor does it matter whether the tax is years old or is currently due. A tax is a tax is a tax... and all can be compromised for pennies on the dollar... once you know how!

This doesn't mean that you're in for a free ride or that the IRS has suddenly turned into a charity. That is not the case. Instead, the IRS's newly liberalized policy acknowledges that a pennies-on-the-dollar settlement may be best for them as well as you, particularly when they won't gain more by seizing your assets or forcing you into an unrealistic installment arrangement that you can never pay.

It also costs the IRS far less to settle quickly for what you can afford to pay rather than endlessly chase you for what you can't pay. And the IRS knows you will be a more productive, tax-generating American if you can live and work free of IRS pressures. In a word, the IRS has become pragmatic and realistic in dealing with its errant taxpayers and this is best seen in its new policy in making Offers in Compromise easier to obtain.

Can the OIC program work for you? It can if you can convince the IRS that your offer in settlement of your delinquent taxes is more than they could obtain through seizure of your assets plus what you can reasonably afford to pay over the next two or three years under a full payment installment agreement. The IRS will welcome your *reasonable* offer that is logical for them to accept given your present and foreseeable financial circumstances. So the OIC is hardly a matter of beating the IRS. Instead, it's a win-win situation that gets the IRS the most money with the least hassle not only for them but also for you by allowing you to pay only what you can afford and wiping the state clean.

Still, the OIC program is only one alternative when you owe the IRS. You do have other options this book will explore. For instance, it may make more sense not to compromise and instead convince the IRS to suspend collection by considering you "uncollectible." Or you may discharge your taxes in bankruptcy. Finally, an installment agreement may be your fastest, most practical answer. This book will help you determine and pursue your best option.

It is not difficult to prepare your own OIC. Nor should you be so intimidated by the IRS that you don't try. I will carefully guide you; explain the law, work you through each step of the OIC process and show you how to complete the required forms.

I will then give you the tips you need to negotiate your very best deal – and, yes, contrary to what you may think, you really can bargain with the IRS! An offer in compromise *is* hard bargaining – often a long and exasperating process before you reach your deal with the IRS. Don't let this discourage or frustrate you. It's the price you pay when you owe taxes and want the opportunity for a fresh tax-free start.

You'll have many other questions as you work your way to and through an Offer in Compromise. How do you stop the IRS from grabbing your assets or your wages? How do you position yourself financially so you have the least wealth exposed and can then negotiate the best settlement? What do you do if the IRS turns down your OIC? What do you do if you default on your OIC? What do you do about overdue state taxes? The answers to these and many other questions asked by every troubled taxpayer can be found in this book.

The Appendix contains all the forms you will need to complete your Offer in Compromise. For your guidance you'll also find many other helpful forms.

The IRS offers considerable assistance and information to its taxpayers. I have listed the toll-free *Tele-tax* numbers as well as their free publications covering a variety of tax subjects.

As a special bonus you will find the *Official IRS Collection Manual*. This difficult-to-find publication is the bible for every collection officer... and now you can be forewarned and forearmed when dealing with the IRS.

Finally, you will find a full glossary of tax terms. This hopefully, will take the riddle out of the IRS vocabulary.

While you can handle your own OIC, do carefully consider hiring a professional. A qualified professional can help you to better weigh your options, design the offer most advantageous to you and negotiate your best deal. Taxpayers can seldom muster the courage to bargain as hard as they must with the IRS. That's why I devote an entire chapter to finding the *right* professional and how you can work with your advisor for the best result. But even if you do hire a professional, you'll find this useful guide will familiarize you with the OIC program, make you more comfortable with the process and more knowledgeable in working with your advisors.

So if you have paralyzing tax problems look at this book as your passport to a new beginning. I'll provide you with all you must know. You must provide the determination, sincerity and willingness to tackle your tax problems so they are finally behind you.

As so many other taxpayers have happily discovered, your tax troubles may soon vanish for pennies on the dollar!

Wishing you every success.

Arnold S. Goldstein, Ph.D.
October 1993

CHAPTER 1

DO YOU OWE THE IRS?

Is the IRS chasing you? Do you have nightmares of losing your home, savings, business and all you worked for? It can happen! No threat to your financial security is as serious as owing the IRS because only the IRS has such awesome powers to extract money from you.

The IRS collection division is tough (it has a tough job to do) but can also be cooperative and reasonable – if you are cooperative and reasonable. While the IRS has powerful collection laws, you as a taxpayer have equally powerful laws to protect yourself from the IRS. You must understand and assert those rights as your first-line defense against the IRS.

HOW THE IRS TRACKS YOU DOWN

Hiding is never the answer when the IRS is after you. The IRS will find you no matter where you go or how often you move. Its weapon? A powerful IRS computer linked to 50 state computers as well as to Social Security and every other federal agency that ever came in contact with you. You are also easily tracked through your state tax agencies, motor vehicle departments, unemployment offices, public welfare agencies, professional licensing boards, and even your voter registration records. It's impossible to hide.

Despite their vast network, the IRS computers work slowly. It can take the IRS years to find you. So while moving around can forestall your day of reckoning, it is not the way to avoid it.

If you owe taxes then deal with the IRS as soon as possible. Delay will only cost you additional interest and penalties and more aggravation and anxiety. You will also face a more hostile IRS if you avoid it. But before you confront the IRS you must protect your assets and position yourself so you can bargain with the IRS more on your terms – not its terms! You will learn these essential survival strategies in the next chapter.

A WORD TO NON-FILERS

Are you one of about ten million Americans who have not filed tax returns for several years? The bad news is that you have little chance of escaping detection. Eventually the IRS catches its scofflaws, and as the IRS computer becomes even more sophisticated, avoidance will be all but impossible.

Don't let the IRS catch you! File your delinquent returns *before* the IRS discovers you're a non-filer. Voluntarily file and you virtually eliminate any possibility of criminal prosecution. On the other hand, if the IRS catches you, it may criminally prosecute you, particularly if your delinquent returns involve sizeable taxable income.

It may take you time to get your tax returns prepared, so at least notify the IRS of your delinquency and your intent to file. The IRS will give you a reasonable opportunity to file, and your notification will usually protect you from criminal prosecution. Nor should inability to pay stop you from filing. File your tax returns even without the tax payment. You will be assessed interest and some penalties for late filing but will avoid those costly penalties imposed on non-filers.

If you do file several years of delinquent returns, then file them about one week apart so the IRS can't easily detect the scope of your non-filing. However, preparing all returns simultaneously allows you to determine the total amount due the IRS and to more intelligently cope with the tax liability. If you file your first returns too soon, the IRS will quickly demand their payment. For that reason you should deal with your delinquent returns collectively and never pay any one IRS return unless you know how all will be paid.

Once your unpaid returns are processed or you otherwise incur a tax liability, the IRS will start the collection process. Expect four increasingly threatening notices from the IRS, each about one month apart. Your unpaid account is then considered delinquent and forwarded to the IRS Automated Collection System (ACS). An IRS collection agent whose job is only to collect the taxes you owe will then phone or visit you.

WHAT THE IRS ALREADY KNOWS ABOUT YOU

The IRS agent will initially want you to complete a *Collection Information Statement* or IRS Form 433-A that requires you to disclose your assets and income. Its purpose? To uncover property and wages available to the IRS for seizure and levy. It also gives the IRS the information it needs to work out an installment plan with you if you can't immediately pay.

If you refuse to cooperate, the IRS can summons you to an IRS office conference, and even have the federal court summons you to appear, as the court can jail you and/or impose a fine for your failure to comply.

The IRS *can* compel your appearance to answer questions, but it *cannot* compel you to disclose financial information or documents. Taxpayers can legally refuse to disclose financial information. It is not even necessary to invoke your rights under the Fifth Amendment. No law requires you to give information to the IRS. This involves technical questions of law, so always follow the advice of your legal counsel in this situation. You certainly can refuse information if you have good reason to suspect you are under criminal investigation by the IRS or any other federal or state law enforcement agency.

Most importantly, protect your assets *before* you give financial information to the IRS. The IRS quickly liens and seizes assets, so timing is critical. Also observe this important rule: Never falsify financial information. Be truthful to the IRS because false statements are perjurious. Remember: It is generally legal to *refuse* information but illegal to *falsify* information. If you refuse information, the IRS can then reconstruct your finances from other sources. The IRS may not find everything but trust it to leave few items undiscovered.

The IRS will want updated financial information about once a year. An IRS agent will meanwhile independently track your financial condition and your ability to pay. You may unknowingly trigger greater IRS collection efforts by showing increased income on you tax return. With the IRS computers, you can't conceal much about your financial affairs.

The IRS is also smothered with other financial information about you from your own and other taxpayers' tax returns. Your own tax return reveals your:

- wages
- interest income
- dividend income
- tax refunds
- rental income
- royalty income
- capital gain distributions
- moving expense payments
- vacation allowances
- severance pay
- real estate taxes
- travel allowances

Through their tax returns or other mandatory reports, others reveal:

- mortgage interest received
- funds received from barter and broker exchanges
- unemployment income
- tax shelters
- fringe benefits received from your employer
- distributions from pension and profit-sharing plans
- cash payments of over $10,000 made to your bank account
- cash payments of over $10,000 received in your business
- gambling winnings above $600
- insurance payments made to as a health care provider
- fees paid to you as an accountant, attorney or entertainer

This vast database lets the IRS reconstruct, with considerable accuracy, your financial past and present. A diligent IRS agent will independently check these and other sources to discover your assets and income. Few rely solely on what you voluntarily disclose. Review your tax records. Review the information others provide the IRS. What do you think the IRS knows about you?

Armed with this information, what can the IRS do to collect from you?

1) Lien and/or seize and sell your assets.

2) Levy your funds held by third parties (such as bank accounts, insurance, wages and accounts receivable).

HOW TO DELAY THE TAX COLLECTOR

Now that you understand some of the IRS's awesome powers, you will wonder how you can delay the tax collector.

Begin with the IRS's massive Automated Computer System (ACS). To stop or suspend further collection action against you, *you* must act to have a "freeze code" entered into the ACS. Simply ignoring the IRS does not stop the collection process.

There are several freeze codes. Each signifies a specific reason for suspending collection, and each code halts collection for a specific time interval, but never for more than one year.

How can you put the tax collector on hold? Try these three strategies:

1) Challenge the accuracy of your tax bill. You do not have to explain

why you disagree with the bill, only that you believe it is incorrect. This one tactic suspends collection against you for weeks, or even months, until the IRS eventually determines you have no reasonable defense and then reactivates the computer.

2)   You can get a 60-day extension just by asking for it. Simply request it on your tax bill and return it to the IRS.

3)   You can also request that your tax file be sent from the local office to the IRS District Office. This automatically suspends collection and also offers two other important advantages: 1) Revenue officers at the District Office level grant more lenient installment plans than do collection agents at local offices, and (2) they are usually more liberal. A District Office also less familiar with your finances, may be slower to garnish your wages or levy your bank accounts. The downside? A District revenue officer may more diligently investigate your finances.

To transfer your tax file to the District Office, you need only question your bill and request transfer. Should your tax agent refuse to transfer your case, then appeal to the supervisor. Persistence is all it takes.

HOW TO COPE WITH A TAX LIEN

The tax lien is the first serious IRS collection remedy. You will get a 10 day notice of the IRS's intent to file a tax lien against you. This tax lien *will* greatly affect you and your lifestyle. First, an IRS tax lien stays in force as long as the IRS can enforce collection, which is ten years under the current statute of limitations. Added to this time is the time a tax claim is in court, you are out of the country or your OIC is under IRS review. Your OIC will also add another year to the statute of limitations.

The immediate effect of the tax lien is to automatically encumber your property. Its practical consequence is to prevent you from selling or borrowing against your major assets. It also makes it virtually impossible to get the credit you need to finance larger purchases, such as a car or a home. Because the tax lien supersedes later encumbrances, a new lender cannot obtain proper security for a loan. One solution is to have your spouse take title, assuming he or she is free of tax problems. This underscores the benefit of filing separate tax returns. Another strategy is to set up a corporation to own your new acquisitions, with others, not yourself, the corporate stockholders.

These maneuvers won't totally solve your problems because a tax lien also destroys your credit. The bottom line is that a lien means you can hold no assets in your name and must rely on others for financing.

Tax liens also encourage foreclosure by existing lenders concerned that the IRS may seize assets they hold as collateral. This commonly occurs with accounts receivable because the IRS gains a superior lien against existing lenders on receivables generated more than 45 days from the lien date. This problem is critical for businesspeople with pledged receivables, since their lenders would eventually lose their priority rights to those receivables. These lenders naturally expect immediate release of the tax lien, which happens only if the taxes are paid, other collateral substituted for the receivables, or a Chapter 11 is filed. Otherwise the lender must foreclose on the pledged receivables to protect itself. This is one reason why many tax-burdened companies are forced to file Chapter 11.

FIVE WAYS TO RECOVER SEIZED PROPERTY

Unless your tax liability is discharged through bankruptcy, or resolved through an OIC or an installment arrangement, the IRS will eventually seize and sell your assets at public or private sale.

The IRS can seize your home, but it will do so only as a last resort. Still, the IRS cannot immediately throw you out. You have about 90 days between seizure of your home and a public auction or sealed bid sale and another 180 days to stay in possession after your home is sold. Within this six-month period you can redeem or reacquire your home for whatever the buyer paid, plus interest. Once this 180-day redemption period passes, you lose all rights to your home and the buyer can evict you, which can take another several months. As a practical matter, you may have up to a year of rent-free living once your home is seized. This is one small consolation to losing your home.

You have no similar right of continued possession of seized personal property. The IRS immediately takes cars, boats and other personal property. Nor have you the right to redeem or reacquire personal property, as you do with your home.

There are five ways to recover seized property from the IRS:

1) *You can file an Offer in Compromise or enter into an installment agreement with the IRS.* The purpose of many seizures is to prod taxpayers to resolve their tax problems. Lax taxpayers do respond when they are about to lose their valued assets.

2) *Show the IRS that release and return of the seized property will facilitate collection.* Business assets, for example, in operation may generate more money for the IRS than they would bring at auction, and this would justify their release.

3) *Your tax liability is satisfied or no longer enforceable.* Full payment obviously discharges your obligation, as does expiration of the ten year statute of limitations. In either instance the IRS must release all seized property still in its possession.

4)   *You file bankruptcy (Chapter 7, 11, 12 or 13).* Any bankruptcy automatically stops further action by the IRS, unless it gets bankruptcy court approval to proceed with the seizure.

5)   *You give the IRS a bond or substitute collateral equal in value to the seized asset.*

Seizure of your assets will not come as a surprise. The IRS gives 30 days' notice of its intent to levy or seize assets. This seizure notice may be given to you in person, mailed, or left at your home or workplace. Never ignore this notice! This is your one final opportunity to submit your OIC or otherwise resolve matters with the IRS *before* you lose your valuable assets.

HOW TO DEFEND YOURSELF AGAINST AN IRS LEVY

The power to levy gives the IRS the ability to attach your money held by third parties. A mailed notice of levy can cause you to lose:

*   Checking and savings accounts
*   Stocks, bonds and other investments
*   Cash value life insurance
*   Keoghs and IRAs
*   Inheritances due to be received
*   Interests in partnerships and certain trusts
*   Accounts receivables
*   Claims against third parties

As with a seizure, the IRS must give you advance notice of its intent to levy. Unless you then pay your taxes, reach an installment agreement, or file an Offer in Compromise or bankruptcy, the IRS can levy these assets without further notice. If the IRS believes your assets are in jeopardy of being concealed or transferred, it can levy *without* prior notice. This is called a "jeopardy assessment."

The IRS may seize or levy your assets in any order or sequence. If some levied assets do not fully cover your taxes, other assets will be levied until your tax bill is paid. You can get the IRS to release its levy if:

*   You fully pay the tax, including penalties and interest.
*   You enter into an installment agreement.
*   You submit an Offer in Compromise.
*   The IRS determines the levy causes extreme or undue financial hardship.

- The value of the property levied greatly exceeds the taxes, and release would not impair collection.

- You file bankruptcy.

SIX DEADLY MISTAKES MOST TAXPAYERS MAKE

Dealing with the IRS is like walking a mine field. You discover your fatal error only when it's too late. While no book can do more than uncover a few of the more numerous mines, beware these six ticking time bombs:

1) *Putting up with an unreasonable or incompetent revenue officer.* If you think you're being overly mistreated or the victim of an incompetent or overbearing revenue officer, then demand transfer of your case to another revenue officer. Yes, revenue officers must be tough to be effective and collect, but they must also act reasonably.

2) *Know where you stand.* Ask the revenue officer what further action you must take *and* what you might expect from the IRS. Never assume you know where matters stand or what should happen next. Avoid nasty surprises. And when the IRS tells you something – get it in writing!

3) *Never admit to violating the tax laws.* If you think a revenue officer is trying to get incriminating statements from you, then terminate the interview and get an attorney. If you are interviewed by a special agent or recited your Fifth Amendment rights, stop talking and run to an attorney.

4) *Never ignore the IRS.* Reply to all IRS correspondence and promptly return any phone calls. Your willingness to communicate will go a long way toward winning IRS cooperation, but don't needlessly volunteer information.

5) *Pay your taxes if you can afford to pay them.* The IRS will incessantly pressure you to sell or borrow against your assets and it *will* be cheaper than having the IRS as a creditor. However, don't let the IRS coerce your spouse to sell assets or lend you money to pay *your* bill. Pay only to the extent the IRS can take your assets.

6) *Never extend the statute of limitations.* The IRS has only ten years from the date of assessment to collect your delinquent taxes. This was extended in 1991 from six years. Once the statute of limitations expires, your liability expires. However, the statute of limitations is extended by:

   - *Waiver:* When you sign a waiver and voluntarily agree to extend the time period for collection.

- *Offer in Compromise:* The period of time an Offer in Compromise is under IRS consideration.

- *Absence from the country:* The period of time you are out of the country for more than six continuous months.

- *IRS lawsuit:* When the IRS starts a lawsuit to enforce collection.

Never extend the statute of limitations voluntarily. The IRS will try to get you to sign a Form 900 Waiver. When the statute of limitation is running out, expect the IRS to become overly aggressive in its collection efforts and offer you a "lenient" payment plan in exchange for the waiver. *Don't sign!* If the IRS couldn't collect from you during all the preceding years, why will it succeed in the short time it has left? Once the statute of limitations expires you are finished with the IRS. Extend the statute of limitations and you extend your IRS problem.

Despite the IRS's great collection powers, it does let thousands of tax claims expire each year. When *your* statute of limitations has expired, have the IRS abate the tax liability which acknowledges you are liability-free. Until you receive your abatement, continue to keep property out of your name. Becoming wealthy at the last moment may be just the fatal mistake the IRS is patiently waiting for.

TAKE ADVANTAGE OF YOUR TAXPAYER'S BILL OF RIGHTS

As a taxpayer, you gained several important rights against the IRS in 1988 when the IRS adopted a Taxpayer's Bill of Rights. Its purpose is to educate taxpayers and to let them know in plain English what the IRS can and cannot do when dealing with taxpayers. You will find the complete Taxpayer's Bill of Rights in the Appendix. Read it carefully!

You can also get help with your tax problems through the IRS Problem Resolution Program. If you have a tax problem that you cannot resolve through normal channels, then you can reach the Problem Resolution Office by calling the IRS taxpayer assistance number in your area.

There are two ways the Problem Resolution Office can help you. They may suggest that you submit Form 911 Application for Taxpayer Assistance. This is in the Appendix. Or you can call (800) 829-1040 to directly speak to a taxpayer ombudsman. If the service believes the IRS action is causing you undue hardship, it may issue a Taxpayer Assistance Order (TAO) to suspend further IRS action against you. These, however, are not commonly issued.

You will also find in the Appendix numerous tax publications that are provided absolutely free by the IRS as well as other sources of assistance to the taxpayer in trouble with the IRS. Order those that cover areas of specific concern. Knowledge is critical when you deal with the IRS.

CHAPTER 2

HOW TO PROTECT YOUR ASSETS FROM THE IRS

As a taxpayer with severe tax problems chased by an ever-zealous tax collector, you must quickly learn how to protect your assets from lien, seizure or levy.

Having few or no assets exposed offers the IRS few or no assets to seize. This not only protects your assets but also significantly reduces what you will eventually pay the IRS under your OIC. This is because your offer to the IRS cannot be for less than your equity in those assets exposed to the IRS. Wealth available to the IRS is wealth you must pay the IRS. Make "poverty on paper" *your* objective. Only when you have very little for the IRS to take can you win those pennies-on-the-dollar settlements.

There are many ways to *legally* shelter your assets from the IRS. You can also quite easily *improperly* shield your assets so the IRS can recover them *and* impose serious criminal sanctions or civil fines. Faulty asset protection will also destroy IRS cooperation on your Offer in Compromise.

Timing is critical. You must protect your assets at the first hint of a tax problem. You can't afford to wait. Delay only jeopardizes your assets.

HIRE AN ASSET PROTECTION PROFESSIONAL

The most important rule is *not* to protect your assets on your own. To avoid trouble the job must be done correctly. Nor should you rely upon your tax professional for asset protection advice. Tax advisors are seldom experts in sheltering wealth. And because they constantly deal with the IRS, they may be too timid and ineffective in what they will do to protect you. You need a good asset protection lawyer who is bold and creative and will aggressively, but legally, shelter your assets using strategies unknown by others less experienced in asset protection.

WHERE DO YOU FIND THIS ASSET PROTECTION PRO?

Talk to a few bankruptcy lawyers. They usually have good asset protection skills. Estate planning specialists are also usually skilled in this area. My IRS Rescue organization maintains a nationwide roster of asset protection specialists and will gladly refer you to one in your area. These lawyers all have considerable experience shielding taxpayer assets from the IRS as well as other creditors. For a no-charge referral call (305) 480-8543.

The best place to start? Become knowledgeable about asset protection. Even before you call a lawyer, read *Asset Protection Secrets*. This unique book, described in the Appendix, gives you 234 perfectly legitimate and proven ways to protect everything you own from any financial threat... including the IRS! And don't think for a moment that you can't legally protect your assets from the IRS. You can. Read *Asset Protection Secrets* and you'll see how!

Why must you proceed knowledgeably? The IRS, like other creditors, can go to court to recover fraudulently transferred property. The IRS may also file a "nominee lien" against property wrongfully in the hands of the transferee. Of course, the IRS must prove in court that the property was fraudulently conveyed. Fortunately, the IRS as a giant bureaucracy seldom goes to such great lengths to recover fraudulently transferred property, unless the tax liability and the value of the transferred property is significant and the transaction a blatant fraud or sham. Asset protection in anticipation of a tax lien comes under the adage of "nothing to lose and everything to gain." Still, transfers best withstand scrutiny and challenge when handled by an asset protection specialist who can oversee the safest disposition of your assets and prevent serious problems for yourself or others involved in the transaction.

ASSET PROTECTION FUNDAMENTALS

There are four basic ways to protect your assets from the IRS:

1) Retitle your assets in the name of another individual or entity.

2) Convert your non-exempt (unprotected) assets into exempt (protected) assets.

3) Place your assets beyond the legal reach of the IRS, such as in offshore havens.

4) Decrease the equity in your exposed assets by encumbering those assets.

You must distinguish between these common tactics and those that are clearly illegal, such as concealing assets upon which a levy has been authorized, e.g., hiding an auto or boat.

A second serious mistake is committing perjury to conceal and thus protect your assets. You must never lie to the IRS, particularly when your statement is under oath. However, with sound asset protection, you can truthfully answer questions concerning your assets, confident the IRS can do nothing to seize them.

No law prevents you from selling, transferring or encumbering your assets. You can sell your property even when it has a tax lien against it. The IRS lien would continue to encumber the property, but the sale would protect any remaining equity from additional liens that may be filed against the property while under your ownership.

ASSETS THAT ARE SAFE FROM THE IRS

When the IRS wants to get paid, it doesn't have to leave you with much, but it still cannot take everything you own. Certain assets are automatically protected from seizure by federal law. Assets exempt from IRS seizure include:

- Fuel, food, furniture and personal effects up to a total of $1,650
- Undelivered mail
- Tools and books needed for your job, business or profession – up to $1,100
- Income needed to provide court ordered child support
- Unemployment, worker's compensation, public assistance and job training benefits
- Clothing and school books
- Pensions

Note that Social Security, IRAs, and Keogh plans are not automatically protected. The IRS seldom and only reluctantly seizes these assets, but if you have a large tax liability then be cautious and protect your IRAs or Keoghs. Tax penalties for early withdrawal on these accounts may be compromised with your existing tax liability. Property owned between husband and wife as tenants by the entirety may also be protected, depending upon your state law. Aside from these few assets, everything else you own can be seized by the IRS.

BEWARE OF STATE ASSET PROTECTION LAWS

Do you think your home is protected from the IRS by your state homestead laws? You will be in for a rude surprise. The IRS is the one creditor that can ignore your state homestead laws and seize your home.

The IRS can also ignore other state exemptions designed to protect certain personal property from creditors. Why does the IRS have this unique power? Because the IRS is a federal agency whose authority supersedes state debtor protection laws. So don't count on your state laws for help. You need other asset protection strategies to protect your assets.

YOUR MOST VULNERABLE ASSETS

IRS collection agents have wide discretion when deciding which assets to seize to satisfy a tax claim. In practice, they consider these factors:

- The amount of the tax liability versus the property needed to pay the tax.

- The ease of seizure and disposal of the various assets.

- The importance of each asset to the taxpayer.

Now you can see why the IRS usually targets these assets, in descending order:

- Bank and checking accounts
- Cars, boats, airplanes, and other recreational vehicles with high equity
- Cash value life insurance
- Accounts receivable
- Stocks and bonds
- Collectibles
- Investment and vacation real estate
- Home
- IRAs and Keoghs
- Wages

The IRS will seize a taxpayer's home, IRAs, Keoghs or wages when the taxpayer is uncooperative or no other assets are available to satisfy the tax. Still, the IRS may threaten to seize a home or levy wages to spur the taxpayer into borrowing or selling assets to pay the tax. IRS agents know that no threat spurs taxpayers to find money faster than the spectre of losing their home or other treasured asset.

TWO WAYS TO SAFEGUARD YOUR BANK ACCOUNT

You must quickly protect your bank account and safe deposit box because the IRS targets these first.

The IRS has a record of your checking and savings accounts and *will* levy these accounts. Any bank account in your name is unsafe as long as you owe the IRS. The IRS routinely and continuously levies bank accounts of delinquent taxpayers. To outflank an IRS levy, you must protect your money using two simple strategies:

- Set up a corporation to hold your personal funds. From this account pay your personal debts. You may transfer money to the corporation as a loan and withdraw it as repayment without incurring a tax. Do keep good records to properly report all income at tax time.

- Alternatively, transfer your money to banks the IRS doesn't know about. Small, distant banks are best because the IRS will "shotgun" or levy every major bank in your area. Since the IRS periodically makes you submit a new financial statement and disclose *new* bank accounts, you must immediately thereafter open new accounts. This tactic is absolutely legal because you were truthful about your bank accounts when you answered!

Your safe deposit box is no safer than your bank accounts. If the IRS suspects you have cash or other valuables in your safe deposit box, the IRS will want to inspect it. This is automatic under an Offer in Compromise. If you refuse, the IRS will seal the box. To gain access to your box, you must permit IRS inspection or the IRS can patiently wait for your rental contract to expire, at which time a bank officer can legally open the box for IRS inspection.

This is why you must store cash or other valuables elsewhere. If you need a safe deposit box for your valuables, then set up a corporation to rent one in its name. Since your corporation is a separate legal entity, the IRS cannot demand access to its safe deposit box for collecting *your* personal taxes. There's another advantage even if you are not a tax delinquent. The IRS can seal and inspect *your* safe deposit box upon your death. But a corporate box has perpetual life. Your death will not bring IRS inspection of the corporate box, which can be opened by your spouse or another trusted individual.

Aside from collecting overdue taxes, the IRS snoops for cash in safe deposit boxes because the IRS considers such cash as undeclared, fully taxable income. You must prove the money is either tax-free or previously reported income.

TRUSTS AND JOINTLY OWNED PROPERTY: TWO DANGER ZONES

Property held in trust cannot be seized by the IRS to pay the tax liability of the grantor except under two circumstances:

- The grantor fraudulently conveyed the property to the trust, or
- The grantor retains control over the trust property or the right to revoke the trust.

If you convey property to the trust *before* you incur a tax liability, you have well-sheltered assets provided you use an *irrevocable* trust and adequately relinquished control over the assets. The IRS will closely examine your irrevocable trust. If it finds you retained sufficient control over the trust, it will be considered your alter-ego and your trust assets will be in jeopardy. Living trusts are popular because these trusts let you avoid probate. They do not, however, protect assets from the IRS or other creditors because they are *revocable* trusts. Cautiously use trusts to protect your assets. Few are trustworthy protectors of your wealth.

Similar problems arise with jointly owned property. If a husband and wife, for example, own a home in joint tenancy, or as tenants by the entirety, the IRS can usually force the sale of the property, even if only one spouse has the tax liability. In some states, property held as tenants by the entirety is completely protected from the creditors of any one spouse, but not creditors of both spouses. This protection usually also applies to the IRS. Do you own property under a tenancy by the entirety? Verify its protection with your attorney.

Legal complications usually discourage the IRS from seizing jointly owned marital property when only one spouse owes taxes. But don't take a chance. Protect jointly titled property *before* a lien is filed. While the IRS may have difficulty seizing the interest of only one spouse, a tax lien will cloud title to the entire property and make it difficult or impossible to sell or refinance.

Joint bank accounts are particularly vulnerable because the IRS levies *all* joint account funds. The non-liable joint-owner must then prove what he or she contributed to the account to recover his or her share. Never participate in a joint account or joint tenancy unless you are absolutely certain your co-owner is free of tax and other creditor problems. However, since you can't be certain whether your joint-owner has or will have legal or financial problems, it is best to avoid these arrangements altogether.

You may now see why you should *not* file joint tax returns with your spouse. You will pay slightly higher taxes when you file separate tax returns, but the IRS cannot seize jointly owned property as easily as individually owned assets when only one spouse has the tax liability. With joint returns you cannot easily protect your assets since neither you nor your spouse can serve as a safe harbor. You must absolutely file individual returns when:

- One spouse has ongoing tax problems, continuing audits or recurrent tax liabilities.

- One spouse's tax returns may cause serious civil or criminal problems.

- One spouse has most of the marital assets in his or her name and the other spouse the greater likelihood of tax problems.

How to Work For The IRS For Below Minimum Wage

The wage levy is the IRS's most devastating power and particularly devastating when you consider the IRS can take everything you earn, except for your paltry personal exemption of $75 a week plus $25 a week for each dependent, including your spouse. One IRS levy automatically garnishes all future wages until your tax liability is fully paid or the wage levy is released.

Because the wage levy is such an extreme IRS collection weapon, it is used only when less drastic collection efforts fail. Not even the IRS can realistically expect a single wage earner with a net salary of $500 a week to give the IRS $425 and continue to work forever for $75 a week. The wage levy therefore chiefly prods the taxpayer to respond when other efforts fail. Avoid this embarrassment and aggravation. File bankruptcy, negotiate an installment plan or submit an OIC with the IRS *before* it resorts to a wage levy. Take the initiative and you will find the IRS more lenient. But you can take two steps to combat an IRS wage levy:

- If you own your own business, you can divert your income to your spouse or adult children who work in your business. They can then gift or loan the funds back to you. Be prepared to prove that your spouse and children actually perform services for the business and can justify their income.

- You can also set up another corporation to subcontract to your primary business, and you can get paid from this subcontractor corporation. The IRS will eventually find out about your new employer, but this can take a year or more. You can then repeat the process with another corporation. This strategy is perfectly legal and workable!

You forfeit this ability to sidestep the wage levy if you work for a large company that must honor the levy. If that's you and you owe a small tax that several paychecks can handle, then just grin and bear it. If your tax liability is too large to be quickly paid, then you must either file bankruptcy, submit an OIC or negotiate an installment plan. Filing an OIC should release the wage levy. Your final alternative? Quit your job. It's not the solution for most taxpayers but is an option if you have other sources of income unknown to the IRS. Collecting unemployment will give your more money each week than what the IRS will leave you.

TIPS TO STALL THE IRS FROM SEIZING YOUR BUSINESS

Do you realize the IRS actually favors certain tax-delinquent businesses? What are they?

- Businesses financed by the SBA or other federal agencies. It's foolish for one federal agency to collect its money at the expense of another federal agency that will, by its action, lose its loan.

- Minority-owned businesses or those that employ a high number of minorities.

- High-profile businesses within the community, such as a major employer.

Is yours such a favored business? Highlight these points to your tax collector. You will see greater restraint. No, it is not official IRS policy to favor these businesses, but *it is* unofficial policy! Leniency still should not be construed as immunity. No matter how important the business, the IRS eventually expects payment of overdue taxes from *everyone*.

If you own such a favored business, you should be able to work out a more lenient installment plan or more easily negotiate an Offer in Compromise.

Another tip: The IRS never seizes businesses with hazardous waste problems. If you have such a problem, let it work for you!

Why else would it be unpleasant for the IRS to seize your business? Would your equipment be difficult to remove? Is vandalism a potential problem? Would your customers hound the IRS for the return of stored goods? Is your business so heavily encumbered there's no equity for the IRS?

Highlight too the positive benefits that result from not seizing your business. Are there important customers counting on your future shipments? Will your assets increase in value with time, perhaps by turning raw material into finished products or receivables? Wouldn't this enhance the value of the business if the IRS waited to enforce its rights?

IRS agents only want *one* good reason for *not* going through the strenuous job of liquidating your business. Find one!

THE FOUR MOST POWERFUL ASSET PROTECTION STRATEGIES

Always assume you won't resolve your difficulties with the IRS. Prepare for the worst by following these four powerful strategies to protect your assets when the IRS is chasing you:

1) Transfer your assets to family limited partnerships.

Although unfamiliar to most Americans, a family limited partnership is usually the safest way to title your home and other assets and protect them from creditors. As the general partner you continue to enjoy complete control over the partnership property while the partnership can be safely owned by other family members, trusts or a variety of other entities. The limited partnership can hold virtually any asset: real estate, CDs, savings, stocks, bonds, and even cars and boats. You will want to isolate your "dangerous" or "liability-creating" assets, such as a business, in a separate corporation so these assets cannot endanger your "safe" assets in the limited partnership. What can the IRS get by chasing your tiny partnership interest? Only your tiny share of the distributed profits and your tiny share of the net proceeds upon liquidation, both of which events remain entirely within your control. A limited partnership protecting your assets leaves the IRS with no meaningful recourse. Discuss this with your lawyer, or see how it works in *Asset Protection Secrets*. Savvy lawyers rank the family limited partnership America's No. 1 asset protector. They're right!

2) Encumber the equity in your property.

Can you borrow another $50,000 on your home, $10,000 on your car or $100,000 on your business? When the IRS is after you, borrow heavily so the smallest possible equity remains exposed. Do you owe a relative or a friend? Secure the debt with a mortgage on your property. Your goal must be to encumber the equity in your assets until there is absolutely no equity available for the IRS to seize. Encumbered assets will also help reduce your OIC settlement because you have less equity.

3) **Liquidate your life insurance cash value, savings, CDs, IRAs, Keoghs, stocks, bonds, annuities or other securities.**

Sitting-duck assets are as good as cash to the IRS. Liquidate them *before* the IRS grabs them. What do you do with the cash proceeds? You'll soon find answers. But before you liquidate these assets, check with your attorney. These assets may already be protected by existing laws or easily sheltered in other ways. For instance, life insurance put into a life insurance trust may protect it against the IRS *and* keep your insurance intact.

4) **Collect what you are owed.**

Your next step? Coax those who owe you money to pay now even if you must heavily discount their bills. It's obviously smarter for you to get less cash now rather than have the IRS collect more later. Similarly settle your lawsuits against others, even if at a bargain price. Your claims against others lose all value to you once levied by the IRS. Finally, are you due a tax refund? File your tax return *before* the IRS computers are fed the fact that you owe *them* money!

HOW TO MAKE CASH DISAPPEAR QUICKLY AND LEGALLY

Sell or refinance your assets and you may wind up with a wheelbarrow full of cash. How do you protect this cash from the IRS?

1) *Buy exempt assets:* For instance, invest as much cash as you can into your pension plan because pension plans are fully protected from the IRS. Or you can take the cash proceeds from a non-exempt asset and buy an exempt asset, such as tools of the trade or furniture. Check your state laws to identify those assets that are exempt. You will find them listed in *Asset Protection Secrets*.

2) *Pay "friendly" creditors:* Do you owe your father for your college tuition? A brother for a past loan? You see the idea. Why not use your cash to pay these "friendly" creditors? If it's a *bona fide* debt the IRS can't complain.

3) *Prepay expenses:* Did you know you can prepay your child's education, even years in advance. Many colleges offer prepayment arrangements. You can also prepay alimony, child support, insurance, medical care and even the legal fees necessary to combat the IRS. Your lawyer will like that. What bills can you prepay?

4) *Use offshore accounts:* When you owe the IRS *big* money and have *big* money to shelter, then an offshore haven may be your answer.

The Cayman Islands and Isle of Man are two havens whose principal industry is to safely shelter money from the IRS and other American creditors. Your money is even safer when titled in a foreign-based asset protection trust, popularly used in these two havens. Offshore banking is perfectly legal, totally effective and neither as difficult nor inconvenient as it sounds. If you have $100,000 or more to protect, then investigate an offshore haven.

5) *Give a gift:* You can gift up to $10,000 per year, per donee without a gift tax. A gift to hinder creditors is a fraudulent transfer; however, the IRS rarely chases small cash gifts to your children or other family members who are logical beneficiaries of your generosity.

HOW TO PHYSICALLY PROTECT YOUR ASSETS FROM THE IRS

Although the IRS code makes it a felony to remove, deposit or conceal property upon which an IRS levy has been authorized with the intention of defeating the collection of taxes, this doesn't mean you must docilely turn over to the IRS those assets subject to seizure. For all their power, IRS agents do not have the authority to force a taxpayer to produce property for seizure.

You may, for example, continuously relocate your car or boat under threat of seizure. But if you volunteer the location of your assets to an IRS agent, your disclosure must be truthful. As with relocated bank accounts, a car, boat or other tangible asset can be similarly moved to defeat seizure. Still, this tactic is not recommended, no matter how desperately you may want to keep your property. The IRS will eventually find and seize your more significant assets. The safer strategy is to sell or encumber your assets *before* the collection process reaches the point of lien and seizure. For example, if you sell your car and lease another, the IRS has no car to chase and you avoid a "hide-and-seek" game you will lose. More importantly, you have cash from the sale which, as you have seen, is so much more easily protected.

Nor can the IRS enter your residence or business premises to seize property unless you voluntarily consent to such entry or the IRS agent has a warrant or a "writ of entry" court order.

You may examine the writ of entry and confine the agent to those premises described in the writ. But this applies only to private premises. The IRS needs no writ of entry to seize assets on public property. An automobile in a public garage, for instance, can be seized by the IRS without a writ of entry, while the same auto in your garage cannot.

Property located in another state can also slow IRS seizure as the local IRS agent must usually transfer your file to an agent in the state where the asset is situated.

As you can see, there are ways to protect your assets from the IRS. This chapter revealed only several of the more basic examples. With the many other possible strategies are other potential pitfalls and dangers. That's why you must read *Asset Protection Secrets* and get the advice of an asset protection specialist as the very first round in your battles with the IRS.

CHAPTER 3

FOUR ALTERNATIVES TO THE OFFER IN COMPROMISE

Before you proceed with an Offer in Compromise (OIC), decide whether an OIC is your best remedy or whether another solution to your tax problems would make more sense in your circumstances. Consider these four alternatives to the OIC:

1) An abatement

2) An installment agreement

3) Remaining "uncollectible"

4) Bankruptcy

HOW TO ABATE YOUR TAX LIABILITY

Under an abatement the IRS cancels all or part of the accrued penalties and/or interest, although they may reduce your base tax liability as well. The OIC, in contrast, compromises the total tax plus interest and penalties for an amount that coincides with your assets, income and general ability to pay.

You should apply for an abatement if you can pay the tax liability but believe you should be excused from penalties or interest for good cause. Most abatements extend to penalties (about 40 percent are granted). Interest abatements are far less common.

You have good reason for an abatement if your tax problems were at least partly due to:

- Illness
- Destruction of your records
- Family problems or divorce
- Incarceration or other significant disruption to your life
- Improper advice from a tax professional.

In sum, an abatement may be granted if you were victimized by factors beyond your control which factors caused your tax delinquency and the penalties and interest.

There are abatements for:

- Civil fraud penalties
- Negligence penalties
- Failure to pay estimated tax penalties
- Failure to file penalties
- Late filing penalties
- Dishonored check penalties

Don't consider an abatement if you can't pay the abated amount (usually the amount owed less penalty). In most cases this is about 75 percent of the unabated or present tax bill.

How do you file for an abatement? You can send a simple letter requesting an abatement; however, it is wiser to use a *Claim for Refund and Request for Abatement* (IRS *Form 843*), you will find this form in the Appendix. Include with your request copies of all documents that support your case. You will need strong and convincing documentation so you can't overbuild your case.

Should you pay the underlying tax in the meantime? If the IRS thinks you will have difficulty paying even that amount, they may be prompted to abate rather than risk receiving less under an OIC or bankruptcy. On the other hand, you will continue to accrue interest (and possibly penalties) while your abatement application is pending. If you foresee the possibility of an OIC or bankruptcy, then it is probably sounder to make no payment until your abatement is acted upon.

The IRS should reply to your abatement request in about 60 days. Call or write the IRS to follow up and then send a copy of your original letter and documentation. Don't let your guard down during this period. The IRS will continue collection activity *until* the abatement is granted and the abated amount is fully paid.

You may appeal a rejected abatement request. This appeal must be in writing and made within 30 days of the rejection. The IRS has brochures available on how to appeal an abatement.

PAYING YOUR TAXES IN INSTALLMENTS

You may owe the IRS more than you can immediately pay but have enough assets or income to fully pay the taxes over time. Many taxpayers are too financially strapped to handle a whopping tax bill with one payment. If you're one of these taxpayers the installment agreement may be your answer.

If you don't have the money to fully pay the IRS, you can request an installment plan. The IRS has a new Form 9465, *Installment Agreement Request*, which you must attach to your return. This is also found in the Appendix. This indicates the amount you can pay each month. The IRS does not require that you disclose any additional financial information to support your request, nor do you have to show the IRS there's no other way for you to make the payment now due. The IRS does not specify what it considers an acceptable minimum monthly payment, nor the duration of the tax payments. Each individual IRS office determines by its own policies whether a proposed payment plan is acceptable or not. If your installment proposal is unacceptable, the IRS will contact you and tell you what they want as a payment schedule.

If you filed your return without the new form, you should send a letter to the IRS explaining your situation and propose a monthly payment schedule. Keep in mind that spreading your payments over time will cost you more interest, currently calculated at 7 percent annually. You may also incur late payment penalties of .5 percent per month. Combined, they equal about 13 percent annual interest, so borrow money elsewhere at a lower rate if you possibly can.

Individual IRS offices can approve installment agreements up to $10,000. Requests for installment payments for amounts in excess of $10,000 will trigger an IRS request for additional financial information. Make your payments on time on an approved installment plan and the IRS will not usually file a federal tax lien.

The IRS guidelines recommend an installment arrangement if it would "facilitate collection" of the owed taxes. Once the IRS agrees to an installment arrangement it must honor it unless:

- You miss a payment.
- You fall behind on other taxes due the IRS.
- You fail to give the IRS updated financial information, when requested.
- You gave the IRS false information when negotiating your installment plan.

If you need more than a year to pay your taxes, then expect the IRS to take a hard look at your income and expenses. The IRS will cooperate – provided they get every dollar above what you absolutely need to support yourself and your family.

And the IRS will pressure you to sell or borrow against assets, or to borrow from friends or relatives. The IRS will agree to an extended installment plan *only* when the IRS does not believe it can retire the liability much sooner through seizure or levy of your assets.

The IRS prefers agreements calling for equal monthly installments. Suggest payment dates that coincide with your payroll dates. An installment agreement for more than two years must be reviewed at its mid-point, but in no event less than every two years.

As a practical matter, installment agreements beyond two years are seldom sensible to the taxpayer. If you owe the IRS more than you can pay within two years, you should either submit an OIC (if you have few assets), or sell or borrow against your assets to pay the taxes sooner.

As with an abatement, you can appeal an IRS rejection of your installment proposal. This appeal may made be by letter and mailed to the agent's immediate supervisor. In fact, the agent must advise you of your right to appeal if you cannot agree on installment arrangements.

STOP COLLECTION BY BECOMING "UNCOLLECTIBLE"

Do you have negligible assets subject to levy by the IRS, and no income beyond that which is absolutely necessary to cover your living expenses? If so, the IRS may temporarily inactivate collection against you under the "hardship" rule or so-called 'Section 53'.

You will continue to owe the taxes and interest will accrue, but once the IRS has earmarked you as uncollectible they will temporarily suspend further collection activity.

The IRS will periodically re-examine your finances to see if your financial condition has improved to the point that some payment can be demanded. This financial review will occur about once a year and you must then complete a new financial statement (Form 433A). The IRS may question you in conference about this updated financial information or simply request that you complete and return the form by mail. As with all information you give the IRS, make certain that what you say is completely truthful.

The IRS may also monitor your financial condition by computerized review of your tax returns. For example, the IRS computer may "trigger" your return if your reported gross income exceeds a pre-established amount.

Millions of Americans have remained "uncollectible" for years and completely avoided paying their back taxes. Obviously, these individuals could not title assets in their name or have significant income available for IRS levy. Still, many of these "uncollectibles" enjoyed relatively comfortable lifestyles.

The IRS has ten years from date of assessment to collect, but if you have no valuable assets in your name, a small income and expect your bleak financial situation to continue, then remaining "uncollectible" may be your most practical remedy.

WILL BANKRUPTCY END YOUR TAX WORRIES?

There are essentially two types of bankruptcies and two types of taxes. The effect of bankruptcy on your tax obligations depends upon both the type of bankruptcy and the type of tax you owe.

First, you may be liable for either personal income taxes or for withholding taxes (usually due from a business that you owned or managed). Withholding taxes are not dischargeable through any type of bankruptcy. Personal income taxes are dischargeable in Chapter 7 bankruptcy, but only if the tax was assessed at least three years prior to the filing.

Next consider the different types of bankruptcy. Income taxes, whether more or less than three years old, are not dischargeable under a Chapter 13 wage-earner plan or Chapter 11 reorganization. Under Chapter 13 you agree to make monthly payments over three to five years to pay either a portion or all of your debts. Because taxes are a priority claim, you generally pay the entire tax claim under a Chapter 11 or Chapter 13.

A Chapter 7 bankruptcy can effectively rid you of old tax claims, but you must move carefully:

- Make certain that the taxes are no less than three years old from the date of assessment. More recent taxes are not dischargeable.

- If you either negotiated a settlement (OIC) with the IRS, or had your tax claim adjudicated, you must wait at least 240 days from that date to file bankruptcy.

- Bankruptcy won't discharge taxes if you understated your income or filed false tax information for the years you want discharged. The IRS can still come after you for any deficiency discovered through audit, so make certain your taxes for these years are accurate.

- Filing bankruptcy does not affect liens presently against your property. The IRS can, with bankruptcy court approval, still sell and seize the property. Your remaining tax obligation will be discharged.

- Don't forget that Chapter 7 bankruptcy will not discharge witholding tax liabilities - but the fact that you are bankrupt may influence the IRS to consider you 'uncollectible'.

A Chapter 11 or Chapter 13 may work well for you if you can fully pay your taxes over time. A Chapter 13 gives you three to five years to pay your taxes and the IRS cannot bother you during this time. In a business or profession? You can elect a Chapter 11 reorganization which generally gives you six years from the date of assessment to fully pay the IRS. A Chapter 13 or Chapter 11 bankruptcy is recommended only if you have assets you do not want to lose. If you have relatively few assets and a substantial income tax liability, then wait the three years and fully discharge the tax under a Chapter 7 bankruptcy.

As powerful as the IRS may be, the federal bankruptcy laws are considerably stronger. Once you file bankruptcy the IRS must stop all further collection action. So bankruptcy can be an effective way to save your assets and stretch out your payments to the IRS. But don't wait too long before you file for bankruptcy.

For example, if you are in business the IRS may have levied your cash and your accounts receivable. Perhaps the IRS seized and closed your business as well. Under Chapter 11 or Chapter 13 you can compel the IRS to return these assets. That, however, can take time to enforce. Your attorney must first file a complaint against the IRS for turnover. The bankruptcy court may take weeks or even months to act. Meanwhile, your business remains closed, employees find new jobs, and customers flock to competitors. Customers who owe you money will find the IRS levy a convenient excuse not to pay. Few businesses can survive so serious a disruption.

Bankruptcy is probably not your best alternative if the IRS is your only significant creditor. If you have a few assets you will do as well with an Offer in Compromise (and probably resolve your claim for very little), or even be classified "uncollectible," thus suspending all collection efforts.

Bankruptcy may be your right remedy if you have many other creditors also pressing for payment *and* your taxes are dischargeable under bankruptcy.

CHAPTER 4

THE OFFER IN COMPROMISE PROGRAM IN A NUTSHELL

Simply stated, the IRS Offer in Compromise Program (IRS code section 7122) authorizes the IRS to compromise outstanding tax obligations with financially burdened taxpayers for less than the full tax due. In essence, the IRS makes a deal with you to pay all you can reasonably afford and forgives any remaining balance.

The Offer in Compromise Program (OIC) is not new. The IRS has compromised tax liabilities for over 80 years. Historically, the IRS discouraged OICs, or at least did little to encourage their use, as seen by the fact that so few taxpayers over the years took advantage of the OIC program. For example, during the 1980s the IRS processed as few as 2,000 offers a year, yet millions of taxpayers who were ideal candidates for the OIC program never tried to compromise their taxes.

In 1992, the IRS adopted new policies and procedures to greater promote taxpayer use of OICs and to streamline the handling of such cases. IRS agents increasingly and more enthusiastically now advise delinquent taxpayers about the OIC program. Many tax professionals agree the IRS is now more lenient and willing to accept reasonable OICs than in the past. Apparently, the IRS has discovered that allowing taxpayers to voluntarily pay a portion of what they owe is preferable to chasing the taxpayer for the full amount and ending up with even less.

WHY THE OIC PROGRAM HAS BECOME POPULAR

It is not surprising that the IRS has found the OIC a more productive solution when dealing with tax-burdened Americans. Too many long-term installment agreements fell into default and too much IRS effort was lost enforcing those agreements. And the heavy hand of the IRS forced too many taxpayers into bankruptcy or made them impoverished to the point they were "uncollectible."

The Offer in Compromise Program, in contrast, provides a realistic way for the IRS to bring in revenue it otherwise would never collect, or at least not efficiently collect, while giving the taxpayer a fresh start.

The IRS's new attitude toward OICs is best summarized in its own policy statement.

"The Service will accept an Offer in Compromise when it is unlikely that the tax liability can be collected in full and the amount offered reasonably reflects collection potential. An Offer in Compromise is a legitimate alternative to declaring a case as currently not collectible or to a protracted installment agreement. The goal is to achieve collection of what is potentially collectible at the earliest possible time and at the least cost to the government.

In cases where an Offer in Compromise appears to be a viable solution to a tax delinquency, the Service employee assigned to the case will discuss the compromise alternative with the taxpayer and, when necessary, assist in preparing the required forms. The taxpayer will be responsible for initiating the first specific proposal for compromise.

The success of the compromise program will be assured only if taxpayers make adequate compromise proposals consistent with their ability to pay and the Service makes prompt and reasonable decisions. Taxpayers are expected to provide reasonable documentation to verify their ability to pay. The ultimate goal is a compromise which is in the best interest of both the taxpayer and the Service. Acceptance of an adequate offer will also result in creating, for the taxpayer, an expectation of and a fresh start toward compliance with all future filing and payment requirements."

The OIC program is detailed in the Appendix. While this and the following chapters highlight the law's key provisions, do turn to the Appendix for more complete and thorough information about the program.

WHO CAN BENEFIT FROM THE OFFER IN COMPROMISE PROGRAM?

Any taxpayer can file an Offer in Compromise. This includes:

- individuals
- married couples
- incorporated businesses

- partnerships
- non-profit organizations
- receivers
- trustees of trusts
- executors of estates

In sum, any person or entity that can in any way incur a federal tax liability can file an Offer in Compromise to settle that liability. That right also extends to the taxpayer's duly authorized agent or representative.

WHAT TAXES CAN BE COMPROMISED?

Just as any taxpayer can file an OIC, the OIC program compromises virtually any personal, estate or business tax, including:

- personal income taxes
- corporate income taxes
- estate taxes
- unemployment taxes
- withholding and employment taxes
- road taxes

These, of course, are taxes most commonly owed by taxpayers.

The IRS can further compromise any civil or criminal case related to the tax laws. It can compromise not only the tax but also all penalties and interest.

Nor does it matter how old the tax may be. The Offer in Compromise may extend to old taxes on which collection has been suspended, recent taxes currently placed for collection, or taxes for the present year which have not even been assessed. You may also combine the various tax obligations, regardless of tax type or age, into one Offer in Compromise. Finally, you can compromise taxes, regardless of the amount.

WHEN YOU CAN COMPROMISE YOUR TAXES

There are only two circumstances when an Offer in Compromise will be considered by the IRS.

1) When the taxpayer is unable to pay the full tax liability and it is doubtful that the tax, penalty and interest can be fully collected through the collection process within the foreseeable future ("doubt of collectibility cases").

2) Where there is doubt about the taxpayer's tax liability ("doubt of liability cases").

A case may involve both doubt of collectibility *and* liability.

Compromises of civil liability do not compromise criminal liability in the same case, and vice versa. Criminal liability may be compromised if: 1) It involves a regulatory provision of the Internal Revenue Code or associated statutes and, 2) if the violations are not premeditated with the intent to defraud.

WHAT YOU MUST PAY THE IRS

IRS policy is to accept an OIC only when it is in its best interests – as well as that of the taxpayer.

In doubt of collectibility cases, the IRS will consider these three questions:

1) Could the IRS collect more from you (through seizure of assets or wages) than you are offering? You must convince the IRS that it's more cost-effective for the IRS to accept your offer rather than enforce collection.

2) Would the IRS be better off to wait for some future date when your financial position may improve? Keep in mind that the IRS will consider your possible *future* wealth as well as your *present* wealth.

3) Would the general public believe that accepting your offer was incorrect and improper?

Answer "no" to each of these questions and your offer stands a very good chance of being approved.

Many OICs are settled for literally "pennies on the dollar," but this does not suggest that the IRS works on the "something is better than nothing" principle. The IRS has ten years to collect – unless you discharge the taxes in bankruptcy – and the IRS frequently takes the chance it will collect more *someday* rather than settle for too little *today*.

HOW THE COMPROMISED AMOUNT IS PAID

You can pay the offered amount:

• In one lump sum payment – upon acceptance of the OIC or a specified time thereafter.

• In installments, but usually not beyond five years.

• Through a combination of a lump sum payment and installments.

You must also submit a small refundable deposit with the OIC. The IRS may additionally ask for collateral agreements that obligate you to pay a portion of your future income or grant to the IRS other concessions. These agreements will be discussed in greater detail.

THREE MORE KEY POINTS IN AN OFFER IN COMPROMISE

Your Offer in Compromise also commits you to:

- Comply with all terms and conditions of the agreement.
- Give the IRS your future tax refunds to cover those unpaid taxes not compromised.
- Comply with all IRS requirements (timely tax filings and payments) for five years.

If you fail on any of these points, the IRS can rescind the OIC agreement and collect the balance due on the original tax liability or that balance due under your OIC.

The IRS takes OIC compliance quite seriously. Many OICs come from chronic tax delinquents and scofflaws, and OICs are not intended to encourage people to disregard the tax laws. The aim of the OIC program is to help troubled taxpayers get back on a straight track with the IRS – if they can stay on a straight track. This explains why the IRS quickly revokes OICs when the taxpayer continues to violate the tax laws.

REQUIREMENTS FOR FILING YOUR OIC

Filing an OIC requires you to complete and submit to the IRS:

- Form 656 *Offer in Compromise*
- Form 433-A *or* 433-B *Collection Information Statement*

With these forms you also submit your deposit and any additional documents that support your case. These forms are contained in the Appendix.

For an OIC to be considered, all tax returns due from you must be filed. You will want your delinquent tax returns filed so you can include *all* outstanding tax obligations in your OIC. This includes not only income taxes but also other outstanding tax liabilities, such as withholding taxes due from a business.

OICs AND CONTINUED COLLECTION

Filing an Offer in Compromise does not automatically suspend IRS collection. However, the IRS usually does not continue collection if you have submitted a reasonable offer. The IRS *will* continue to enforce collection if it appears you are using the OIC only to delay collection or fraudulently transfer your assets or in some way diminish the IRS's ability to collect. Notwithstanding a filed offer, the IRS will file a lien against your property and *will not* release the lien until your OIC has been fully paid.

ADVANTAGES AND DISADVANTAGES OF AN OIC

This overview of the Offer in Compromise Program should help you determine whether an OIC is *your* best solution to your tax problems.

The obvious advantage of the OIC is that it gives you the chance to begin your financial life anew without pressing tax claims. While you must pay the IRS something, this amount may represent a very small fraction of what you owe. The OIC provides a systematic and rational way for you and the IRS to agree on a fair, equitable and realistic way for you to end your tax difficulties.

There are several small disadvantages to an OIC:

- An accepted OIC is public record for one year. Anyone can examine considerable personal information about you and your finances. Such disclosures may hurt you in the future. Unaccepted offers remain confidential and are not public record.

- Filing the OIC extends the 10-year statute of limitations for collecting taxes one additional year plus the time the OIC is under IRS review. This extension occurs even if your OIC is rejected. This can be a disadvantage as OICs frequently take a year or two for the IRS to review. This is particularly true when amended OICs are filed. If you offer installment payments, this added year doesn't begin until your final payment is made.

- An OIC also requires you to agree not to contest in court nor appeal the amount of your tax liability *if* your offer is accepted. But this would become a disadvantage only if the OIC was later rescinded by the IRS because *you* violated the agreement, *and* the IRS tried to collect the original disputed amount.

- You will lose all tax overpayments (refunds) for all future tax periods, including the current year, to the extent such application of refunds is necessary to pay the uncompromised liability. Even without the OIC, the IRS could automatically offset and apply these refunds to your tax liability so this is not a true disadvantage.

- Finally, the OIC process requires you to fully disclose to the IRS your entire financial history. This, however, is no more information than is provided for an installment agreement. If your offer is rejected, the IRS *will* know more about your assets, and your disclosures may even prompt an IRS audit; however, this seldom occurs as a result of an OIC.

The opportunity to end your tax problems on terms you can afford should clearly outweigh the several disadvantages of an Offer in Compromise. The Offer in Compromise Program is an opportunity every troubled taxpayer must seriously consider!

PLANNING YOUR OFFER

The success of your OIC rests on your ability to propose an offer that is:

1.   Acceptable to the IRS, and

2.   Within your ability to pay.

The IRS is very strict when considering the adequacy of an offer on doubt of collectibility cases. An offer viewed as adequate and fair by the average taxpayer may not be acceptable to the IRS.

As an overview, an Offer in Compromise must represent the taxpayer's *maximum* capacity to pay. This means all that can be reasonably collected from the taxpayer's equity in assets and income, whether present or prospective. This also includes amounts that may be recoverable through transferee assessment, as well as exempt assets beyond the reach of the government and other income, such as inheritances, available to the taxpayer.

ESTIMATING YOUR MAXIMUM CAPACITY TO PAY

In doubt of collectibility cases, the IRS focuses on your maximum capacity to pay. This is unlike doubt of liability cases where your offer must be based on the estimated degree of liability rather than the collectibility of what you owe.

In determining your maximum capacity to pay, decide first whether your offer at least equals the quick sale value of your assets.

The quick sale value is that amount that can be realized from the sale of an asset when financial or other pressures force the taxpayer to sell quickly.

For offer purposes, the taxpayer's equity in assets represents the quick sale value of an asset less those encumbrances which have priority over the federal tax lien.

The "quick sale" value is a unique method of appraisal used almost exclusively in the OIC program. This method recognizes the taxpayer and the IRS are in opposition and must negotiate a middle ground valuation.

The two typical appraisal methods are fair market value and forced liquidation value. The first, the fair market value, is the price between a willing seller and willing buyer for an asset reasonably marketed over a sufficient period of time. This is normally the maximum price obtainable for the asset. The second, liquidation value, represents what the IRS can get from a distress sale of the taxpayer's assets. This usually means a public auction. The "quick sale," then, is a compromise between a low liquidation value and the high fair market value. Obviously, a variety of values within this range can be adopted by the IRS and taxpayer and often are. The negotiation process thus involves you and the IRS reaching agreement on asset valuations. However, when making the offer, the taxpayer should use liquidation values but expect the IRS to modify the valuation upwards to a quick sale value.

There is no one formula to compute the quick sale value of an asset. Quick sale values vary depending upon supply and demand, availability of financing, the local economy and even the time of year. Unusual or hard to sell assets may have an exceptionally low quick sale value. These variables encourage the IRS to use considerable discretion when negotiating asset valuations with the taxpayer, and those values can be quite low if the taxpayer knows how to bargain effectively. The IRS will not normally set a quick sale value below 70 percent of the fair market value, but a lower value can be accepted when the lower value can be shown to be in the best interests of the IRS. An example of this is hazardous waste property which makes the property difficult, if not impossible, to sell.

HOW TO VALUE SPECIAL ASSETS

Certain assets present special valuation problems. Use these IRS guidelines when evaluating:

- **Joint ownership property:**

  If you own property with others, your offer must reflect the value of your interest in the property. Where a taxpayer owns property as a tenant by the entirety with an innocent (no tax liability) spouse, the IRS considers the taxpayer's interest to be no more than 50 percent and usually as low as 20 percent of the overall value of the property. Twenty percent is the amount that should be offered because the IRS will have difficulty reaching assets owned as tenants by the entirety. Joint tenancy and tenancy in common properties are normally valued on the full basis of the taxpayer's interest in the property because the IRS has full recourse to these ownership interests.

- **Pensions:**

   Pension plans also present special valuation problems. The IRS manual suggests the following guideline for valuing a taxpayer's pension plan:

   1) "Where under the terms of employment, a taxpayer is required to contribute a percentage of his/her gross earnings to a retirement plan and the amount contributed, plus any increments cannot be withdrawn until separation, retirement, demise, etc., this asset will considered as having no realizable equity.

   2) If the taxpayer is within five years of retirement (including early retirement) and the plan permits the taxpayer to take the pension in a lump sum, a collateral agreement must be secured whereby the taxpayer agrees to request the lump sum and to pay over to the Service the amount of the lump sum when received. This is required because if the taxpayer had access to the funds at the time of submitting the offer, the full amount would have been considered an asset and therefore payable in full as part of the offer.

   3) Where the taxpayer is not required, as a condition of employment, to participate in a pension plan, but voluntarily elects to do so, the realizable equity for compromise purposes shall be the gross amount in the taxpayer's plan reduced by the employer's contributions. However, in these situations each case should stand on its own merits.

   4) If the taxpayer is permitted to borrow up to the full amount of his/her equity in a plan, this should be taken into consideration in the computation of realizable equity.

   5) The current value of property deposited in an Individual Retirement Account (IRA) or Keogh Act Plan Account should be considered in the computation of realizable equity. Cash deposits should be included at full value. If assets other than cash are invested (e.g., stock, mutual funds), the IRA should be valued at the quick sale value, less expenses. The penalty for early withdrawal should be subtracted in computing net realizable equity." [IRC § 57(10)8.4.]

Because negotiations concerning the terms and requirements of pension plans will require extensive information from the employer, you should obtain this information as soon as possible.

Recent Supreme Court decisions protect pensions from creditors and this would bar the IRS from seizure of your pension, but the IRS will nevertheless take it into account for purposes of your OIC.

- **Exempt assets:**

  Other exempt assets, like pensions, are also technically protected from the IRS, but the IRS argues that since the taxpayer has access to them, they should be in the equation of what should be paid the IRS. This seems to contravene the intent in legislating these assets as exempt; however, it is IRS policy to count them. From a strategy viewpoint, you should exclude your pension and other exempt assets (listed in Chapter 2) from your offer. Let the IRS demand they be included.

- **Closely owned corporations:**

  Taxpayers who own family owned corporations or unincorporated businesses will find them particularly difficult to value.

  While a taxpayer should argue the value of the business equals the liquidation value of its assets less outstanding liabilities, the IRS believes an offer should reflect the company's "going concern value" rather than the liquidation value of its assets.

  To obtain a quick sale value of your business that will be acceptable to the IRS usually requires a professional appraisal. A written estimate of this value may be obtained from a local business broker if you own a small business. Larger companies should be appraised by a certified business appraiser. For the names of certified appraisers in your area, call the Institute for Business Appraisers at (407) 732-3202.

- **Jewelry and Collectibles:**

  The IRS will want to inspect your home for art, antiques, jewelry, coin and stamp collections and other collectibles. If these assets have a value above $1,000, they too should be professionally appraised.

- **Your home:**

  It is not difficult to obtain a quick sale valuation on your home. Get several written appraisals from local real estate brokers and use the *lowest* appraisal.

OTHER FACTORS THE IRS CONSIDERS

While there is no formal IRS policy on these points, the IRS does consider factors beyond the quick sale value of your assets when measuring your net worth and your maximum capacity to pay.

- Do you have a close, wealthy relative, particularly an innocent spouse who is not responsible for your taxes? The IRS may want you to borrow what you can.

- Do you own exempt or unreachable property that can be sold or borrowed against to increase your offer?

- Do you have property that may rapidly escalate in value?

- Do friends or relatives hold mortgages against your property? The IRS will want you to ask them to accept less than the amount owed so the equity available to the IRS can be increased.

- Do you have recently transferred property that the IRS considers fraudulent?

- Do you anticipate an inheritance?

HOW TO MINIMIZE YOUR NET WORTH

You want to show the lowest possible asset values because that is how the IRS mainly evaluates the adequacy of your offer. How do you minimize those values? Try these five strategies:

1) *Use liquidation values rather than quick sale values.* Yes, the IRS may want to use quick sale values – but make the IRS fight for the point. Submit your offer based on liquidation values.

2) *Get two or three appraisals on major assets and use the* lowest *appraisal.* You have no obligation to show the IRS the highest appraisals, so build your case on the *lowest* appraisals. If the IRS wants to challenge your appraisals, it can hire its own appraiser.

3) *Deduct from the liquidation values all costs and expenses of liquidation.* Will the IRS need to insure the property, protect it from vandalism, or heat it? What will it cost to advertise the property for sale? What about auctioneer fees? These costs can reach 20 percent or more of the liquidation value of the property. Deduct these costs.

4) *Use convincing evidence to support your low value.* For instance, have comparable homes in your area been recently foreclosed upon? What did *they* sell for? What is the assessed value of your property for real estate tax purposes? Is this assessed value lower than your appraisals?

- *Use photos to show defects in the asset or to substantiate its poor condition.* A home, boat or car may vary considerably in value based on its physical condition. Let pictures tell the story and have inspection reports confirm poor mechanical condition.

- *Have you tried to sell the asset?* Can you show you were unsuccessful in obtaining a higher price than the amount used in your offer?

5) *Exclude from your offer exempt assets and pensions.* Another point worth repeating. You know the IRS will want exempt assets included, but let the IRS press the point. Quite frequently it won't.

HOW TO FIGURE YOUR NET WORTH

It is not difficult to calculate your net worth. Use the *Net Worth Worksheet* in this chapter.

Notice that the worksheet allows you to estimate your net worth based upon both the quick sale value *and* the liquidation value of your assets. While you will base your offer on liquidation value, be prepared to also demonstrate your net worth based on the quick sale value of these assets if the IRS so insists.

List all assets on the worksheet, but when planning your offer *exclude*:

- exempt assets

- protected assets, such as those in irrevocable trusts or offshore havens

- assets not listed on the *Collection Information Statement* (Form 433-A)

- assets owned entirely by your spouse

WILL YOUR INCOME LET YOU PAY MORE?

Net worth is only one test. The IRS also considers the taxpayer's present or prospective income or earning capacity, or in the case of a business, its present and prospective profits.

Income analysis:

The IRS evaluates *all* sources of taxpayer income and deducts those expenses that are reasonable and necessary. Those expenses are called the "exclusions." The difference between your total income and exclusions is added to what you can pay the IRS toward your offer.

Since the IRS will want to know about every source of income, use the *Income/Expense Worksheet*, which also includes your spouse's income. The IRS may not have a claim against your spouse but will expect your spouse to contribute to the common expenses, such as rent and utilities, thus leaving you more disposable income for your offer.

The IRS will also check whether your income matches your earning power, considering your age, education, occupation, health and experience. If you are, for instance, a physician earning two-thirds less than similar physicians, then why? If your income dropped from a steady $80,000 a year to $30,000, the IRS will again ask why.

The IRS also estimates your prospective income. If your income may substantially increase, the IRS may want a collateral agreement to share in that increase. This will be discussed in greater detail later.

Your goal is to underscore to the IRS why your earning capacity is low and limited in the future.

- Is your health poor? If so, fully document your medical problems. Will your illness become progressively worse and further decrease your ability to work or force you to work fewer hours? Does it limit the type of work you can do? Is it a psychiatric problem? How does that translate into decreased earnings? Detailed and persuasive medical reports are critical to your OIC.

- Do you work in a distressed business or occupation? Show the IRS why your job or business has an unstable income or future. If you own a business, then poor financial statements will be helpful. Do you plan to change jobs? Submit your OIC while you are unemployed. Remember: Poverty is an ally when you negotiate with the IRS.

- Do you have family problems? There are endless factors the IRS can consider, and contrary to popular belief, the IRS can be quite understanding and very lenient with taxpayers who have problems in life other than their tax troubles. You may, for example, be going through an emotionally draining divorce. Perhaps you have a sick spouse or child. If situations within your family impair your ability to earn money, then let the IRS know about them.

- Do you have criminal problems or serious lawsuits against you? Do you face the possible loss of a professional or occupational license? This shows economic instability which can also convince the IRS to accept less.

- What about your age? The IRS seldom demands installment payments or collateral agreements from taxpayers over 60. Some IRS officers show age consideration to taxpayers over 50.

Expense analysis:

"Reasonable expenses" or the "exclusion" you are allowed must always be aggressively negotiated with the IRS. The IRS will want you to survive on a "bare bones" budget. You must insist upon a reasonable living standard, which means enough money to:

- cover all present expenses.
- pay foreseeable future expenses.
- cover inflation.
- provide a margin of error for contingencies and change in circumstances.

In your calculations you must include *all* your expenses. The IRS will uncover all sources of income but forget many expenses. The *Collection Information Statement* includes only the basic expenses and ignores those smaller expenses we all have and must pay from our incomes.

That's why you must use the *Income/Expense Worksheet* in this chapter to insure no expense is overlooked. Also go through your own records. What other expenses do you have that are not covered in the worksheet?

Your goal is to have your expenses equal or exceed your income, so you can show no excess income available to the IRS. The IRS, in turn, will challenge many expenses to lower the exclusion and thus raise the income available for collection.

For your offer use the highest expenses you can reasonably justify. Even a six-figure income can have matching expenses, so few taxpayers should have trouble showing expenses to match their incomes.

The IRS will try to disallow some expenses as unnecessary and decrease as excessive other expenses. Be firm. Stand strong. Defend your expenses. Don't let the IRS intimidate you into a life of poverty. To make your strongest case, be prepared:

- Why is each expense necessary? Are there less costly alternatives?
- What have you historically spent on each expense? Can your records prove it?
- Have you included foreseeable expenses? What about inflation? Do you have sufficient reserves for contingencies? You need a margin for error because you do not want to default on your OIC.

Unless you are a very high (usually a six-figure) income taxpayer, "income" should not be considered in your offer. Base your offer instead *only* on the net value of your assets. Let the IRS raise the question of income and why it should be included in your offer.

HOW YOU WILL PAY THE IRS

The total amount you offer the IRS may be paid in the following ways:

- a lump sum payment and/or
- installments.

The IRS wants to get paid quickly, so it may favor a lower lump sum over a larger offer paid over time. The IRS wants to close its cases and not spend its time monitoring long-term installment plans.

If possible, satisfy this important IRS objective and pay whatever you can as an immediate lump sum payment – while still paying as little as possible.

The IRS will rightfully demand a down payment to match what you can generate from your assets. For instance, the IRS will expect you to:

- Liquidate all cash, savings, CDs, cash value insurance and other easily cash-converted assets.
- Borrow whatever you can on any assets with equity – such as a home or car.
- Sell all luxury items – such as a vacation home, boat or recreational vehicle to extract all the equity from these non-necessities.

Turn as many assets as you can into cash *before* you submit your OIC. This shows the IRS you are serious about settling your tax bill. A larger down payment can also significantly reduce your overall settlement, and you will find it cheaper to borrow from other lenders rather than pay the IRS interest. Finally, if the IRS does *not* settle, you will want your net worth in the form of cash rather than easily seized tangible assets.

An installment arrangement can be used to pay "net worth" that cannot be sold or refinanced. Installment payments usually are used to cover disposable income available to the IRS.

Installment offers should not exceed five years. The IRS discourages longer agreements. Offer a payment schedule that coincides with your cash flow or payroll dates, thus reducing the chance of default under your OIC.

You can always discount an installment obligation through prepayment. For instance, if you owe the IRS $500 a month for the next three years, the IRS will accept something less than $18,000 – if you pay today. Just as you must pay interest on your installment payments, the IRS will offer you a discount for prepayment. Discounts of 20 percent to 50 percent are not unusual – particularly if the IRS thinks you may default on your OIC and cannot fully recover the balance owed.

COLLATERAL AGREEMENTS

Collateral agreements should not be part of your offer to the IRS; however, they are frequently required by the IRS and then become a part of the overall OIC settlement.

There are several types of collateral agreements, which may be used individually or collectively.

The IRS may require a collateral agreement if:

- You expect a substantial increase in income, an inheritance or investments likely to significantly increase in value.

- You are a corporate taxpayer with a net operating loss carry-forward.

- You are a business owner with accounts receivable.

- You own real estate or investment property with a "high" basis.

- You owe the taxes together with others, who are not parties to your offer.

Future Income Agreements

The future income agreement is the most common collateral agreement. It obligates the taxpayer to pay to the IRS a graduated percentage of future income *above* a negotiated annual income exclusion. The future income agreement normally covers five years. This should not be confused with an installment agreement, which represents disposable current income. The collateral agreement involves substantial *increases* in income.

Obviously, you must not portray too bright a future. Poor health, advancing age, generally declining income or business conditions, high future bills (college tuitions or medical costs) may convince the IRS your financial future is not too bright and a *Future Income Agreement* is unnecessary.

Future Income Agreements are becoming less frequently demanded as the IRS dislikes long-term arrangements. As with an installment agreement, you can "buy-out" a collateral agreement for a lump sum payment, often for a nominal amount if your future income looks bleak.

Future Income Agreements can also apply to corporate taxpayers, but it is usually difficult to estimate the right "future income" threshold for corporations because neither the IRS nor the business can easily predict future profits, cash flow, the capital needed for growth or the contingencies that strike every business.

HOW TO SETTLE WITH THE IRS FOR PENNIES ON THE DOLLAR

Waiver of Losses and Investment Credits Agreements

This agreement applies only to businesses that agree not to offset net operating losses or unused investment credits against future profits. This increases their future taxes and profits.

Waiver of Bad Debt Agreements

This agreement similarly requires businesses not to deduct uncollectible accounts receivable as bad debts. This again increases taxable income.

Reduction of Basis Agreements

If you own real estate, investment property, or other valuable tangible assets, the IRS may have you reduce the "taxable basis." When you sell these assets you will then incur a higher capital gain tax.

Co-Obligor Agreements

This agreement gives the IRS the right to continue collection against other liable taxpayers not discharged under your OIC. Some state laws automatically also discharge other taxpayer-obligers without this type of agreement. Common examples of this situation are when some, but not all, business partners seek to settle a 100 percent penalty or when ex-spouses attempt to separately settle a joint tax liability.

HOW TO PUT YOUR OFFER TOGETHER

Let's review the five steps in planning your offer:

Step 1. Get your information.

Assemble all your financial records, appraisals, deeds, bills of sale, mortgages and other documents you and the IRS will review.

Step 2. Calculate your net worth in assets.

Use the *Net Worth Worksheet* to list *all* of your assets. Estimate your net worth in each item based upon its liquidation value less all prior encumbrances and liquidation expenses. Assign fractional values if you co-own property. Obtain appraisals to confirm the value of key assets.

Step 3. Determine your disposable income.

Use the *Income/Expense Worksheet*. Give yourself every benefit of the doubt so you eliminate excess income.

Step 4. Add your net worth and disposable income.

Your total offer should equal both 1) your net worth (from the *Net Worth Worksheet*) and any net disposable income projected five years ahead. This sum represents the **maximum** amount offer to settle all taxes you owe the IRS.

Step 5. Calculate how this amount will be paid.

Offer to pay as much as possible upon acceptance by selling unessential items and borrowing against other assets. Installments necessary to pay the balance, plus interest, should be paid as soon as possible – but in no event beyond five years.

SOME CASE EXAMPLES

Case No. 1

Mary and Sam, both in their early 70s, owed the IRS about $45,000. Having filed bankruptcy several years earlier because of a failed business, they had only a small equity in a modest home and lived on Sam's $1,200 a month pension.

Because they had only enough income to live on (Sam had health problems and couldn't work), Mary and Sam decided to offer the IRS $4,500 to settle their $45,000 tax liability. They correctly reasoned they had too little equity in their home for the IRS to seize it, and after nearly a year the IRS accepted the $4,500 cash offer.

Case No. 2

Tony, a single 28-year-old entrepreneur, owed the IRS $50,000 covering two years' income taxes. Tony's major assets included a sports car with $10,000 equity and 50 percent interest in a sailboat worth about $40,000.

When the IRS pressed for payment, Tony filed an OIC offering $5,000 down and $2,000 a year for the next five years. This offer was rejected by the IRS, which insisted upon at least $25,000 cash plus a collateral agreement whereby the IRS would get 50 percent of Tony's income above $60,000 a year over the next five years.

Tony then amended his offer to $15,000 down and a collateral agreement of 50 percent of earnings over $50,000. After several more amended OICs, Tony and the IRS finally settled for $20,000 down, $2,000 a year for the next five years and a collateral agreement of 50 percent of all income over $60,000 a year for five years.

Case No. 3

Harry and Lois owed the IRS $65,000 from a failed business venture. Harry, now employed as a machinist, and Lois, a nurse, together earned about $60,000 a year.

Their assets included their home worth $80,000, but with a $40,000 mortgage. Their other assets were worth less than $10,000.

The couple offered the IRS a total of $40,000, payable with $15,000 down (from second mortgage refinancing) and $5,000 a year for five years. The IRS refused since their assets would possibly allow the IRS to recover more through seizure.

On appeal, Harry and Lois pointed out that they had five children, one with serious medical problems. This persuaded the IRS appeals officer to accept their original offer, but only after several threatened seizures by the IRS. The appeals officer agreed with Harry and Lois that the IRS could *possibly* get more through enforced collection, but that under the circumstances the offer was fair to both parties.

Case No. 4

Sally, a retired 68-year-old schoolteacher, owed the IRS $16,000 arising from some disallowances of deductions on her tax return.

Sally had no assets except for her pension, household furniture, a used car and less than $500 in savings. Sally's offer to settle for $500 was rejected and the IRS officer suggested instead that Sally be classified as "temporarily uncollectible" because of her negligible assets and income. Sally never again heard from the IRS.

Case No. 5

Through numerous business adventures and misadventures, Greg ran up a $600,000 tax liability.

Greg's assets consisted of a $700,000 home with only a small mortgage, a fully paid Cadillac and investments worth $400,000.

Greg proposed to settle for $100,000 with $50,000 paid upon acceptance and $50,000 paid over five years. The IRS summarily rejected this as frivolous considering Greg's financial situation. He then amended his OIC to $150,000 in installments with the same $50,000 down. The IRS insisted upon the full $600,000 because Greg had the assets to fully satisfy the tax and there were no mitigating circumstances to either settle for less or accept payment over time. When Greg failed to satisfy the tax obligation, the IRS seized and sold his home and several other assets and fully collected the tax.

CHAPTER 5 • PLANNING YOUR OFFER

Case No. 6

Martha and John, both aged 55, struggled with their small restaurant that ran up $100,000 in unpaid withholding taxes.

Their restaurant had negligible value. Their personal assets consisted of a $150,000 home with a $90,000 mortgage, $10,000 equity in two cars and $20,000 in other miscellaneous assets. Working at the restaurant full time, Martha and John together earned only $50,000 a year.

Martha and John figured they could borrow $20,000 against their home, refinance another $6,000 on their autos and sell some of their remaining assets to raise another $10,000. This would give Martha and John about $36,000 toward the taxes. They figured they could scrimp by on $30,000 to $35,000 a year, and thus pay the IRS about $5,000 a year from their future net earnings. This, they proposed, would be paid over three years for a total settlement of $51,000 plus interest. The IRS accepted.

After the first year, Martha and John lost their business and their earning dropped to $30,000 a year. They then amended their original OIC and offered the IRS an immediate $4,000 to discharge the remaining $10,000 due under the OIC. Because Martha and John had acted in good faith to resolve their tax problems, the IRS accepted this second compromise, despite Martha and John having sufficient assets to satisfy the taxes outstanding.

Case No. 7

Pedro, a victim of "tax shelter deal-gone-wrong," owed the IRS about $200,000.

His only asset was his condominium worth $90,000. Moreover, Pedro had only sporadic earnings as a chef because he suffered from recurrent manic depression. He seldom earned more than he needed to live on.

Pedro offered and the IRS accepted $50,000 to settle. Pedro would raise this money by refinancing his condo with a 20-year mortgage. Pedro knew he could manage these payments and the IRS felt the $50,000 was close to what they would get through a forced sale of the condo. Considering Pedro's health problems and his sporadic earning, the IRS did not press for future installments or a collateral agreement.

DOUBT OF LIABILITY OFFERS

Unlike "doubt of collectibility" cases, offers based on "doubt of liability" center on whether the IRS can sustain a claim against the taxpayer. This involves a careful assessment of the applicable law or the facts of the case – depending upon whether the dispute involves one primarily of law or facts.

The IRS can usually assess its chances of winning a disputed tax case with considerable accuracy. Therefore, an offer that does not coincide with the IRS case assessment is likely to be turned down.

It is almost always necessary to employ a tax professional to assess the merits of a tax case and suggest an appropriate offer. Moreover, the tax professional may correctly recommend that instead of an OIC to resolve the issue (invariably turned down by the IRS), the taxpayer instead pay the tax and then start refund litigation or even go to tax court where the taxpayer's odds are greatly improved.

INCOME / EXPENSE WORKSHEET

1. INCOME
List monthly income of (both spouses, if married). Disclose all sources of income. Income should be monthly averaged when received in different periods.

	HUSBAND	WIFE		HUSBAND	WIFE
Salary/Wages	$ _____	_____	Veterans Adm. Payments	$ _____	_____
Commissions	$ _____	_____	Royalties	$ _____	_____
Tips	$ _____	_____	Disability/Workers Comp	$ _____	_____
Dividends	$ _____	_____	Unemployment Benefits	$ _____	_____
Interest	$ _____	_____	Public Assistance Payments	$ _____	_____
Alimony	$ _____	_____	Other income	$ _____	_____
Child Support	$ _____	_____		$ _____	_____
Annuity Income	$ _____	_____		$ _____	_____
Pension Income	$ _____	_____		$ _____	_____
Social Security	$ _____	_____		$ _____	_____
Business Profits	$ _____	_____	**TOTALS**	$ _____	_____

2. EXPENSES
Use this Expense list to complete your monthly expenses. It is more complete than the IRS Form 433A. This information can be summarized and included on Form 433A, or it can be attached to the Form. Use monthly averages.

Housing			Eyeglasses	$ _____
Rent or Mortgage payment	$ _____		Other	$ _____
Second Mortgage payment	$ _____		**Retirement**	
Repairs and Maintenance	$ _____		Pensions	$ _____
Electricity and gas	$ _____		IRA	$ _____
Water and Sewer	$ _____		Keogh's	$ _____
Telephone & Cable	$ _____		Other	$ _____
Rubbish Removal	$ _____		**Installment Payments**	
Other	$ _____		Motor Vehicle	$ _____
Food			Credit card/Rental charges	$ _____
Groceries	$ _____		Student/Personal Loan	$ _____
Meals out	$ _____		Other installment payments	$ _____
School lunches	$ _____		**Miscellaneous Expenses**	
Other	$ _____		Child support	$ _____
Clothing			Alimony	$ _____
New clothing	$ _____		Child care & day care	$ _____
Laundry & cleaning	$ _____		Tuition	$ _____
Other	$ _____		Accountant	$ _____
Transportation			Attorney	$ _____
Public Transportation	$ _____		Personal items	$ _____
Gas	$ _____		Charitable contributions	$ _____
Repairs	$ _____		Entertainment	$ _____
Parking and tolls	$ _____		Recreation	$ _____
Other	$ _____		Subscriptions	$ _____
Medical			Household products	$ _____
Doctors & Dentist	$ _____		Other	$ _____
Prescriptions	$ _____		**TOTAL MONTHLY EXPENSES**	$ _____
Hospital bills	$ _____			

NET WORTH WORKSHEET

Use this worksheet to determine your equity (or net worth) in the various assets you own. If you own only a partial interest in that asset then use that proportionate share. Use a 20% value for property held as tenants by the entirety.

	Quick Sale Value	Liquidation Value	Less Encumbrances	Equity At Quick Sale	Equity At Liquidation Value
Home	$_____	_____	_____	_____	_____
Vacation Home	$_____	_____	_____	_____	_____
Rental Property	$_____	_____	_____	_____	_____
Vacant Land	$_____	_____	_____	_____	_____
Farm	$_____	_____	_____	_____	_____
Time Share	$_____	_____	_____	_____	_____
Automobile	$_____	_____	_____	_____	_____
Boats	$_____	_____	_____	_____	_____
Profit sharing plans	$_____	_____	_____	_____	_____
Pension plans	$_____	_____	_____	_____	_____
Retirement accounts	$_____	_____	_____	_____	_____
Individuals Retirement Account	$_____	_____	_____	_____	_____
Life Insurance cash value	$_____	_____	_____	_____	_____
Checking and Saving accounts	$_____	_____	_____	_____	_____
Certificates of Deposit	$_____	_____	_____	_____	_____
Money Market Funds	$_____	_____	_____	_____	_____
Mutual Funds Annuities	$_____	_____	_____	_____	_____
Stocks and Bonds	$_____	_____	_____	_____	_____
Partnership Interests	$_____	_____	_____	_____	_____
Closely Held corporations	$_____	_____	_____	_____	_____
Trusts	$_____	_____	_____	_____	_____
Antiques	$_____	_____	_____	_____	_____
Art	$_____	_____	_____	_____	_____
China and Silver	$_____	_____	_____	_____	_____
Jewelry	$_____	_____	_____	_____	_____
Furs	$_____	_____	_____	_____	_____
Sporting or hobby equipment	$_____	_____	_____	_____	_____
Collections	$_____	_____	_____	_____	_____
Furniture and Furnishing	$_____	_____	_____	_____	_____
Mortgages and notes receivable	$_____	_____	_____	_____	_____
Contract rights	$_____	_____	_____	_____	_____
Liens and judgements held	$_____	_____	_____	_____	_____
Livestock and pets	$_____	_____	_____	_____	_____
Tax refunds due	$_____	_____	_____	_____	_____
Other	$_____	_____	_____	_____	_____
	$_____	_____	_____	_____	_____
Total	$_____	_____	_____	_____	_____

HOW TO PREPARE AND SUBMIT YOUR OFFER TO THE IRS

Read this chapter carefully *before* you complete and submit your OIC. Many OICs are returned or rejected, not because the offer was unacceptable, but because the forms were improperly or inadequately completed. Sloppy preparation only delays the process and encourages the IRS to press its collection efforts while you scramble to correct the problem under undue stress.

The OIC forms are comprehensive but not too difficult to prepare. The key is to answer each question *fully and truthfully*! The IRS will closely scrutinize and investigate each point, so false or incomplete statements are a bad idea. Even inadvertent errors can lead to serious civil or criminal fraud charges, and the IRS will automatically reject or rescind any OIC found to be materially incorrect, even if discovered years later.

ASSEMBLING YOUR DOCUMENTS

Begin by carefully assembling all your financial records. Don't guess or estimate amounts. Reconstruct your assets, liabilities, income and expenses from checks, deposits and other records. If your records were destroyed or lost then document the reason for their loss, such as with fire, police or other casualty reports. Bear in mind that IRS agents, like customs agents, have a keen sixth sense of when you're trying to hide something.

Later in this chapter you will see the various documents that may be requested by the IRS. Assemble these documents in advance. It's even proper to submit many of these documents with your OIC. Never give the IRS your originals, only submit copies.

You will need Form 656, *Offer in Compromise*. A blank copy is in the Appendix. You must submit with it a Form 433-A *Collection Information Statement for Individuals* or Form 433-B *Collection Information Statement for Business*, both also found in the Appendix. Before using them, make certain that they are the most current forms by calling the IRS at (800) 829-1040, or ask your IRS agent.

ENLIST THE IRS TO HELP YOU PREPARE YOUR OFFER

If an IRS agent has already been assigned to your case, you can request the agent's assistance in completing your forms. Do not be discouraged by an agent who suggests your OIC attempts will be unsuccessful. Whether your OIC succeeds is not the decision of the IRS collection officer but that of the Special Procedures staff which ultimately reviews your offer.

Moreover, you *do not want* the IRS officer to help you establish your offer. As mentioned in the prior chapter, the IRS officer will invariably urge you to offer more than you should. The chicken should not turn to the fox for comfort. All you want from the IRS officer is assistance in correctly completing the forms and recommendation to the Special Procedures staff that your OIC be accepted.

SEVEN STEPS FOR COMPLETING YOUR OFFER

There are seven key steps for completing the OIC documents:

1)   Form 656, *Offer in Compromise*, must be used to submit your offer. The form must be prepared in triplicate and filed in the district office of the Internal Revenue Service in your area.

2)   If you have been working with a specific service employee on your case, file the offer with that employee. You may make triplicate copies of Form 656 in this book (front and back) or obtain triplicate copy forms directly from the IRS. Form 433-A, *Collection Information Statement for Individuals* and/or Form 433-B, *Collection Information Statement for Business*, must accompany Form 656, If the offer is being submitted on the basis of doubt of collectibility. These forms are not needed on "doubt of liability" cases. For the offer to be considered, all blocks on Forms 433-A or 433-B must be completed. In those blocks that do not affect you indicate by writing "N/A" (not applicable). With Form 433-A and/or 433-B, you should submit documentation to verify values of assets, encumbrances and income and expense information listed on the collection statement.

3)   Your full name, address and taxpayer identification number must be entered at the top of Form 656. If this is a joint liability (husband and wife) and both wish to make an offer, both names must be shown. If you are singly liable for a tax liability (e.g. employment taxes) and at the same time jointly liable for another tax liability (e.g. income taxes) and only one person is submitting an offer, only one offer must be submitted. If you are singly liable for one tax liability and jointly liable for another and both joint parties are

submitting an offer, two (2) Forms 656 must be submitted, one (1) for the separate tax liability and one (1) for the joint tax liability. If you want to compromise both your personal taxes and business (if a corporation or partnership), you must make separate offers for each.

4) You must list all unpaid liabilities to be compromised in item (4) on Form 656. The type of tax and the period of the liability must be specifically identified. This includes:

- Income Tax
- Trust fund recovery (previously called 100-percent penalty)
- Withholding and federal insurance contribution taxes (social security)
- Federal unemployment tax
- Other taxes – may include estate tax, road tax, excise taxes, inheritance tax or any of the various federal taxes.

If you owe more than one type of tax, then list all the outstanding taxes on the form. If you need more space, then detail the taxes an a seperate page and attach it to the OIC.

Be certain to include **every** tax you could possibly owe the IRS. If it is not listed, it will not be compromised under the OIC.

5) The total amount you are offering to compromise (the liability) must be entered in item (5). The amount must not include any amount which has already been paid or collected on the liability. Generally the starting place for the amount you offer should be the amount shown in item 2 column (d) in Form 433-B or line 37 titled "Equity in Assets" on Form 433-A.

If any amount is to be paid on notice of acceptance of the offer or at any later date, you must include in item (5) as follows:

a) The amount deposited at the time of filing this offer.

b) Any amount deposited on a prior offer which is to be applied on this offer. (This does not include any amount you previously authorized the Service to apply directly to the tax liability).

c) The amount of any subsequent payment and the date on which each payment is to be made.

Example:

$30,000 with $5,000 deposited with the offer and $25,000 to be paid within ten (10) days from the date of acceptance.

Example:

$103,000, of which $13,000 is deposited with the offer and $10,000 is to be paid within ten (10) days from the date of acceptance and $10,000 paid on the 15th of each month following the month in which the offer is accepted.

The offer should be liquidated in the shortest time possible. Under no circumstances should the payment extend beyond five (5) years from the date of acceptance to the date of full payment. Interest is due at the prevailing Internal Revenue Code rate from the date of acceptance to the date of full payment.

6)   You must state in item (6) why the Service should accept your offer. Attach additional pages as necessary. It is legally sufficient to simply say, "Doubt of collectibility of the full amount of tax, interest and penalty owed," or "Doubt of liability." Where there is both doubt of liability and collectibility, then check both reasons.

7)   You must sign and date the offer in the lower right hand corner of Form 656. If you and your spouse are submitting the offer on a joint liability both must sign. If the offer is to be signed by a person other than the taxpayer, a valid power of attorney must be submitted with the offer.

UNDERSTAND WHAT YOU ARE SIGNING

While Form 656 is easy to complete, it does create a legally binding contract between you and the IRS and obligates you to certain conditions even if your offer is *not* accepted. Read the entire reverse side of the OIC.

In sum, it's key points provide:

•   That by your making the offer you agree that the IRS can retain all payments, or credits previously paid on the taxes to be compromised. Keep in mind that you cannot apply these earlier payments to what you agree to pay under the OIC. For this reason, you should never pay anything toward delinquent taxes unless it is part of an OIC or an installment agreement with the IRS.

•   Your offer automatically lets the IRS keep any future refunds not in excess of what you owe. But this is not significant as the IRS would offset and keep your refunds anyway. If your OIC is based on doubt of liability, then you should delete this provision.

•   That payments will usually first apply to taxes and penalties *before* interest. This is disadvantageous to you because interest is a deductible expense whereas penalties are not. This means you will have to wait for your final payments to take an interest deduction, assuming you shall pay in installments.

- That you will not contest the tax liability in court while the IRS is considering your OIC. Further, if you are making a deferred or installment offer, you must punctually make each payment or the IRS will: 1) sue for the balance due on the offer, or 2) sue for the full amount of the liability, less payments made, or 3) disregard the OIC and proceed with their collection remedies.

- That you agree to extend the ten-year statute of limitations on collection for one additional year plus the period of time the IRS spent considering your offer, including the time period installments have not been paid.

- That you understand the IRS is under no obligation to stop its collection efforts while your OIC is pending (although it generally does).

COMPLETING THE COLLATERAL AGREEMENT

The *Collateral Agreement* (Form 2261) is primarily used if you offer to pay the IRS a percentage of your future income.

The *Collateral Agreement* (Form 2261-B) also can be used to reduce the basis of assets. This means you will pay more taxes in the future and therefore add to what the government can recoup in addition to your compromise payment.

Collateral Agreement (Form 2261-C) is primarily used to waive net operating losses, capital losses and unused investment credits.

There are two points you should remember about collateral agreements:

1) Never submit a collateral agreement voluntarily. Even if you are willing to concede some points on a collateral agreement, you should let the IRS insist upon a collateral agreement.

2) Never sign a collateral agreement unless approved by a tax professional. These agreements can become quite technical and you will need a careful explanation about each point and what it means to you in financial terms.

Your offer documents, therefore, should initially include only:

- Form 656 *Offer in Compromise*
- Form 433-A *Collection Information* (individual), or
- Form 433-B *Collection Information* (business)
- Any supporting documents
- Your deposit

Do not submit:

- Collateral agreements
- Authorization to apply OIC deposit to liability

MAKING A DEPOSIT WITH YOUR OFFER

A small deposit with your offer shows good faith and is required. You will get your deposit refunded, without interest, if your offer is rejected.

What deposit is suggested? About five to ten percent of your total offer is a good yardstick. The larger the offer, the smaller the percentage. If money is scarce make a smaller deposit but offer to make your first installments sooner. Attach your deposit directly to Form 656. Keep in mind there is no *minimum* deposit. If you can afford only $500 or $1,000, then deposit that amount or whatever you can afford.

HOW THE IRS PROCESSES YOUR OIC

If the offer is for "doubt of collectibility" you may submit it directly to the collection division of the IRS. This will probably be through the IRS officer assigned to collect your overdue taxes.

Offers for "doubt of liability" are submitted to the examination division, not the collection division. You may, for instance, give the OIC to the tax auditor assigned to your case. It can be submitted any time during the audit period or anytime before a court determines it is duly owed.

Once the IRS receives your OIC, it will thoroughly search its computerized records to recap your tax history. What other taxes do you owe? What tax returns are still delinquent? Have you filed an OIC before? This review process takes about two or three months.

The IRS will simultaneously determine whether your offer is completed correctly and acceptable to process. What will the IRS look for?

- Does your OIC include your full name, address, social security or employer identification (EID) number?
- Is there a complete list of *all* outstanding taxes of *all* types? (Remember: it is your responsibility to determine your total unpaid tax obligation.)
- Is your offer specific as to the amount of your offer and how it will be paid?
- Have you stated why the IRS should accept your offer? The more detail you provide, the more convincing your case, however, a simple reason such as "I can't afford to pay," or "I have insufficient

assets or income to fully pay," is perfectly acceptable. It's always persuasive to explain *why* the IRS cannot collect more through normal collection procedures.

- Have you submitted fully completed and signed collection information statements (Forms 433-A or 433-B)?

- Are there proper signatures by each party submitting the offer? If someone is signing for you, does a proper power of attorney accompany the OIC, or was one previously filed with the IRS?

- Is there a deposit with the offer?

HOW THE IRS CHECKS YOUR FINANCES

With your OIC accepted for processing, the IRS will next thoroughly verify and investigate your OIC *and* your finances. The IRS does not work on blind trust. It goes to great effort to make certain that your representations are true.

Unless they are already submitted, the IRS will ask for these documents and records:

- Bank statements and canceled checks for the last 12 months.

- Documents relating to all real estate interests (deeds, mortgages, contracts, leases, real estate tax bills). The IRS will be particularly interested in your property appraisals and how you appraised your real estate for purposes of formulating your offer.

- Earnings records (pay stubs)

- Bank books (Savings, CDs)

- Insurance policies

- Copies of tax returns for the past three years. (The IRS can retrieve them if you don't have copies.)

- Titles and registrations for all vehicles (cars, trucks, boats, and planes).

- Stocks, bonds or other securities you own.

- Documents showing your debts and other obligations (mortgages, notes, bills, judgments, lawsuits, state or municipal tax claims). The IRS will specifically want to know their incurred dates, the original amount, present balance, how each debt is paid and the security pledged to each creditor.

Next the IRS will next closely investigate whether any assets or funds are held for you by a "straw." The agent will want to know what unlisted assets you recently owned and how and when you disposed of or transferred them by asking you these questions:

- Have you sold or transferred any real estate, vehicles, stocks, bonds or other assets within the past two years?

- Do you have access to a safe-deposit box?

- Are you a grantor, trustee or beneficiary of a trust?

- Are you an officer, director or stockholder in a business or corporation?

- Are you a plaintiff in a lawsuit?

- Do you have any insurance claims pending?

- Do you own any paintings, jewelry, fur coats, heirlooms or similar valuables?

- Does anyone owe you money?

- Is anyone holding money or other property on your behalf?

- Do you anticipate receiving an inheritance within the next year?

These same questions are sometimes answered by having you complete an *IRS Data Sheet*. Although similar to a *Collection Information Statement* Form 433-A or 433-B, the *Data Sheet* allows the IRS to more closely examine your finances from a slightly different perspective. By comparing answers, the IRS can better assess your truthfulness.

Finally, the IRS will verify all encumbrances against your property. To the extent an encumbrance decreases the equity available to the IRS, the IRS will question the validity of the debt. The IRS mostly inquires about recorded mortgages or security interests that have priority over their own lien. The IRS will also closely check the relationship between you and your creditor, the nature of the debt and whether there was good consideration for the mortgage.

If the IRS determines a mortgage is not "arms-length" or that an asset was fraudulently transferred, then the IRS will require you to increase your offer by an amount equal to the mortgage or the equity in the fraudulently transferred asset.

Because OICs are complex, expect more than one IRS agent to be involved in your case. For instance, the IRS Service Center will put together an *OIC Control Document* (Form 2515) containing your name, address, social security or EID number, the tax liabilities involved, terms of your offer, deposits received and a tax history transcript, which includes any prior offers. IRS investigators also may interview employees, friends, relatives and others who can verify the information the IRS relies upon to decide whether to accept your offer.

During this investigation period the IRS District Office will check for outstanding or pending:

- Criminal investigations
- Tax appeals
- Bankruptcies
- Civil suits by or against you
- Federal and state tax liens
- Prior or pending IRS seizures or levies

Meanwhile the IRS's vast computers will instantly verify your driver's license, social security, real property, corporation records, motor vehicles, professional licenses and virtually your entire financial, credit, civil and criminal background. There is little about you the IRS won't know!

The new IRS policy is to reduce paperwork and simplify the handling of OICs, so the IRS now chiefly relies upon the data or information you furnish and will ask you only for such additional documentation as is reasonable.

OICs based on inability to pay, or "doubt of collectibility," are eventually sent to the IRS's Special Procedures Division for review by an Advisory Revenue Officer. If the Advisory Revenue Officer in Special Procedures concludes that your offer is unsatisfactory, the officer will recommend a summary rejection letter.

If the officer recommends accepting your offer, this will then be reported to a superior who, in turn, will transmit this recommendation to the District Director for final approval. However, any IRS employee in the chain of review may return the OIC to the Revenue Officer for further investigation or clarification.

Aside from the outright acceptance or rejection of your OIC is a third possibility: the Request for Amendment. This may occur when your offer is unacceptable, but you are reasonably close to what the IRS may accept. Here, the Revenue Officer may suggest an amended OIC and indicate what the IRS will accept. This will be discussed more fully in the next chapter.

It is important to remember that the entire IRS evaluation focuses on one issue: Does your offer represent your "maximum ability to pay," as discussed in the prior chapter. If they conclude it does, you are on your way to resolving your tax problems.

PROCESSING 'DOUBT OF LIABILITY' CASES

Offers in Compromise not based on collectibility, but based on doubt of liability, follow a slightly different procedure.

These cases are ordinarily assigned to the Examination Division of the IRS, but if it is a 100-percent penalty case (i.e. non-payment of withholding taxes), then the case is turned over to collections.

The Revenue Officer handling the 100-percent penalty case will accumulate evidence concerning your responsibility for non-payment of withheld payroll taxes. At this point you probably had an earlier hearing on your protest before an Appellate Hearing Officer, so it is up to you to provide additional information to justify reassessment of your liability. The Revenue Officer can completely overturn the assessment, declare it partially valid or decide that "a definite determination cannot be made."

When your liability is in doubt, the IRS will compromise based on the degree of doubt rather than your financial condition or the ability of the IRS to enforce collection.

The question of liability will most frequently arise from an audit when issues of what constitutes taxable income or a deductible expense become contested.

Considering the complexity of the tax code its remarkable that there are not many more OICs based on "doubt of liability." Too many taxpayers simply pay the disputed tax, perhaps because they don't know about the OIC program or don't think an OIC is worth pursuing for the money involved.

The burden is on you to show the IRS why there is a basis for mutual doubt on the liability. Provide the IRS with applicable and persuasive case law to support your position if you disagree on legal interpretation or questions of law. This usually means the assistance of a lawyer qualified to present a legal case.

More frequently the IRS disputes factual issues, such as whether losses or expenses were actually incurred. The burden is still yours to provide tangible evidence (receipts, diaries, logs, pictures) that at least create a reasonable doubt about the claimed liability, with the evidence sufficiently significant to raise the level of doubt beyond a mere suspicion. Of course, the stronger the doubt of liability, the less you need to offer the IRS who will begin to appreciate the weakness of its position.

HOW TO STOP IRS COLLECTION DURING THE OIC

The OIC should not be used merely as a device to forestall collection. But the IRS usually will suspend collection efforts while your OIC is pending if they believe you submitted your OIC in good faith, it has a reasonable chance of acceptance and that the IRS will not be prejudiced by delaying collection.

Generally, the Revenue Officer assigned to your case decides whether to suspend collection activity. The Revenue Officer will complete Form 657 which includes the Revenue Officer's evaluation of collectibility and the officer's determination of whether to continue or suspend collection.

You should specifically request that collection activities against you be suspended and, to support your case, point out your cooperativeness and diligence in submitting the OIC.

The Revenue Officer will nevertheless file all notices of lien in all localities where you have assets. Filing tax liens while an OIC is pending is standard policy; however, the IRS may agree not to file a lien if you can show that your offer was made in good faith, that withholding a tax lien will not harm the IRS, *and* a tax lien will impair your ability to pay the IRS, such as when it prevents you from borrowing. While suspending collection is normal during an OIC, it is unusual for the IRS *not* to file a tax lien, as the IRS can always lift its lien to allow borrowing or a sale of assets that will pay the IRS.

EIGHT MORE TIPS FOR FILING YOUR OIC

1) Expect the IRS to take about a year to review your offer. Nor can you prod the IRS to move faster. Remember, your OIC must undergo thorough investigation and work its way through many channels. Be patient. You will eventually receive an answer to your offer.

2) If your offer calls for installment payments, do not pay them *until* your offer has been formally accepted by the IRS. Do, meanwhile, file your tax returns on time or request an extension. If your current taxes are more than you can afford, you may want to include them in a new or amended OIC.

3) The IRS works slowly but expects taxpayers to react quickly to its demands. If the IRS asks you for additional documents or information, then submit it promptly or at least explain the reasons for any delay.

4) The IRS loves documentation. You can never give them too much paper to support your case. Do you claim poor health and poor earning capacity? Then submit ample medical reports to substantiate it. Nor should you wait to be asked for this documentation. Put yourself in the IRS's position. What documents or evidence would you want to see before you accepted a taxpayer's statement or representation?

5) Avoid comments or gestures that can be misconstrued as a bribe. Slang such as "I'll make you an offer you can't refuse," can get you into trouble. Put as much as possible into writing and work only through official channels so there are no misunderstandings.

6) Alert those who can corroborate your financial circumstances that they may be contacted by the IRS. It's probably smart to tell them about your pending OIC so you dispel their concerns or suspicions that you may have more serious IRS problems.

7) Reconsider your offer if your financial circumstances change significantly while the OIC is pending. If your fortunes improve, you do not have to increase your offer – provided your financial information was accurate when disclosed. The IRS, of course, will reject your offer *if* it becomes aware of your improved financial condition. On the other hand, if your financial condition deteriorates, then amend your offer downward or withdraw your offer in favor of bankruptcy or a determination that you are "temporarily uncollectible."

8) Expect hassles. Working with the IRS is never easy and your OIC can be a long and tortuous process. It takes patience and tenacity to settle for pennies on the dollar.

Sample of Form *Offer in Compromise*

Form 656
(Rev. Sept. 1993)

Department of the Treasury—Internal Revenue Service

Offer in Compromise

▶ See Instructions Page 5

(1) Name and Address of Taxpayers

John Taxpayer
123 Main Street
Anytown, Anystate 01234

(3) Employer Identification Number

(2) Social Security Number
111-22-3333

For Official Use Only

Offer is (Check applicable box)	Serial Number
☐ Cash (Paid in full)	(Cashier's stamp)
☐ Deferred payment	
Alpha CSED Ind. _____	
Amount Paid	
$	

To: Commissioner of Internal Revenue Service

(4) I/we (includes all types of taxpayers) **submit this offer to compromise the tax liabilities plus any interest, penalties, additions to tax, and additional amounts required by law (tax liability)** for the tax type and period checked below: (Please mark "X" for the correct description and fill-in the correct tax period(s), adding additional periods if needed.)

☒ Income tax for the year(s) 1992___, 19 93___, 19_____, and 19_____

☐ Trust fund recovery penalty (formerly called the 100-percent penalty) as a responsible person of _____ (enter business name) for failure to pay withholding and Federal Insurance Contributions Act taxes (Social Security taxes) for the period(s) ended ___/___/___, ___/___/___
 __/___, ___/___/___, ___/___/___ (for example - 06/30/92)

☐ Withholding and Federal Insurance Contributions Act taxes (Social Security taxes) for the period(s) ended ___/___ __/___, ___/___/___, ___/___/___ (for example - 06/30/92)

☐ Federal Unemployment Tax Act taxes for the year(s) 19_____, 19_____, 19_____, and 19_____
 __/___, ___/___/___

☐ Other (Be specific.) _____

(5) I/we offer to pay $ 20,000

If you aren't making full payment with your offer, describe below when you will make full payment (for example – within ten (10) days from the date the offer is accepted): See the instructions for Item 5. $6,000 is to be paid upon $2,000 to be paid with this offer as a refundable deposit; $6,000 is to be paid upon acceptance; and $4,000 to be paid annually in three (3) years, payable in monthly installments.

As required by section 6621 of the Internal Revenue Code, the Internal Revenue Service (IRS) will add interest to the offered amount from the date IRS accepts the offer until the date you completely pay the amount offered. IRS compounds interest daily, as required by section 6622 of the Internal Revenue Code.

(6) I/we submit this offer for the reason(s) checked below:

☒ Doubt as to collectibility ("I can't pay.") You must include a completed financial statement (Form 433-A and/or Form 433-B).

☐ Doubt as to liability ("I don't believe I owe this tax.") You must include a detailed explanation of the reason(s) why you believe you don't owe the tax.

IMPORTANT: SEE REVERSE FOR TERMS AND CONDITIONS

	Under penalties of perjury, I declare that I have examined this offer, including accompanying schedules and statements, and to the best of my knowledge and belief, it is true, correct and complete.	Date
I accept waiver of the statutory period of limitations for the Internal Revenue Service.	(8a) Signature of Taxpayer-proponent	
	John Taxpayer	Jan 4, 1994
Signature of authorized Internal Revenue Service Official	(8b) Signature of Taxpayer-proponent	Date
Date		Form **656** (Rev. 9-93)
Title	Cat. No. 16728N	

Part 1 IRS Copy

Dispose of prior issues.

Information completed on this form is illustrative only

CHAPTER 7

IF THE IRS REJECTS YOUR OIC

Before the IRS liberalized its OIC program in 1993, more OICs were rejected by the IRS than were accepted. It is difficult to estimate how many more OICs will be accepted now that the IRS more strongly encourages OIC settlements to enforced collection; however, it is reasonable to assume that you have a far greater chance of reaching agreement on an OIC than you would at any time before.

WHY THE IRS MAY REJECT YOUR OFFER IN COMPROMISE

There are many reasons why the IRS may reject your offer, but these are the seven most common:

1) *The amount offered is less than what the IRS believes they can collect through enforced collection.* Remember, the OIC program is not designed to let taxpayers escape taxes they can afford to pay. If the IRS rejects your OIC for this reason it will usually suggest that you amend your offer. This is by far the most frequent reason for rejection and will be further discussed in the next section.

2) *The IRS believes you cannot or will not comply with the terms of your offer.* This may occur when you have a history of chronic delinquency or have repeatedly fallen behind on earlier arrangements agreed to by the IRS. This may also happen if the IRS thinks you can't possibly honor the terms of your offer because of inadequate assets or insufficient income.

3) *You are delinquent in your tax filings or in paying other tax obligations not covered by your OIC.* It is important to keep in mind that the IRS will not consider an OIC unless you have filed *all* tax returns due.

4) *The taxpayer died before the OIC is accepted.* The IRS will automatically turn back an OIC under these circumstances.

This does not mean, however, that the executor of the estate cannot resubmit the OIC or a new OIC. The executor's OIC may also include any estate taxes together with past due income taxes.

5) *The IRS doesn't believe the taxpayer was honest in disclosing assets or income.* Even suspicions of dishonesty can cause the IRS to reject your OIC. If you think that may be the reason for rejection (the IRS seldom volunteers their suspicions), then it is up to you to candidly review the situation with the IRS so you can explain matters of concern and restore their confidence in your honesty.

6) *The taxpayer is not cooperative or proceeding with reasonable diligence and good faith.* If the IRS thinks you are stalling (particularly to delay collection) then they will reject your OIC. Proceed diligently. Stay within IRS timetables for submitting follow-up documents. If you do need more time, then request an extension from the IRS and explain why additional time is needed.

7) *Public policy considerations discourage acceptance by the IRS.* This may occur, for instance, if the taxpayer has a recent or tax-related criminal record. The IRS will cut deals with honest, law-abiding taxpayers who for one of a variety of reasons fell behind on his or her taxes. The IRS does not want to portray the image of cooperating with less-than-honest taxpayers.

Sometimes the IRS will issue a "summary rejection." This is a denial without weighing the merits of your offer because your OIC is (1) considered frivolous, or (2) your financial information is incomplete, or (3) you have outstanding tax returns.

HOW TO HANDLE THE REQUEST FOR AMENDMENT

The IRS rejection letter will state with some detail the reason the IRS refused your offer. Several reasons may be cited. Some factors may be easily remedied, such as a rejection because you incorrectly completed your OIC.

More commonly, the IRS will reject an OIC and thus prod the taxpayer to increase the offer. This is done through a request for amendment. It is important to remember that the IRS may not counteroffer nor tell you what they *will* accept. Instead, they tell you what they won't accept by simply rejecting your offer.

In practice, IRS agents *may* hint a "range" of what the IRS may accept. You must inch your way toward that "range," realizing the IRS may well accept something less.

You are entitled to see the report that lists the factors behind the rejection. The Special Procedures Officer will give you a copy or you can get it by making a request under the Freedom of Information Act.

If your OIC was rejected because it was "too low," the agent must also tell you what amount definitely would be accepted.

Here a seasoned professional is most helpful. With many OICs behind you, you develop an instinct for where to start – where you will probably end – and how you will get there. This usually means several "amended" OICs until one is finally accepted.

Regardless of how low your offer may be, the IRS cannot refuse to consider it, although it can be summarily rejected as frivolous.

If you do submit a good faith offer but the offer was too low to be accepted, you must be granted the continuing opportunity to resubmit amended offers.

The IRS cannot capriciously or arbitrarily refuse your offer. There must be a reasonable basis for denial, and this usually means that the IRS has some reasonable basis for believing it can collect more from you through its normal collection powers.

This does not mean that OICs aren't arbitrarily rejected. Many IRS agents and District Officers have a history of arbitrarily refusing to entertain OICs, and there is a marked inconsistency in the number of OICs between Districts. This invariably reflects the attitude of their personnel toward the OIC program.

You can simply amend your offer by letter if the new offer is not significantly different and there is no material financial or personal change. If your new offer is substantially different – or if there are new financial or personal circumstances – then complete a new OIC Form 656 and financial statements (Form 433A).

Never withdraw your OIC.

Once you file your OIC firmly wait for either all acceptance, rejection or request for amendment. Never withdraw your offer.

IRS officers oftentimes encourage taxpayers to withdraw their OICs on the basis that the IRS will most likely turn it down and the taxpayer will have a greater chance of success with a new OIC if they were not turned down on an earlier OIC.

There is no basis for this. You can be turned down any number of times and it does not adversely prejudice subsequent offers.

More importantly, be forcing the IRS to issue a written rejection, you learn why your OIC is being turned down and discover what the IRS will accept. Without this information you are "shadow boxing."

HOW TO APPEAL YOUR CASE

You always have the right to appeal a rejected offer. If you do receive a rejection letter you should file a written appeal within 30 days unless you plan to submit an amended or new OIC. Missing an appeal deadline is never fatal because you can always submit a new OIC – on slightly different terms – and file a timely appeal when that OIC is rejected. This procedure follows closely the procedure for appealing an audit.

Your rejection letter will include detailed instructions for filing an appeal. Follow these instructions carefully. They will be stated in IRS Publication 931 which will accompany your rejection.

If the taxes you owe exceed $2,500, your appeal must be in writing, but no particular form is required nor is it difficult to appeal.

Your letter need only refer to the date of your OIC, the date of the rejection letter and that you wish to take an appeal and now request a conference.

Keep the 30 day filing period in mind. This applies to all appeals, except that you are allowed an additional 15 days if the IRS rejected your OIC because of insufficient information. This effectively gives you 45 days to provide new information concerning your case.

If you do appeal, your appeal and the written report and evaluation of the IRS agent handling your case will be sent to the appeals officer.

The agent's report is a critical document to examine because it explains why the IRS agent did not accept your offer. More importantly, it may indicate what amount and terms *would* be accepted by the IRS. You do have the right to inspect the agent's report which can be insightful in preparing an amended OIC that the IRS will accept.

Many OIC cases are ultimately resolved upon appeal. The appeals officer frequently bridges the difference between taxpayer and agent and concludes an OIC on terms acceptable to both the taxpayer and the IRS. Still, you must not appeal with expectations of complete victory. Taxpayers seldom win OIC appeals. Nor can you be certain the appeals officer will suggest settlement terms. The IRS staff may simply affirm or overturn an agent's decision concerning an OIC. In these instances the decision almost always favors the IRS agent.

Unfortunately, once your appeal is decided at the appeals conference, you have no further right to appeal. Nor can you appeal to the tax court.

Even though your odds of winning an appeal are slight, you have nothing to lose by trying. At the least you will forestall collection until you put one of your other options into play.

GETTING YOUR DEPOSIT REFUNDED

If your offer is rejected the IRS *must* return your deposit. In fact, the IRS must escrow your deposit in a special fund so it is available for immediate return. But you must still be careful. The IRS agent may try to get you to apply the deposit to your tax bill even though the IRS rejected your offer. Always refuse this request. Despite IRS bluffs to the contrary, the IRS *cannot* apply your deposit unless you agree to it in writing! Unfortunately, you do not get interest on your deposit.

RECONSIDER YOUR OPTIONS

What do you do if you have offered the IRS as much as you reasonably can and the IRS still turns you down on appeal?

One option is to carefully reconsider what you think is a reasonable offer. You may have approached the OIC expecting more leniency than the IRS was willing to extend.

Closely examine the IRS's reasons for rejecting your offer.

Has the IRS misinterpreted certain information? Does the IRS question the validity of some information and need more documentation? Does the IRS know things about you that you didn't think they knew?

Perhaps your professional advisor misled you and painted too optimistic a picture about what the IRS would accept. Have one or two other professionals review your file. Do they consider your OIC reasonable? Do they see another proposal that may satisfy you and the IRS? And, yes, you can run into an exceptionally unreasonable IRS agent, or one who gets along poorly with you or your advisor and becomes as tough as possible.

Once you have dismissed these possibilities and find the IRS still insists on more than you can afford to pay, you must again reconsider your options. These are the same options you should have considered *before* you submitted your OIC. And because a rejected OIC means the IRS will quickly resume collection, you must move swiftly to protect yourself before they seize or levy your assets.

If you have insignificant assets and only modest income, why not go for "uncollectible" status? If you do have assets, then talk to a good bankruptcy lawyer. A Chapter 11 or 13 bankruptcy (giving you several years to pay the taxes) or a Chapter 7 (to completely wipe out the taxes if they are more than 3 years old) may be the right remedy for you.

You may also play the game once again. For instance, you may relocate and submit a new OIC through a different IRS office. You may also hire a new tax pro who is situated nearer another IRS office. This may prompt transfer of the file and dealing with a new – and hopefully more lenient – agent. There are any number of reasons to justify transfer of your file to a new IRS office and when personalities and politics become a factor, it is a strategy to consider. The new IRS office will know about your prior OICs; however, you will be dealing with new IRS agents who may be more reasonable. Also play for time. An OIC rejected today may be accepted tomorrow. Perhaps your financial situation changed for the worse so your new OIC is now more attractive to the IRS. You may even succeed with an OIC that gives the IRS less than you offered before.

Solving your tax problems frequently means shifting gears and parlaying several different strategies. A strategy that originally seemed correct may give way to another solution that, with time, appears more logical. You see, a rejected OIC does not mean you are necessarily without other solutions to your tax problem.

CHAPTER 8

WHEN THE IRS ACCEPTS YOUR OFFER

Congratulations! Your tax troubles may soon be behind you. Start by carefully reviewing the IRS's acceptance of your offer. Once the IRS officially accepts your OIC it will issue an *Offer Acceptance Report* (IRS Form 7249). The acceptance should clearly set forth the taxes that are compromised and all terms of the settlement. Specifically review the acceptance for these three points:

1)   Does the acceptance specify *all* the taxes you owe and that are subject to compromise?

2)   Does the acceptance accurately summarize all major terms of your settlement?

3)   Is the acceptance duly signed by a revenue official authorized to bind the IRS?

If you are represented by a professional he or she will have the responsibility to review the acceptance. If you are not represented, then it may be wise to hire a professional for this one specific task. Remember: The acceptance is the legal document that binds the IRS to your OIC, and you're not fully safe until you have a legally binding acceptance that specifies the exact terms you bargained for.

IF YOU DEFAULT ON YOUR OIC

If your OIC calls for installment payments, you may eventually find yourself in default of your agreement and unable to make the payments as promised. After all, you too face the same financial problems we all encounter from time to time – unemployment, unexpected or unavoidable bills, divorce, illness or a host of other problems that may make payment difficult or impossible.

If you anticipate a default then contact the IRS *beforehand*. Do not default and make the IRS come to you looking for your payment. You can expect little cooperation unless you accept your responsibility to notify the IRS of your problems. Only then will the IRS feel that you take your OIC obligations seriously.

Whenever possible, contact the agent who handled your case. State your problem in writing so there can be no question that you took the initiative in alerting the IRS to your default.

Start by detailing the circumstances for you non-payment. Show why these problems will leave you with too little money to pay the IRS, and why the debts you are paying demand priority over IRS payments.

Use common sense. The IRS will not be sympathetic that you lost your job if you are still making payments on your expensive sports car. However, the IRS will work with you if you alert them to your problem, have a good excuse for non-payment, and are completely truthful. This last point is most important. Never lie to the IRS. The IRS may check your story! To corroborate your excuse supply documentation (such as a job termination notice or medical bills). Keep in mind, that like yourself, the IRS has also invested considerable time and effort to reach a settlement and they don't want to cancel your agreement any more than you do.

What options are available to you if you do foresee a default on your OIC? You may ask the IRS to:

- Temporarily reduce or abate your payments
- Extend the payment schedule
- Accept alternate forms of payment

If your default will be temporary (less than one or two months) then request a temporary abatement or a reduction in payment. The IRS is more cooperative if you offer small interim payments because this shows your good faith.

Clearly state what you are proposing to the IRS. Let them know what interim payments you can make, when you expect to resume full payment, and when the IRS will be updated on your financial circumstances if you don't know when you can get back on schedule.

In effect, you are compromising an already compromised debt by asking for a further extension of time to pay. It is even possible to offer to settle an already compromised tax liability for a fraction of what you originally agreed to pay under the OIC. For instance, your financial situation may have deteriorated since your OIC so the IRS may now doubt whether it can collect even the compromised amount.

There is no required form to compromise the balance owed under an OIC. You can do this by a simple letter request. However, as with an original OIC, you must state why it is in the best interests of the IRS for them to cancel all or part of what you owe under the OIC. Rather than completely cancel the remaining obligation, it is more likely the IRS will simply determine you temporarily uncollectible and suspend further collection.

You will have a far easier task convincing the IRS to defer payments rather than cancel or further compromise what you owe.

If the IRS agrees to your request for an extension, modification or further compromise, it will notify you by formal reply letter. Until you receive such a notification you are bound by the agreed terms of your OIC.

If the IRS decides not to extend, modify or further compromise your obligation, they will immediately try to:

- Collect the entire balance due under the OIC, or
- Collect the original tax liability and interest, less any payments made.

Notice that your default under the OIC can reinstate your original tax liability (less payments made). This is because the IRS agreed to compromise your tax liability *conditional* upon your performing under the OIC. Your default allows them to rescind their end of the agreement.

If you do plan to file bankruptcy after a default, then let the IRS know of your plans. They will probably suspend collection until you have had a reasonable opportunity to file and this will save both you and the IRS wasted efforts and aggravation.

WHEN THE IRS CAN CANCEL THE AGREEMENT

The OIC is a binding agreement between you and the IRS, but like all contracts it can be rescinded if the agreement was based upon misrepresentation, fraud or mutual mistake.

The IRS does encounter taxpayers who are dishonest and fail to disclose assets or income as required. Should the IRS later discover these misrepresentations they can rescind the OIC and pursue the original tax liability. This generally occurs when the misrepresentation was intentional and significant and wrongfully induced the IRS into a settlement they otherwise would not have agreed to.

This once again underscores the importance of accuracy and truthfulness when dealing with the IRS. Your agreement with the IRS is meaningless unless the IRS remains bound to it. That means you need an honest agreement.

That's why it's a good idea to have your accountant or someone else familiar with your financial affairs review the financial statements that accompany the OIC. It is easy to misinterpret a question or overlook an asset that must be disclosed. Even innocent errors can cause problems far greater than a cancelled OIC agreement.

KEEP RECORDS OF YOUR PAYMENTS

Hopefully you will faithfully and punctually fulfill your agreement with the IRS. It will certainly benefit you if you should run into future tax troubles.

It is important to keep meticulous records of all payments under the OIC so you can prove to the IRS that you have made all the payments due under the OIC. The IRS sometimes misplaces payments or credits payments to incorrect accounts. So keep a ledger that accurately documents each payment. Your checks should be clearly marked with your account (Social Security or EIN) and the installment the check represents.

If your agreement calls for deferred payments, then it is a good idea to periodically have the IRS confirm your current balance. If there are bookkeeping problems between yourself and the IRS they can then be resolved more easily.

HOW TO GET YOUR TAX LIEN RELEASED

Once you have fully paid what was due under the OIC, the IRS must send to you a *Certificate of Release of Federal Tax Lien* (Form 668Z). You must receive a certificate for each office that has a lien on file. This may include the clerk of your city, town or county, the Federal District Court nearest where you reside and wherever real estate transactions for your locale are recorded. If you have moved, there may be liens filed where you originally lived. There may also be several liens for the same tax liability filed in the same place. This commonly occurs if your tax problems have extended for a number of years. To ensure that you obtain a Certificate of Release of Federal Tax Lien for *each* lien filed, you must conduct a complete lien search. This can be done in several ways:

- *Ask the IRS agent for copies of every lien the IRS filed against you.*

- *Have a commercial lien search service comb the public records.* These firms know how and where to look for liens, but do be certain they know everywhere you lived or worked from the very beginning of your tax troubles. Also let them know of any change of name. I recommend Docu-Search. Their toll-free number is (800) 332-3034. They give good reliable nationwide service at a reasonable cost; however, there are many other excellent firms who provide the same service.

- *Review your credit report.* This may disclose outstanding tax liens, but don't rely upon your credit report alone. A credit report may easily overlook some tax liens. You'll see in the next section how to get your credit report.

- *Conduct your own lien search.* It's not as difficult as you may think. The clerk at the public recording office is usually cooperative and will assist you in your search.

Once you're satisfied you identified all the recorded liens, then make certain the IRS does file a Certificate of Release for each lien. Don't assume the IRS will do this on their own. Frequently they don't. You must be diligent in following up on this or you'll have outstanding tax liens that will haunt you for years. Remember: Even *one* outstanding tax lien can ruin your chances for credit.

Don't, however, expect the IRS to release its lien until all conditions of your OIC have been satisfied. This includes all initial and installment payments as well as transfer or assignment to the IRS of any other properties or rights due the IRS under the agreement.

The IRS *will* discharge its lien *before* the collateral agreement is fully satisfied if a lien may hamper your earning power, especially if the IRS is counting on sharing any increase in your future income.

HOW TO CLEAR YOUR CREDIT

As underscored before, a tax lien on your credit report will definitely hurt your chances for significant credit, such as a loan to buy a home, business, car, boat or any other major purchase. It may also prevent you from obtaining credit cards.

Unfortunately, the fact that you had tax liens may not be erased from your credit report for several years. However, a *past* lien isn't nearly as damaging as a current tax lien. That's why you must be certain *every* credit bureau updates your credit history to show that your outstanding tax liens have been fully paid and discharged.

Start by requesting a copy of your credit report from the three major credit reporting agencies:

TRW	TRANS UNION	EQUIFAX
Complimentary	P.O. Box 7000	Box 740241
Credit Report	N. Olmstead, OH 44070	Atlanta, GA 30375
Box 2350	(313) 689-3888	(800) 759-5979
Chatsworth, CA		
(800) 392-1122		

These bureaus will send you a copy of your credit report for a nominal amount (about $20). They may also refer you to a local office.

Review your credit reports. For each recorded lien (not noted as discharged) you must insist that the reporting agency contact the IRS or check the public records to confirm that the lien(s) have been released. You may also send the credit bureaus copies of the Certificate of Release of Federal Tax Lien. Follow up to make sure your credit report reflects the discharge of all tax liens against you.

Credit bureaus can be slow to update your credit report. You can easily be penalized with poor credit for many years only because the credit bureaus stubbornly show outstanding liens. So it is up to you to clear your credit profile and again rebuild your credit. One way to do it quickly and conveniently is with *The E-Z Credit Repair Kit* available by order in the back of this book.

You can also help your credit picture if you are only in the process of resolving your tax problems. For example, if you are mailing your payments in installments then at least have your credit report reflect the fact that an agreement has been reached with the IRS and discharge of your lien is anticipated. You can submit up to a 100-word statement to that effect to the credit bureau and insist that it accompany your credit report.

STAY OUT OF TROUBLE WITH THE IRS

Once your tax problems are behind you, your goal should be to steer clear of future tax troubles. Here are five tips for avoiding surefire IRS problems:

1. *Don't try to beat the system.* We must all file tax returns and failure to file will eventually catch up to you and cause you even bigger tax problems.

2. *Hire a good accountant to stay on top of your taxes.* If you lack the discipline to comply with your tax obligations, hire an accountant who will prod you into compliance.

3. *Keep good records.* Many taxpayers get into deep trouble with the IRS only because they failed to keep adequate records. If you are audited, you'll need good records or you may be hit with a larger tax bill than you can afford to pay.

4. *Don't play games with Uncle Sam.* We all want to save on our taxes, but the IRS can severely penalize you if they find you are less than honest.

5. *Stay abreast of the tax laws.* Yes, our tax laws can be complicated, but by understanding the laws you can frequently alter your financial strategies to significantly lower your taxes. Perhaps you will find that you have overpaid your taxes and that the IRS now owes *you* money!

CHAPTER 9

HOW TO GET THE PROFESSIONAL HELP YOU NEED

At this point you may feel that handling your own OIC is too complicated a task and that you need professional assistance. Let's see whether this is your best option and, if so, how to find and use the right professional.

SHOULD YOU HANDLE YOUR OWN CASE?

Let's start with the disadvantages of representing yourself because they are far more numerous than are the advantages:

- *You lack the professional's expertise on how to get your very best deal.* Odds are that on your own you will offer the IRS far too much to settle. You may also overlook alternatives to the OIC that would be more sensible in your situation. I have reviewed many taxpayer-negotiated OICs and found that these taxpayers consistently offered the IRS much more than was necessary to settle – sometimes two or three times more. It's false economy to save a few dollars on professional fees only to needlessly pay the IRS many times that amount in an overly generous settlement.

- *You may be too frightened, frustrated or intimidated by the IRS to effectively or comfortably handle your OIC.* Most taxpayers are far happier to keep their distance from the IRS and prefer to leave the sparring to their advisors. If you're uncomfortable with an IRS confrontation, then hiring a professional beats tranquilizers! Still, dealing with the IRS is not always as painful as you may imagine. In fact, most IRS agents are reasonable and helpful, particularly when they see you are making an honest effort to resolve your tax problems.

- *You may slip up and make statements that can get you into even more trouble – perhaps an audit or even criminal prosecution.* You must always be careful about what you say to the IRS.Professionals know where to draw the line. You may, for instance, volunteer incriminating information involving undeclared income. You may inadvertently reveal assets or sources of income that can sabotage a favorable settlement. You may make statements that can create tax liability for your spouse or business associate. One careless comment can get you into even bigger trouble! Yes, you should be honest with the IRS. But it's difficult to know precisely how candid you can be unless you are that seasoned tax professional.

- *You take valuable time away from your work or other more pleasant pursuits when you must wrestle with your own case.* This is probably the least important reason for handling your own OIC. After all, it's unlikely you will earn as much from your other pursuits as you will need to pay a professional. But for a good many taxpayers that statement is untrue. Physicians, dentists, lawyers, executives, successful business owners and other high-income taxpayers will do appreciably better paying a tax professional while they more profitably ply their own occupations.

HOW TO SAVE PROFESSIONAL FEES

The one big advantage of representing yourself, of course, is that you will save big fees. And for most taxpayers this is no small matter.

Tax professionals can be costly. Their fees range from $25 per hour for an enrolled agent or new accountant in a rural area to $300 or more per hour for a seasoned tax lawyer in a major city. And most tax consultants won't agree to a fixed fee to handle your OIC. They can't possibly anticipate how many hours will be required because they can't foresee the numerous contingencies nor IRS stubbornness in negotiating a final agreement.

But do ask for a rough estimate or a fee range. Unless you have an exceptionally large tax liability or a very hostile agent your fee should be under $5,000 and is more often about $2,000 to $3,000 for a simpler OIC. Any OIC involves too much paperwork to expect substantially lower fees.

Some tax professionals will agree to a contingent fee or a fee that's a percentage of the savings. This makes sense because it gives the professional a strong incentive to cut the very best deal. A contingent fee, while it may be reasonable in relation to the savings, may be excessive compared to an hourly fee. Consider this proposition very carefully. Your best alternative may combine a nominal hourly fee with a bonus based on results.

Don't hesitate to negotiate fees. Tax professionals seek new clients and do negotiate lower fees or at least additional time to pay the fee. Also avoid large retainers. You won't know if you're satisfied with your advisor at first so reserve the flexibility to change advisors without having to chase the return of a hefty retainer.

Regardless of your fee arrangement, there's much you can do to keep your fees to a minimum:

- *Request monthly statements.* This will alert you to overcharges or extensive fees you cannot afford *before* they accumulate.

- *See if a lower-priced associate in the professional's firm can handle the more routine aspects of your OIC.* And handle yourself whatever you can. Delegate only the critical parts of the case that you cannot handle yourself.

- *Cooperate.* Get your financial information together quickly and orderly. Don't make your professional chase you for information. That's a wasted expense.

- *Keep communication with your professional to the essential minimum.* Phone calls add up. Call sparingly, get to the point and hang up!

Most importantly: *Shop fees!* Yes, you need a competent professional, but you will find fees range widely among professionals of equal competence and background.

Here's another fee-saving option: Why not hire a tax professional to serve only as your consultant? The professional need not officially represent you before the IRS, but would answer your specific questions and guide you generally through the OIC process. If you don't mind facing the IRS and have the patience to handle the paperwork, this option will save you most of the fee and still keep you fully guided on the important points.

TAX PROFESSIONALS TO CONSIDER

You can choose among three types of tax professionals to represent you on your OIC:

1) Attorneys
2) Certified Public Accountants
3) Enrolled agents

Attorneys

An attorney in good standing in a state bar may represent taxpayers on IRS matters. This doesn't mean all lawyers are qualified to handle an OIC. Obviously, you need one with experience. A lawyer inexperienced with OICs has little value because they have yet to develop the "feel" of what the IRS will accept and are unfamiliar with the OIC procedure.

Your best bet is to call a tax lawyer. They are easily found by contacting your local or state bar association, or your family lawyer may refer you to one. Some states offer special certification to tax specialists which attests to their competence. Tax attorneys frequently have the LL.M. degree (master of laws), which is a post-graduate degree in taxation.

If you owe substantial taxes, or have significant assets, then strongly consider a tax lawyer. You will certainly want a tax lawyer if the IRS suspects fraud, is threatening criminal prosecution or if an appeal to tax court is likely.

Certified Public Accountants

As with attorneys, most CPA's are permitted to practice before the IRS and handle OIC cases, however, as with attorneys this is no assurance of their competence. Call your state association of Certified Public Accountants. They can tell you how to find accountants in your area who are experienced with OIC cases. Your best choice may be your regular accountant – if he or she has solid OIC experience. After all, your accountant is already familiar with your finances and can more quickly and easily put together the information than can another professional unfamiliar with your finances. Contrary to popular belief, the majority of CPAs have little direct involvement with the IRS. Even those who routinely prepare tax returns may have had little exposure to OICs. If that is your accountant, then move on.

Enrolled Agents

Enrolled agents are generally neither attorneys nor accountants. They are usually former IRS agents or examiners who are now in practice for themselves and are permitted to represent taxpayers before the IRS. EAs earn their designation by having a minimum of five years experience practicing before the IRS or by passing a rigid qualifying exam administered by the IRS. EAs must also participate in annual continuing education. There are about 24,000 active EAs, 6,000 of whom belong to the National Association of Enrolled Agents.

To find enrolled agents in your area call the National Association of Enrolled Agents at (800) 424-4339.

How do you decide which type professional is best for you?

There is no easy answer because there are good and bad practitioners within each group. Still, there are some factors to consider.

A tax attorney is likely to be more expensive than either a CPA or EA. On the other hand, you enjoy confidentiality with an attorney as all written and verbal communication between you and your attorney is privileged. This means you can freely disclose your deepest secrets to your attorney in complete confidence. Moreover, if you must go to court with the IRS only an attorney can represent you. Start with an attorney and you will not have to change advisors.

The one big advantage of an accountant? He or she is already familiar with your finances and tax history. But don't let your accountant handle your OIC for this reason alone. You need an accountant with a good track record with OICs. You will find CPAs are usually mid-priced between lawyers and enrolled agents.

Enrolled agents are sometimes your best candidate because they frequently worked for the IRS (sometimes handling OIC cases exclusively) and best know the inner workings of the IRS and how to strike your most favorable deal. An EA is also likely to be less expensive than an attorney or accountant. While these may appear to be compelling reasons to hire an EA, remember that some EAs cannot completely shed their IRS past and don't fight as hard as they could for their taxpayer-clients.

There are also several firms that specialize in OICs. These firms either employ attorneys, accountants or EAs or refer their cases to qualified specialists. Due to their high volume of cases, these firms are oftentimes more economical, and because they handle only OICs and related cases, they offer considerable expertise. One firm that handles OIC cases nationwide is IRS Rescue, Inc. Their services are described in the Appendix.

HOW TO FIND A TAX PRO

It is not difficult to find the tax pro who is right for you:

- *Ask your professional advisors.* Your accountant or attorney may not excel in OICs but may refer you to another professional who does.

- *Personal referrals.* Do you have a friend or acquaintance who has gone through an OIC with good results? Perhaps their advisor will do equally well for you.

- *Professional associations.* Your local bar or accounting association may have a referral panel, but their referral does not necessarily insure competence as they may loosely categorize their specialists, such as under "taxation."

- *Advertising.* Yellow pages and newspapers feature tax professionals, however few advertise as OIC specialists. You have to screen these specialists to see if they have the requisite experience with OICs.

HOW TO SELECT AND WORK WITH YOUR PROFESSIONAL

Don't hire too quickly. Your *right* advisor must convince you that he or she has strong experience with OIC cases. This means at least 10-15 prior cases.

How aggressive is your candidate? Does he or she discuss or recommend other options to the OIC such as abatements or bankruptcy? What approximate outcome does he or she foresee? Does the result seem reasonable and realistic or only puffery to get you as a client?

Does the prospect give you confidence? Is it someone who appears sufficiently aggressive to stand up to the IRS? You don't need a timid tax pro on your side, or one who is intimidated by the IRS.

Shop around. You may have to talk to several prospects before you decide. Only by talking with several candidates can you assess each.

Can your prospect give your case the needed time? This is one chronic problem with accountants. They are so busy during tax season that they have little time for OIC cases. Delays in following through on a case does not sit well with IRS agents always anxious to resolve cases. But this may be an advantage if you need time to rearrange your financial affairs, although it's usually best to work promptly with the IRS and not stall.

Finally, consider the "chemistry" between you and your prospect. You need a pro who can offer more than technical capability. You may also need empathy and emotional support from your advisor. When you battle the IRS you need a strong ally in every sense of the word!

CHAPTER 10

50 ANSWERS TO COMMON QUESTIONS ABOUT THE OFFER IN COMPROMISE PROGRAM

Q: How likely is it that the IRS will accept an Offer in Compromise?

A: In the past, the chances of acceptance were poor – only about one in four. The odds of settling with the IRS are now far better because the IRS has liberalized its OIC policies. Taxpayers and their advisors, in turn, have also become more realistic in their offers to the IRS. The IRS now approves about one out of two OICs.

Your chances will greatly depend upon your IRS District. Some district offices accept many more OICs than do others, a reflection of the attitude of district office supervisors toward OICs. However, if you closely follow the instructions in this book, you stand an excellent chance of reaching a fair and workable settlement with the IRS.

Q: How difficult is it to get the IRS to classify me as "temporarily uncollectible?"

A: The IRS must determine that you have no assets worth chasing and your present and foreseeable income does not exceed what you need to sustain a basic lifestyle. If the IRS decides, however, that you have even $50 in surplus income each month, it will expect that $50 to be applied to your tax liability. There are many more "Section 53" or "temporarily uncollectible" determinations made each year than there are approved OICs. If your assets are negligible, the IRS may even suggest you withdraw your OIC so you can be classified as uncollectible. But keep in mind that "uncollectible" is only temporary. The IRS can always resume collection. With an accepted OIC, your tax problems are forever behind you, provided you comply with its terms.

Q: When should an Offer in Compromise be considered?

A: When your taxes are 1) more than you can pay either through selling or borrowing against your assets or from income above what you need to support yourself and your family; and 2) you have too many assets and/or income to be classified as temporarily uncollectible, and 3) you have no other debts or your taxes are not dischargeable in bankruptcy thus disqualifying you as a bankruptcy candidate. Stated differently, you are a good OIC candidate when your assets are less than the taxes you owe and taxes are your primary financial problem.

Q: Can property of a spouse without the tax liability be used by the IRS to determine the capacity to pay of the tax-liable spouse?

A: While the IRS cannot legally claim your spouse's assets, the IRS when negotiating settlements nevertheless considers spousal assets and will make every effort to have you *borrow* from your spouse so you can increase your offer. Your spouse has no obligation to disclose *his or her* separate finances on matters involving *your* taxes. Most spouses cooperate, whether from misunderstanding their rights or hoping their cooperation will facilitate a settlement with the IRS.

Q: Can penalties be compromised under an OIC?

A: Penalties and interest can both be compromised in the same way as the underlying tax liability. However, if penalties are your major concern, then consider an abatement, particularly if you have reasonable grounds for the IRS to waive the penalty. The abatement process is far simpler than an OIC, and it is your proper remedy when you can pay the tax but believe you have justification for being excused from the penalties.

Q: Can the IRS refuse to consider an OIC?

A: No. It is your right as a taxpayer to submit an OIC, and the IRS cannot stop you.

Many IRS officials remain opposed to the OIC program and discourage OICs or refuse to consider them in good faith as is required. However, the

IRS cannot reject your offer capriciously or in bad faith. If you believe that is happening in your case, you can appeal to a supervisor and demand an explanation as to why your offer has been rejected.

The IRS can summarily reject OICs that they believe are filed frivolously or submitted solely for purposes of forestalling collection.

Q: What should a business owner do who owes delinquent payroll taxes?

A: The first step is to stay current from this point forward. The IRS will close your business immediately rather than let you fall further behind.

If you are still in business, the IRS agent's actions will depend on 1) whether you pay your current taxes, 2) your prospects for paying the tax arrears, 3) the difficulty and time involved in liquidating your business, and 4) the money the IRS would get from a liquidation. That's why a heavily encumbered businesses can more confidently deal with the IRS than can a business with a large equity exposed to the IRS.

As a business owner, you have the same rights as an individual taxpayer to negotiate an installment agreement. Twelve-month agreements are routine and longer installment plans are possible. A Chapter 11 bankruptcy can also stop IRS seizure and automatically give you six years from the date of assessment to pay the back taxes.

Finally, you can submit an OIC to settle the back taxes. Business OICs are far less common than personal OICs, but when your business has fewer assets than tax liabilities, it can be a viable alternative.

Q: Can I settle state taxes as I do federal taxes?

A: Taxpayers commonly owe both IRS and state taxes and do negotiate simultaneous settlements. Most states have tax compromise programs similar to the IRS's. Other states compromise with delinquent taxpayers as a matter of practice, if not official policy.

You should pro-rate your offers to the IRS and the state, paying each their proportionate share. Parity is important. Payment dates and other terms of your offer should also coincide, as should your financial disclosures. Finally, make certain each agency knows you owe the other and that settlement with each is conditional upon settlement with both.

Q: Are offers in compromise open to public inspection?

A: Yes, accepted OICs are public record for one year. And it's wise to inspect OICs that have been approved in your district within the past year for an idea of what the IRS may accept in your case.

Q: Can you file an OIC if your bankruptcy does not discharge your taxes?

A: Bankruptcy does not always discharge your taxes. Payroll taxes and income taxes less than three years old are two taxes not dischargeable in bankruptcy. You can file an OIC to compromise these or any other taxes not dischargeable in bankruptcy.

The time you were in bankruptcy is added to the IRS's statute of limitations to collect from you. Taxpayers emerging from bankruptcy with undischarged taxes should try to be classified "temporarily uncollectible" because the bankruptcy should convince the IRS that the taxpayer presently has no assets.

Q: What types of payment plans can you offer the IRS in a Chapter 13 bankruptcy?

A: There are four possible plans that usually extend payments over three to five years:

1) You can offer a *standard* or *uniform installment plan* that calls for constant payments over the term of the plan.

2) A *step-up plan* increases your payments as your income increases.

3) *Variable* or *seasonal plans* vary your payments to coincide with your cash flow or cyclical income.

4) *Balloon plans* obligate you to pay any remaining tax balance with your finally payment and may be used with any of the other plans.

Q: Is bankruptcy an option if I owe both old and current taxes?

A: According to a recent Supreme Court case, you can file Chapter 7 bankruptcy to fully discharge all taxes over three years old, and *then* file a Chapter 13 bankruptcy to discharge your current taxes under a plan. This is referred to as "Chapter 20" because it combines the double benefit of a Chapter 7 and Chapter 13! Discuss this with an experienced bankruptcy lawyer.

Q: What should I do if I discover an error in the information I provided the IRS as part of my OIC?

A: For material errors, amend your Form 433-A or explain the error in a letter to the IRS. Always put it in writing. Ignore small, immaterial inaccuracies. Notifying the IRS will needlessly delay the process and prompt the IRS to reconsider your application. If you are uncertain whether the error is significant, then correct the information.

Q: What can you do if a tax lien was erroneously filed against you?

A: You may appeal an erroneous tax lien by filing an administrative appeal, although you cannot use an administrative appeal to decide the underlying tax liability.

Erroneous tax liens commonly occur when 1) a tax lien is filed *after* the tax liability was paid, 2) the taxpayer was in bankruptcy, 3) an examination assessment was improperly made, or 4) the statute of limitations for IRS collections has expired.

Q: Can the IRS seize or levy a taxpayer's property without advance notice?

A: Yes, but it is unusual. For it to occur the IRS must believe it would be in jeopardy if it did not act quickly and without notice. A jeopardy assessment would occur, for instance, if the IRS suspects you of transferring assets or planning to take your money out of the country. Jeopardy assessment taxpayers automatically have the right to IRS administrative review and judicial appeal; however, the lien or levy will remain in force pending its outcome.

Q: When will the IRS release a levy?

A:
1) When the tax, penalties and interest are fully paid.
2) When the statute of limitations has expired.
3) When you reach an installment agreement or OIC with the IRS.
4) When the release will facilitate collection.
5) When the levy is causing extreme hardship.
6) When the taxpayer has other assets to satisfy the tax.

Q: What is the IRS's Problem Resolution Program (PRP)?

A: PRP assists taxpayers who are unable to resolve their tax problems on their own through ordinary procedures. Contact PRP only *after* you exhaust all resolution possibilities with IRS collection employees and their supervisors.

PRP also offers a convenient avenue of appeal when you disagree with the tax assessed or a collection procedure, or believe some other taxpayer right has been abridged.

Use Form 911, *Application for Assistance to Relieve Hardship* in the Appendix. A PRP representative will review your application and may issue a Taxpayers Assistance Order (TAO) directing the IRS-involved employees to correct their actions. IRS employees are available to help you complete the application. A word of caution: Don't be optimistic. Few TAOs are actually issued so PRP has not been particularly helpful to taxpayers.

Q: How do I know if I am legally obliged to give information to the IRS?

A: The Privacy Act of 1974 and Paperwork Reduction Act of 1980 requires that the IRS tell you, when you're asked a question, whether your response is voluntary, required to obtain a benefit, or mandatory. As a strict legal matter you can always refuse to answer IRS questions or refuse to turn over documents.

Under these laws, the IRS must also tell you 1) why it wants the information, 2) its legal authority in asking for it, and 3) what could happen if the IRS does not receive it.

Of course, without full disclosure of information and an attitude of complete cooperation, you have virtually no chance of having your OIC accepted. However, if you believe the IRS is asking improper questions, then decline to answer until you seek professional advice.

Q: Can politicians influence the IRS?

A: Many politicians intercede on behalf of their taxpayer constituents, particularly when they believe their constituents have been unfairly treated by the IRS. Contact your congressman only after you have tried and failed to get satisfaction through normal IRS channels.

Your congressman will need your complete file, a letter stating your grievance and how you tried to resolve it, and the results you want. Your congressman will also need a signed *Power of Attorney* (Form 2848) or *Tax Information Authorization and Declaration of Representative* (Form 2848D), both available at your local IRS office.

Q: What is the difference between a revenue officer and a special agent?

A: A revenue officer is a regular IRS employee responsible for the collection of taxes using standard procedures.

A special agent investigates possible *criminal* violations of the IRS code. If you are contacted by a special agent (who must disclose his or her status), then immediately terminate the interview and hire a lawyer.

Q: What will happen if I fail to file a delinquent tax return after repeated demands to do so by the IRS?

A: One possibility is that you will receive a federal summons compelling you to bring either the completed tax return or your books and records to the IRS office. This summons is backed by the power of the federal courts which can hold you in contempt if you fail to do so.

Another possibility is that the IRS will prepare your tax return for you. This is guaranteed to result in a much greater tax than had you prepared your own return.

Q: What if my tax return is due but I don't have the money to pay the tax?

A: Submit your tax return on the date due (or extension date), even if you can't pay the tax. You will be charged interest on your late payment but avoid a hefty late-filing penalty. Most taxpayers in this situation delay filing because they don't want the IRS dunning them. That's understandable. Nevertheless, whether or not you expect to eventually pay the tax, do file on time.

Q: Does the IRS share tax information with state taxing agencies?

A: Yes. In fact, this is standard practice but it must follow strict guide lines. The IRS also shares information with the Department of Justice, other federal agencies and even certain foreign jurisdictions.

Q: Will banking in offshore havens save me taxes?

A: It's a myth that you can avoid U.S. taxes through foreign banking. American citizens must declare income earned anywhere in the world. Foreign banks do not issue Form 1099s on interest income, so the IRS must necessarily rely more on your honesty.

Offshore havens *can* effectively protect your money from IRS seizure. The Isle of Man, Cayman Islands and Gibralter are best for this purpose. Switzerland offers significantly less protection. Want more information? Read *Asset Protection Secrets* and *Offshore Havens*, both available from Garrett Publishing.

Q: Is conversation with my accountant privileged?

A: No. The IRS, the courts and others can compel your accountant to testify about your conversations and turn over letters and other correspondence between you. Only communication with your lawyer is privileged and protected. That's one advantage to having a lawyer represent you rather than an accountant. A solution is to have your attorney hire your accountant to handle your tax matters. Your accountant, working for your lawyer, would then come under the attorney-client privilege. Since confidential documents with your accountant can be subpoenaed, you should have them and all copies immediately returned to you.

Q: Can I deduct from my current tax bill the IRS refunds that are due me from prior years?

A: Yes. If you owe the IRS $5,000 this year and the IRS owes you a $1,500 refund from last year, you can pay only the $3,500 difference. Explain the reason for the reduced payment. The IRS discourages this because it prefers to close its files promptly, which only happens when you make full payment.

Q: What is meant by an "innocent spouse"?

A: When you and your spouse file a joint tax return, both you and your spouse are "jointly and severally" liable for any taxes due.

If it is later shown, for example, that one spouse had unreported income, the other spouse may try to escape civil and/or criminal liability for the tax on that unreported income under the "innocent spouse" rule (IRS 6013(e)). To claim this protection, the innocent spouse must neither have known about the understated income (or other tax) nor could have reasonably known about it. The "innocent" spouse not only avoids tax liability but also provides a safe harbor for the family assets.

Q: When a bank account is levied by the IRS, when must the bank turn over the money to the IRS?

A: Since June 30, 1989, banks have 21 days from date of levy to turn over funds to the IRS. This gives the taxpayer time to resolve the tax problem or settle disputes concerning ownership of funds in these accounts. The "21 day rule" applies only to banks. Other parties holding your funds must turn them over within the time provided for in the levy. Accounts receivable are paid to the IRS in accordance with their original credit terms.

Q: What steps are routinely taken by the IRS to collect delinquent taxes?

A: The standard collection process includes:

- First notice and demand for payment on the unpaid tax.

- Three more payment due notices sent about a month apart.

- 10-day notice of intent to lien.

- 30-day notice of intent to levy (final notice) by certified mail.

- Enforcement action (seizure or levy).

Q: How can I check on a tax refund that is due me?

A: Call *Tele-tax* (listed in the Appendix). *Tele-tax* is a convenient way to get information on 140 different tax topics. You can listen to up to three topics with each phone call. Interestingly, the OIC Program is not one of the 140 topics covered by *Tele-tax*. Could the IRS *still* be trying to keep the OIC program a secret?

Q: Does the IRS offer free publications?

A: Yes. And most of their publications are worth reading. They are listed in the Appendix and are available from the IRS at (800) 829-3676.

Q: What is an "Automated Collection System"?

A: Several years ago, the IRS set up an automated collection system (ACS) to improve efficiency. This systematized process helps IRS collectors contact delinquent taxpayers by mail and phone. It has enormously increased IRS productivity.

Q: How can taxpayers claim a tax refund?

A: Taxpayers who believe they overpaid their taxes may file a claim for refund directly with the IRS. If the claim is denied, the taxpayer can file a lawsuit for the refund in either the U.S. Court of Claims or U.S. District Court.

Q: Can a taxpayer demand to see his or her tax files?

A: Yes. In most instances the IRS will show you your own file. If it refuses, the taxpayer can demand access to his or her files under the Freedom of Information Act.

Q: How does the IRS keep track of each taxpayer?

A: The IRS maintains a taxpayer account for each taxpayer. This IRS computer record contains your tax history, tax assessments, penalties, interest and credits for payment.

To help manage the system, the IRS also issues to each taxpayer a taxpayer identification number (TIN). This is usually the taxpayer's Social Security Number, but for corporations and trusts, it is a separate 13-digit number.

Q: What are the most common reasons for the large tax liabilities that force taxpayers to file Offers in Compromise?

A: Large tax liabilities are generally caused by unpaid withholding taxes. Owners and other responsible parties within a business are personally assessed the unpaid trust portion, or taxes actually deducted from the employees. This is called the 100 percent penalty assessment.

If business owners cannot pay the full withholding tax, they should at least pay the trust portion – that amount withheld from the employees – and designate that the payment be applied *only* to the trust portion liability. The business will owe its share of the payroll taxes due, but its officers and other responsible parties will have no personal liability.

Q: Who can file an Offer in Compromise?

A: Any "taxpayer" may file.

- Individuals
- Married couples
- Trusts
- Corporations
- Limited partnerships
- Limited liability companies
- Foundations, associations and other non-profit organizations
- Estates

In each instance, the OIC must be signed by a duly authorized individual.

Q: How does the IRS determine the "minimum bid price," or what the IRS will sell seized property for at public auction or private bid?

A: The IRS starts with an estimated fair market value. This is then reduced by 25 percent. The minimum bid price is 80 percent of that amount. Of course, the IRS must pay all prior encumbrances and expenses of the sale from the sale proceeds received.

Taxpayers can object to the minimum price bid on their property and request that a new professional appraisal be obtained by the IRS.

Q: What can the IRS do if I fraudulently transfer my assets?

A: The IRS may:

1) Sue in U.S. District Court to set aside the transfer.
2) Sue the transferee for the value of the transferred property.
3) File an administrative claim against the transferee for the value of the transferred asset.

Because of limited staff, the IRS seldom pursues fraudulent transfers.

Q: What can a business owner do to protect business assets from IRS seizure?

A: The business, to the extent practical, should be divided into separate corporations so if one corporation has a tax problem the IRS has no recourse to the remaining corporations.

The business should also be heavily mortgaged or encumbered leaving little or no equity for the IRS to seize.

Q: Do incorporated businesses commonly file Offers in Compromise?

A: Few businesses file OICs. Most OICs are filed by individuals. Businesses with severe tax troubles usually also owe other creditors and file Chapter 11 so they can compromise all their liabilities under one comprehensive reorganization plan.

Q: Do all IRS offices welcome OICs?

A: No. There is a difference in attitude and policy toward OICs between IRS offices and personnel. While it is clearly against the law, some district offices summarily reject all OICs or ultimately approve very few.

If your district office is hostile toward OICs, then write your congressman, or hire a tax representative outside your district and transfer your OIC case to your representative's district.

IRS attitudes toward OICs are improving as they become more widely used and encouraged by top IRS officials.

Q: How does the IRS value property held between husband and wife as tenants by the entirety?

A: This type of tenancy presents legal problems to the IRS, so it evaluates the interest of each spouse to be less than half the total value of the property. Twenty percent of the total value is generally considered each spouse's net worth in the property.

Property held as tenants in common or joint tenancy are fully valued based upon the taxpayer's percentage interest.

Q: Can a revenue officer demand to inspect my house?

A: Yes. Under an OIC this is an absolute IRS right and inspection of the taxpayer's personal goods and household effects is usually a condition for accepting the OIC. Works of art, jewelry, coins, stamp collections, silverware, china, antiques and other collectibles of value will be of particular interest.

This right to inspect applies only to an OIC. The IRS cannot otherwise enter your home without your permission or a warrant.

Q: How does the IRS compute the value of a taxpayer's ownership in a family business?

A: It is always difficult to appraise a small business, however, the IRS will attempt to value it as a "going concern" rather than as assets to be liquidated. If the IRS and the taxpayer cannot agree on this value, the IRS and taxpayer each can have the business professionally appraised.

Q: Can a taxpayer compromise some taxes and not others?

A: Your Offer in Compromise must include *all* owed taxes, plus penalties and interest. It must also include potential or contingent taxes and *every* type of tax, e.g., income taxes, highway taxes, employment taxes, and interest and penalties for each.

Q: Can you delete or modify preprinted provisions on Form 656 Offer in Compromise?

A: No. Deletions or revisions on the preprinted sections of Form 656 are not allowed. You may, however, attach items that modify or clarify your offer.

Q: Will the IRS accept an OIC from a taxpayer with a recent criminal record?

A: That depends on the crime, its notoriety, the taxpayer's reputation in the community and the taxpayer's compliance with the tax laws before and since the crime. If the IRS suspects that the crimes are ongoing, it will obviously deny the OIC for public policy reasons.

Q: Will the IRS inspect a taxpayer's safe deposit box before accepting an OIC?

A: Usually. Refusal to allow inspection will cause summary rejection of the offer.

Q: How does the IRS determine whether a "collateral agreement" to share in the taxpayer's future income is needed?

A: The IRS considers the taxpayer's:

- age
- earning capacity
- education
- health

- profession
- experience

Taxpayers should underplay these factors when presenting an offer.

Q: When can a taxpayer sue the IRS for damages?

A: It's difficult but not impossible to sue the IRS. The taxpayer must show the IRS action to have been frivolous, malicious or wantonly groundless. This means something more than that the IRS "guessed wrong" in determining the correct action.

Frivolous or malicious acts may cost the IRS up to $10,000. While there are undoubtedly numerous IRS abuses, few legal actions are ever commenced by taxpayers against the IRS and far fewer are won.

Taxpayers who encounter IRS abuse should contact the National Coalition of IRS Whistleblowers, 6255 Sunset Blvd., Suite 2020, Los Angeles CA 90028, or P.O. Box 65471, Washington DC 20035. This group includes numerous present and past IRS employees as well as concerned citizens and politicians working to expose IRS abuses and pave the way for reform.

IRS TERMS

This glossary includes those terms most commonly used in the Offer in Compromise program. There are many other tax terms this glossary does not include.

A

Abatement – A partial or complete cancellation of taxes, penalties or interest owed by a taxpayer.

ACS – See Automated Collection System.

Adjustment –Changes to your tax liability.

Amended Tax Return – A tax return filed within three years to make changes to a previously filed tax return.

Appeal – The IRS administrative process for taxpayers to contest decisions within the IRS. The denial of an installment agreement or offer in compromise cannot be appealed.

Assess – The recording of a tax liability against a taxpayer. The IRS does not assess taxes until the appeal period passes.

Asset – Any owned property.

Audit – An IRS review of the accuracy of a tax return. The IRS term for an audit is "examination".

Auditor – An IRS Examination Division employee who audits tax returns.

Automated Collection System – A computerized collection process for IRS collectors to contact delinquent taxpayers by telephone and mail. Often abbreviated as ACS.

B

Basis (Tax Basis) – The cost of an asset, which may be adjusted downward by depreciation or upward by improvements.

C

Collection Division – Tax collectors who work out of the IRS Service Center, Automated Collection or District Office.

Commissioner of Internal Revenue – The head of the IRS.

Criminal Investigation Division (CID) – The branch of the IRS that investigates tax crimes.

Delinquent Return – A tax return not filed by the due date (April 15) or by the dates allowed through the IRS extension periods (August 15 and October 15).

D

Depreciation – A tax deduction allowed for the wear-and tear on an income-producing asset, such as rental real estate or business equipment.

District Office – Local IRS offices that includes auditors, collectors, criminal investigators and Problems Resolution Officers.

Documentation – Written proof.

E

Enrolled Agent (EA) --An EA is a tax accountant or tax preparer allowed to practice before the IRS.

ExaminationOfficial – IRS term for an audit. See Audit.

Exemption – Exemption may refer to the number of dependents (including themselves) or refer to assets that the IRS cannot take if it levies on your property to satisfy your tax debt.

Extension – An extension to file gives a taxpayer more time to file a return but not to pay the taxes owed. A taxpayer can obtain an automatic extension until August 15 and can request a second extension until October 15 by filing with the IRS. The second extension is discretionary. A taxpayer can also request an extension to pay taxes, but they are rarely granted.

F

Failure to File Tax Return – The most common tax crime. Intentionally failing to file a return when you were obligated to do so is a misdemeanor. The maximum prison sentence is one year in jail and $25,000 for each year not filed.

Fair Market Value – The price a willing buyer and seller of property would agree on as fair.

Fifth Amendment – A right guaranteed by the U.S. Constitution that protects people from being forced by the government to incriminate themselves. You can assert your Fifth Amendment right against the IRS by refusing to answer questions or provide them documents.

Freedom of Information Act – A federal law giving citizens the rights to see governmental documents, including their IRS files.

G

Gift – Transfers of property without any payment.

Group Manager – The immediate superior of tax a collector at a District Office.

I

Income – All monies and other valuables receive, except items specifically exempted by the tax code.

Information Return – A report filed with the IRS showing income paid to a taxpayer. Form W-2 (wages) and Form 1099 (other income, such as interest paid by a bank, stock dividends or royalties) are examples.

Installment Agreement (IA) – An IRS monthly payment plan for past taxes.

Internal Revenue Code – The official tax laws of the U.S. as enacted by Congress. Also called the "tax code".

Internal Revenue Manual – IRS handbooks which set forth the internal operating guidelines for IRS personnel.

Internal Revenue Service – The tax law administration branch of the U.S. Treasury.

J

Jeopardy Assessment – An expedited procedure by which the IRS imposes a tax liability without notifying you first. A jeopardy assessment is rare and used when the IRS believes the taxpayer is about to leave the country or hide assets.

Joint Tax Return – An income tax return filed by a married couple.

L

Levy – An IRS seizure of property or wages to satisfy a delinquent tax debt.

Lien – See Tax Lien.

Limitation on Assessment and Collection – See Statute of Limitation.

M

Market Value – See Fair Market Value.

N

Non-Filer – A person or entity who does not files a tax return when require to do so.

Notice of Deficiency – See 90-Day Letter.

Notice of Tax Lien – See Tax Lien.

O

Offer in Compromise – A formal written offer to the IRS to settle your tax for less than the amount you owe or the IRS says you owe.

Ombudsman – An IRS troubleshooter who acts for taxpayers with problems not solved through normal IRS channels. Ombudsman's are Problems Resolution Officers who work in Problems Resolution Programs located in District Offices and Service Center. See also Problems Resolution Officers, Problems Resolution Program.

P

Payroll Taxes – Federal income tax and FICA contributions including both Social Security and Medicare. These are also called Trust Fund Taxes. See also 100% Payroll Penalty.

Penalties – Civil fines imposed on taxpayers who violate tax laws.

Personal Property – All property other than real estate-such as cash, stock, cars.

Petition – A form filed with the U.S. Tax Court requesting a hearing to contest a proposed IRS tax assessment.

Power of Attorney – A form appointing a tax representative to deal with the IRS on your behalf.

Problems Resolution Program – An IRS program to assist taxpayers with problems not solved in normal IRS channels. The program is administrated by Problem Resolution Officers. See also Ombudsman.

Property – See Personal Property, Real Property.

Protest – A written or oral request to appeal a decision within the IRS.

R

Real Property – Real estate is land and improvements to that land.

Regulations – IRS additions to the Internal Revenue Code.

Representative – See Tax Representative.

Return – See Tax Return.

Revenue Officer – An IRS tax collector.

S

Seizure – See Levy.

Service Centers – Ten regional IRS facilities where tax returns are filed and processed.

Special Agent – An IRS officer who investigates suspected tax crimes. See also Criminal Investigation Division (CID).

Statue of Limitation – Legal limits imposed on the IRS for assessing and collecting taxes, and on the Justice Department for charging taxpayers with tax crimes.

Summons – A legal order issued by the IRS or a court to compel a taxpayer or other person to appear provide financial information to the IRS.

T

Tax Attorney – A lawyer who does tax-related work including IRS dispute resolution and tax return.

Tax Code – See Internal Revenue Code.

Tax Court – The only federal court where a taxpayer can contest an IRS tax assessment without first paying the taxes.

Tax Law – The Internal Revenue Code, written by Congress. Internal Revenue Code.

Tax Lien – If you owe money to the IRS, the IRS has a claim against your property by "operation of law" this is done be recording a Notice of Federal Tax Lien at the county recorder's office or Notice to the public with your Secretary of State's office.

Tax Representative – A tax professional qualified to represent you before the IRS. See also Enrolled Agent, Tax Attorney.

Tax Return – A form individuals, partnerships and corporations must file each year with the IRS.

Taxpayer Account – An IRS computer record containing your tax history, and including all tax assessments, penalties and interest, and credits for payments.

Taxpayer Assistance Order – An order that a Problems Resolution Officer can issue to override an action taken by another division of the IRS. See also Ombudsman, Problems Resolution Officer, Problems Resolutions Program.

Taxpayer Identification Number (TIN) – An IRS assigned number used for computer tracking of tax accounts. For individuals, it is their Social Security number. For other entities, such as corporations it is a separate 13-digit number.

Taxpayer's Bill of Right – A 1988 federal law which sets behavior standards on the IRS and establishes taxpayer rights in dealing with the agency.

Tele-Tax – IRS pre-recorded tax topics information, available by telephone.

Trust Fund Taxes – See Payroll taxes.

W

Waiver – Voluntarily surrendering a legal right, such as the right to have the IRS collection period on a delinquent tax debt expire. The IRS may require waivers in exchanges for granting installment agreements.

100% – Payroll Penalty Assessed unpaid payroll taxes against "responsible" individuals involved in a business owing taxes. See also Payroll Taxes.

APPENDICES

APPENDIX A

- IRS OFFER IN COMPROMISE PROGRAM

- IRS COLLECTION MANUAL

- YOUR RIGHTS AS A TAXPAYER

APPENDIX B

- IRS FORMS

INTERNAL REVENUE SERVICE OFFER IN COMPROMISE PROGRAM

The following are excerpts from the Internal Revenue Service Manual (IRM) Section 5700 (Special Procedures) concerning IRS policies on Offers in Compromise. This manual is used by all IRS employees in the administration of the Offer in Compromise Program.

Read this material carefully. It will help clarify the chapter information.

57(10)0

OFFERS IN COMPROMISE

57(10)1
INTRODUCTION

The Service, like any other business, will encounter situations where an account receivable cannot be collected in full or there is a dispute as to what is owed. It is an accepted business practice to resolve these collection and liability issues through a compromise. Additionally, the compromise process is available to provide delinquent taxpayers with a fresh start toward future compliance with the tax laws.

57(10)1.1
OFFER POLICY

Policy Statement P-5-100 sets forth the Service's position on using compromises.

"The Service will accept an Offer in Compromise when it is unlikely that the tax liability can be collected in full and the amount offered reasonably reflects collection potential. An Offer in Compromise is a legitimate alternative to declaring a case as currently not collectible or to a protracted installment agreement. The goal is to achieve collection of what is potentially collectible at the earliest possible time and at the least cost to the government."

"In cases where an Offer in Compromise appears to be a viable solution to a tax delinquency, the Service employee assigned the case will discuss the compromise alternative with the taxpayer and, when necessary, assist in preparing the required forms. The taxpayer will be responsible for initiating the first specific proposal for compromise."

"The success of the compromise program will be assured only if taxpayers make adequate compromise proposals consistent with their ability to pay and the Service makes prompt and reasonable decisions. Taxpayers are expected to provide reasonable documentation to verify their ability to pay. The ultimate goal is a compromise which is in the best interest of both the taxpayer and the Service. Acceptance of an adequate offer will result in creating, for the taxpayer, an expectation of a fresh start toward compliance with all future filing and payment requirements."

57(10)1.2
COMPROMISE OBJECTIVES

1)   To resolve accounts receivable which cannot be collected in full or on which there is a legitimate dispute as to what is owed.

2)   To effect collection of what could reasonably be collected at the earliest time possible and at the least cost to the government.

3)   To give taxpayers a fresh start to enable them to voluntarily comply with the tax laws.

57(10)1.3
PUBLIC POLICY

1)   There are rare circumstances where acceptances of an offer may not be in the best interests of the government. Consequently, an offer may be rejected even though it can be shown conclusively that the amount offered is greater than what could be collected in any other manner. This will generally be limited to situations where public knowledge of the accepted offer would be seriously detrimental to voluntary compliance. A decision to reject an offer for public policy considerations should be rare and should be made only where a clear and convincing case can be made for the detrimental effects of acceptance. The authority is (to) reject Offers in Compromise for public policy reasons is restricted to District Directors.

2) If an offer is to be rejected for public policy reasons, the specific reasons should be fully documented in the case file.

57(10)1.4
TAXES, PENALTIES AND INTEREST CONSTITUTE ONE LIABILITY

A compromise is effective for the entire liability for taxes, penalty, and interest for the years or periods covered by the offer. All questions of tax liability for the year(s) or period(s) covered by such Offer in Compromise are conclusively settled. Neither the taxpayer nor the government can reopen the case unless there was falsification or concealment of assets, or a mutual mistake of a material fact was made which would be sufficient to set aside or reform a contract.

57(10)1.5
COMPROMISE OF EXPIRED TAX LIABILITY

The Service will not accept an Offer in Compromise of a tax which has become unenforceable by reason of lapse of time unless the taxpayer is fully aware of the fact that the collection of the tax is barred. Where such a situation exists, the offer itself (or a separate letter over the signature of the taxpayer) should show that he/she has been advised of the expiration of the statutory period for collection, but, notwithstanding such fact, still desires to have the offer accepted. In this type of case, no collateral agreement is necessary.

57(10)1.6
COMMISSIONER'S DELEGATION OF AUTHORITY TO ACCEPT OFFERS IN COMPROMISE

Delegation Order No. 11 redelegates the compromise authority vested in the Commissioner.

Regional Commissioners, Regional Counsel, District Directors, Assistant District Directors, Service Center Directors, Assistant Service Center Directors, Division Chiefs, Regional Directors of Appeals, Chiefs and Associate Chiefs, Appeals Offices have all been delegated Offer in Compromise acceptance and rejection authority. The authority delegated to Division Chief may not be redelegated. Service Center Directors and Assistant Service Center Directors may redelegate their authority but not lower than to Chief, Compliance Division and Chief, Collection Division (Austin Compliance Center). Chiefs, Field Branch and Chiefs, Special Procedures are delegated authority to accept Offers in Compromise in cases in which the unpaid liability (including any interest, penalty, additional amount or addition to tax) is $100,000 or less and to reject Offers in Compromise regardless of the amount of the liability sought to be compromised. The authority to reject Offers in Compromise for public policy reasons is restricted to District Directors.

57(10)1.62
WITHDRAWAL AUTHORITY

District Directors, Assistant District Directors, Regional Counsel, Regional Directors of Appeals, Chiefs and Associate Chiefs, Appeals Offices are delegated authority to reject and are authorized to acknowledge withdrawal of any offer regardless of the amount of the liability sought to be compromised. The Chief, Field Branch and Chief, Special Procedures are delegated authority to acknowledge withdrawal of any offer regardless of the amount of the liability sought to be compromised. The authority delegated to Chief, Field Branch and Chief, Special Procedures may not be redelegated.

57(10)1.7

JURISDICTIONAL RESPONSIBILITY

57(10)1.71
DISTRICT COLLECTION FUNCTION

1) District Collection functions have jurisdictional responsibility for the following:

   a) Consideration of all Offers in Compromise based on doubt as to collectibility as well as preparation of the necessary documents and letters. This includes offers to compromise proposed liabilities which are still the subject of settlement negotiations in the district Examination function or Appeals Office.

   b) Consideration of penalty only offers. The service center will normally handle these except, in cases where service center management believes they should be considered in the district. The district also has jurisdiction on penalty offers where the issue is in doubt as to collectibility.

   c) Consideration of all offers to compromise 100-percent penalty assessments based either on doubt as to liability or doubt as to collectibility.

d) Consideration of all offers in default, regardless of whether the basic offer was based on doubt as to liability or doubt as to collectibility.

e) Offers in Compromise based on both doubts as to liability and doubt as to collectibility will be assigned initially to the Collection function for a collectibility determination. If it is determined that the taxpayer may be able to pay an amount in excess of the amount offered, processing of the offer should be discontinued. The offer and copies of related documents should be forwarded through district channels to the service center and/or transferred to the Examination function as a doubt as to liability case. In either case the service center will be notified of the change in jurisdiction and the Form 2515 so notated.

57(10)1.72
DISTRICT EXAMINATION FUNCTION

1) The district Examination function has jurisdictional responsibility for investigation and processing of tax offers based solely on doubt as to liability, including preparation of the necessary documents and letters to effect their disposition.

2) Offers in Compromise received in the district Examination function will be processed in accordance with established Examination procedures. Any requests for information from Collection records should be coordinated through the appropriate Collection function. This may include information on liens, suits, judgments, bankruptcy or decedent estates.

57(10)1.8
DETERMINATION OF LIABILITY

1) Liability Less than Offer – If during the investigation of an offer, the liability is found to be equal to or less than the offer, the amount of the assessment in excess of the liability should be abated, and the taxpayer should be request to withdraw the offer, or the offer should be rejected. The taxpayer will be advised to pay the correct liability.

2) Liability Greater than Offer – If during the investigation of an offer, liability is found to be greater than the offer, but less than the amount assessed, the excess amount of the assessment should be abated. The taxpayer will be informed of the redetermined liability and be advised to pay the correct liability.

3) Definite Determination Cannot be Made — If a definite determination of the liability cannot be made, but there is doubt about the liability, the degree of doubt may be measured and the case closed by compromise. The amount acceptable will depend upon the degree of doubt found in the particular case.

4) The Examination function will dispose of completed offer investigations in essentially the same manner as the Collection function, except that:

a) The processing performed in the Collection function will be performed by the Quality Review Staff in accordance with existing Examination procedures.

b) Cases shall be referred to the Criminal Investigation function for concurrence if the following conditions exist:

1. The merits of the ad valorem fraud or negligence penalty are involved;

2. The case if one in which the Special Agent had recommended assertion of such a penalty in the final report in the case and;

3. The district Examination function is recommending acceptance of the offer.

c) If the Criminal Investigation function concurs in the recommended disposition of the case, concurrence should be made and by memorandum the entire file returned to the district Examination function for processing. If the Criminal Investigation function does not concur and no agreement can be reached with the Examination function as to the disposition of the offer, the entire file shall be forwarded to the district director for resolution. Thereafter, the case will be processed in accordance with established procedures. This is applicable only to cases in which no prosecution has been recommended or the question of prosecution has been settled and the criminal case closed.

d) In those offers accepted by the Examination function, the appropriate Form 7249, Offer Acceptance Report, should be forwarded to Collection for inclusion in the public inspection file.

e) If the offer was rejected or withdrawn, Form 1271, Rejection and Withdrawal Memorandum, and accompanying memorandum should be forwarded to Collection.

57(10)1.9
CASES PENDING IN DISTRICT EXAMINATION FUNCTION

When an offer to compromise a proposed liability is submitted on the basis of inability to pay during the examination process, the offer should be considered by the district office in the same manner as any other inability to pay case. If it appears to be an acceptable amount based on a preliminary analysis of the taxpayer's financial statement, the Examination function will secure from the taxpayer conditional agreement on a definite liability. The agreement form should be held in escrow pending final action on the offer. If the offer is accepted by a delegated official, action will then be taken to have the tax assessed. The acceptance letter should not be mailed to the taxpayer until the assessment has been made. It should be noted that if a statutory notice of deficiency has been sent, the period for filing a petition with the Tax Court is not suspended.

57(10)1.10
JURISDICTION OF THE APPEALS OFFICES

1)   When an offer is based in whole or in part on doubt as to liability and the Appeals Office has determined the liability or the case is pending before the Appeals Office, the district director will forward the offer to Appeals for consideration.

2)   If an Offer in Compromise based on doubt as to liability is pending in the Appeals Office, the Appeals Office may call upon the district director to conduct any investigation deemed necessary to reach a conclusion on the merits of the case. These investigations should be conducted as expeditiously as possible.

3)   If any offer is submitted only on doubt as to collectibility and the liability was previously determined by Appeals, the acceptability of the offer will be determined by Appeals, the acceptability of the offer will be determined by the district office.

4)   If an offer is submitted only on doubt as to collectibility and the liability is pending in Appeals, the Appeals Office will be notified and asked whether there is any objection to consideration. The Appeals Office will respond within 30 days. The actual investigation of the offer will be deferred during that period pending the response of the Appeals Office. The Appeals Office will inform the district director of any objection by memorandum.

5) If there are no objections and the offer is to be investigated, the Appeals Office will normally secure the taxpayer's conditional agreement to the liability or to the revised amount determined to be due. If the offer is accepted, the Appeals Office will be notified and it will arrange to have the liability assessed. The acceptance letter should not be mailed until the assessment has been made.

6) If the offer is rejected, Appeals will be notified so that they can again consider the merits of the liability.

7) It should be noted that the filing of an offer does not stay the running of the 90-day period set forth in a deficiency notice.

57(10)1.11
TAX COURT CASES

1) If an offer is submitted on a Tax Court case and it is based on doubt as to liability, the offer will be forwarded to the appropriate Appeals Office for consideration. It will be Appeals responsibility to work that offer.

2) If an offer is based solely on doubt as to collectibility, the procedures for handling Appeals cases will be followed.

3) When an offer is to be investigated, Appeals will normally secure a stipulation agreement to the proposed liability. This will normally be held in escrow.

4) If the offer is recommended for rejection, Appeals will be notified. Appeals will have 10 days to provide the district office with any information that should be weighed in making the final decision. However, the district office will decide whether to reject the offer and provide the taxpayer with the necessary appeal rights.

5) If the offer is accepted by the district office, Appeals will take the necessary action to get the stipulation filed with the Tax Court. The Appeals Office will then take steps to have the tax assessed. The acceptance letter should not be issued until the tax is assessed.

57(10)1.12
APPEAL OF REJECTED OFFERS

1) When Appeals decides that an offer is to be accepted, Appeals will take all the appropriate acceptance procedures. After the required reports have been signed by the delegated official, the case will be returned to the district office for processing.

2) When Appeals sustains the proposed rejection of the offer, Appeals will notify the taxpayer and the offer file will be returned to the district office for processing.

57(10)1.13
CASES UNDER JURISDICTION OF DEPARTMENT OF JUSTICE

1) The Service does not have the authority to accept an Offer in Compromise in the following types of cases:

   a) An offer covering a liability "in suit."

   b) Cases where the liability has been reduced to judgment.

   c) Cases in which recommendation for prosecution is pending in the Department of Justice or United States Attorney's Offices including cases in which criminal proceedings have been instituted but not disposed of.

   d) Cases in which a recommendation for prosecution is pending in the Office of the Chief Counsel, and in related cases in which Offers in Compromise have been submitted.

   e) Cases in which the acceptance of an offer by the Service is dependent upon the acceptance of a related offer or upon a settlement under the jurisdiction of the Department of Justice.

   f) The Chief Counsel will ordinarily be called upon for views and a recommendation on the acceptability of an offer on a liability under the jurisdiction of the Department of Justice. The district director will usually be requested to conduct an investigation of the taxpayer's financial condition and to make a recommendation regarding acceptance. Any amounts received by the district in payment of an offer or related collateral agreement accepted by the Department of Justice should be forwarded directly to the appropriate service center for posting.

57(10)2

MANAGEMENT OF THE OFFER PROGRAM

57(10)2.1
GENERAL

1) Management has the following responsibilities under the offer program:

    a) To ensure that the spirit and intent of Policy Statement P-5-100 are adhered to.

    b) To establish a procedural plan for reviewing Forms 656, Offer in Compromise, received directly from taxpayers to determine whether they are processable before sending them to the service center for processing. This could be accomplished either by each revenue officer doing the review or having the review centralized.

    c) To establish a procedural plan most appropriate for the district for handling the investigation, review and approval of offers. The issues to be covered include the following:

        1. Receipt of Form 2515, Form 656 and Form 433A/B from the service center.

        2. Receipt and distribution of transcripts.

        3. Research of Special Procedures files.

        4. The assignment of offer investigations.

        5. Review and processing of completed investigation.

        6. Maintenance of information necessary to complete Form 4196, Collection Quarterly Report of Offer in Compromise Activity.

        7. Input of status 71 and storage of TDAs when collection is being withheld.

        8. Prompt resumption of collection action when an offer is rejected using information developed during offer investigation.

        9. Reversal of all status 71.

d) The procedural plan should be designed to ensure the following:

1. Timely processing, to ensure offers are competed within a reasonable time frame. Absent unusual circumstances it is the expectation that offer investigations be completed within six months.

2. Quality investigation limited to what is actually necessary.

3. Limited review.

There is no requirement that the Special Procedures function be involved in this process.

e) The Service Center Collection Branch should be advised by each district of the organizational unit to receive all offer referrals and questions for that particular district.

57(10)2.2
FOLLOW-UP PENDING OFFER

No later than February first of each year, the service center will prepare and forward to the office having jurisdiction, a list of all pending Offers in Compromise more than six months old. The receiving office will report whether the case is opened or closed, returning a copy of the list to the service center within 30 days of its receipt.

57(10)3

POST REVIEW OF OFFERS IN COMPROMISE

57(10)3.1
REGIONAL REVIEW OF COLLECTION ACTIVITY ACCEPTANCES, REJECTIONS AND WITHDRAWALS

1) The Assistant Regional Commissioner (Collection) will establish a system of regional post reviews annually to sample a cross section of all types of offer cases. The sample size, mix of open and closed cases and methodology will be determined based on regional needs.

2) In those cases where regional post review discloses a substantial error in fact or judgment on the part of a Collection employee, the region will prepare an advisory memorandum to the appropriate office. A periodic digest or compendium of review findings may also be prepared by the region and sent to district offices and/or service centers in the region.

A copy of the digest, when prepared, should also be sent to the National Office, Assistant Commissioner (Collection), Attention: CO:O. All memoranda and digests should be edited to comply with disclosure regulations. See IRM 1272, Disclosure of Official Information Handbook, texts (12)70 through (12)75.

3) During the post review of completed offers, the regional reviewer also may identify unique cases and prepare an abstract of each such case. These abstracts together with recent IRM changes should be included in the digest of findings, if one is prepared.

4) The review should also look for uniform application of Policy Statement P-5-100.

57(10)3.2
NATIONAL OFFICE REVIEW OF OFFERS

The National Office will conduct periodic reviews as they relate to performance under the Annual Business Plan.

57(10)3.3
REGIONAL REVIEW OF EXAMINATION ACTIVITY ACCEPTANCES, REJECTIONS AND WITHDRAWALS

1) The Assistant Regional Commissioner (Examination) will establish a system of regional post review of all offers (acceptances, rejections and withdrawal) with liabilities of $5,000 or more (Chief Counsel cases are excluded from all post reviews). In this post review, documents for cases requiring review will be screened and, if required, the files on the cases may be requisitioned. This activity should be combined with the regular Examination post review program. Technical, accounting and procedural phases should be emphasized during the post review of all cases.

2) In those instances where regional review discloses a substantial error in fact or in judgment, the Regional reviewer will prepare an advisory memorandum to the office concerned. A copy or a digest may be sent to all other district offices in the region. All memoranda and digests should be edited to comply with disclosure regulations. See IRM 1272, Disclosure of Official Information Handbook, texts (12)70 through (12)75.

57(10)4
COLLECTION ACTIVITY REPORTING INSTRUCTIONS OF OFFER IN COMPROMISE ACTIVITY

In order to evaluate the Offer in Compromise program and disposition of cases, the National Office requires quarterly reporting on Form 4196, Collection Quarterly Report of Offer in Compromise Activity (report Symbol NO-5000-108). Instructions for the preparation and submission of the form are contained in IRM 5872.5.

57(10)5

ADVISING TAXPAYERS OF OFFER PROVISIONS

57(10)5.1
GENERAL

1) When criminal proceedings are not contemplated and an analysis of the taxpayer's assets, liabilities, income and expenses show that a tax liability cannot be realistically collected in full, the possibility of an Offer in Compromise will be discussed with the taxpayer (see 7(10)1 of LEM V).

2) The taxpayer will be advised what an offer is, what the Service procedures and policies are with respect to offers, what forms must be completed, and what benefits the taxpayer will receive from an offer acceptance. The taxpayer should be instructed to read the entire Form 656 including the instructions carefully. When necessary, the Service employee will assist the taxpayer in preparing the required forms.

3) Taxpayers will also be advised that collection will normally be withheld unless it is determined that the offer is delaying tactic and collection is in jeopardy. However, if the taxpayer is making payments under an installment payment agreement, the taxpayer should be told to continue the payments.

4) Before an offer is submitted, the taxpayer will not be told what specifically to offer. The taxpayer will be responsible for initiating the first specific proposal for compromise. However, the taxpayer should be advised that the proposal should not be a "fishing expedition" but a legitimate compromise proposal based on the ability to pay. The taxpayer should be advised that the service does not operate on the theory that "something is better than nothing."

5) The taxpayer should be encouraged to submit a deposit as a sign of good faith. The taxpayer should be advised that if the offer is rejected, the service will return the deposit unless the taxpayer authorizes in writing that the deposit may be applied to the liability.

6) The Revenue Officer should determine what information (e.g. evaluation, bank statements) is still needed to verify the ability to pay. The taxpayer should be encouraged to submit the information with the offer since the sooner this information is available the sooner the Service can make a decision.

7) The taxpayer should be advised that submission of an offer does not constitute acceptance. No offer is accepted until the appropriate delegated official approves acceptance and the taxpayer is notified by letter that the offer has been accepted.

8) The taxpayer will be advised that no abatement will be made or tax liens released until the total amount offered, including interest on any deferred payments, has been paid in full.

9) The taxpayer will be advised that acceptance will require the taxpayer to comply fully with all filing and paying requirements of the law for five years. The taxpayer will also be advised that default of the condition shall be treated the same as default in payment under paragraph (7) on Form 656.

10) The taxpayer will be advised that they waive certain refunds or credits they may otherwise be entitled to receive.

11) The taxpayer will be advised that after the offer amount is paid the accrued interest must also be paid. Interest is due from the date of acceptance until the amount offered is paid in full. The interest provision of deferred payment offers should be explained and that Letter 277(C) will be sent reflecting the amount of interest due and a request for payment.

57(10)5.2
SOURCES OF OFFER FUNDS

1) When discussing offer possibilities with the taxpayer, sources of potential funds should be discussed. Some potential sources could be:

   a) A non-liable spouse who has property which he/she may be interested in utilizing to secure a compromise of a spouse's tax debt.

   b) Relatives or friends

   c) Lending institutions

   d) Employers

   e)   Suppliers

   f)   Customers

57(10)5.3
LIENS ON PENDING ASSESSMENTS

If the offer is to provide for deferred payments and no lien has been filed, it is advisable to inform the taxpayer that to protect the government's interest, a lien will be filed after a proposed liability is assessed. This will avoid any misunderstanding. However, care should be taken to ensure that the lien will not adversely impact the taxpayer's ability to raise the funds necessary to satisfy the offer. See Policy Statement P-5-47.

57(10)6

PREPARATION OF THE OFFER (FORM 656)

57(10)6.1
NAME AND ADDRESS OF TAXPAYER

The full name, address, Social Security Number, and/or Employer Identification Number of the taxpayer must be entered on Form 656. If the liability is joint and both parties wish to make the offer, both names must be shown. If the taxpayer is singly liable for a liability (e.g., employment taxes) and jointly liable for a liability (e.g., income taxes) and only one person is submitting the offer, only one offer must be submitted. If the taxpayer is singly liable for one liability and jointly liable for another and both joint parties are submitting the offer, two offers must be submitted, one for the separate liability and one for the joint liability.

57(10)6.2
TOTAL LIABILITY ON FORM 656, OFFER IN COMPROMISE

   1)   A taxpayer must list all unpaid tax liabilities sought to be compromised in item (1) on Form 656. The type of tax and the period of the liability must be specifically identified. Examples of the most common liabilities involved and the proper identification are as follows:

       a)   Income tax for the year(s) 19XX...

       b)   Withholding and Federal Insurance Contributions Act taxes for the period(s) ended 9/30/XX, 12/31/XX...

       c)   Federal Unemployment Tax Act taxes for year(s) 19XX...

d) 100-percent penalty assessment incurred as a responsible person of Y Corporation for failure to pay withholding and Federal Insurance Contributions Act Taxes for the periods ended 9/30/XX, 12/31/XX...

e) Penalty for failure to file income tax return(s) for the year(s) 19XX.

57(10)6.3
AMOUNT OF OFFER

1) The total amount offered should be shown. If any amount is to be paid on notice of acceptance of the offer or at any later date, the taxpayer must include in item (2) as follows:

a) The amount, if any, deposited at the time of filing the offer.

b) Any amount deposited on a prior offer which is to be applied on the offer. (This does not include any amount the taxpayer previously authorized the Service to apply directly to the tax liability.)

c) The amount of any subsequent payment and the date on which each payment is to be made.

57(10)6.4
TERM OF PAYMENT

1) A cash offer is one where the total amount offered is paid with the offer.

2) A deferred payment offer is one where any part of the amount offered is to be paid at any date(s) after submission of the offer.

3) The terms of a deferred payment offer should be precisely stated so there can be no doubt as to the taxpayer's intent if the offer is accepted. The due date of each payment should be specified, as in the following examples:

a) $5,000.00 deposited with the offer and the balance of $25,000.00 to be paid within 30 days after the date of notice of the offer's acceptance.

b) $3,000.00 deposited with the offer and the balance of $25,000.00 to be paid at the rate of $1,000.00 per month, beginning on the 15th day of the month after the date of notice of the offer's acceptance and on the 15th day of each month thereafter.

4) In cases where deferred payment offers are submitted, the payments may begin immediately upon the submission of the offer especially if they come from current income, or upon notice of acceptance. Payments should be monthly on a deferred payment offer. The offer should be liquidated in the shortest time possible. If the balance of the offer is to be paid in one sum or in a series of installments which involve borrowing or liquidating certain assets, deferred payments should begin at or within a specified time after notice of acceptance. It is not practical to have a taxpayer liquidate assets where values may fluctuate, without knowing that the offer is accepted.

5) The Designated Payment Code 09 will be used for payments made on an Offer in Compromise.

57(10)6.5
GROUNDS FOR OFFER

1) Item 9 of Form 656 is to be used for giving the facts and reasons why the Offer in Compromise should be accepted. If the offer is based only on doubt as to collectibility, the taxpayer must submit a detailed statement which describes why the Service cannot collect more than offered from his/her assets and present and future income, taking into consideration that the Service has ten years to collect liability.

2) If the taxpayer has assets or income that are available to him/her but no available to the Service for collection action, the taxpayer must also explain why the Service should not expect some portion of these assets or income to be paid to the Service if the Service is to compromise the tax liability for less than is owed.

3) If the offer is based on doubt as to liability, the taxpayer must submit a detailed statement as to why the liability is not owed.

57(10)6.6
SIGNING THE OFFER

1) Where a husband and wife seek to compromise a joint liability, both must sign to ensure that the waiver and other provisions bind both parties. In the case of a corporation, the corporate name must be entered on the first line and the signature of the president or other authorized officer on the second line.

2)   An offer submitted by a qualified fiduciary of the estate of a deceased taxpayer will be binding on the taxpayer's estate to the extent that it would be binding on a taxpayer who submits an offer on his/her own behalf. The fiduciary should submit evidence of his/her qualifications.

3)   A Form 2848 is sufficient to allow complete representation for an Offer in Compromise with the exception of Appeals. (See Circular 230 for complete representation requirements of Appeals.) Form 2848 does not have to specifically grant the authority to execute Form 656.

57(10)6.7
OVERPAYMENTS

1)   The taxpayer waives certain refunds or credits he or she may otherwise be entitled to receive. These overpayments of any tax or other liability, including interest and penalties, cover periods that end before, within, or as of the end of the calendar year in which the offer is accepted. Offset of any overpayment would be limited to the difference between the tax liability, including statutory additions, and the amount paid on the offer.

2)   The overpayment of one spouse may not be applied against the separate liability of the other spouse unless a written consent to credit is obtained. Often consents to credit or the waiver of refunds are executed by related taxpayers with the express condition that they be made only if the offer is accepted.

3)   Under no circumstances will this waiver provision be deleted in the case of a taxpayer who seeks a compromise on grounds of doubt as to collectibility.

4)   When a tax offer is based solely upon doubt as to liability, and if the amount of the offer reflects such doubt and equals the apparently correct liability, including penalty and interest to date, then the waiver of refunds, included in subdivision (b), Item 4 of Form 656, should be eliminated. Otherwise the waiver of refunds would compel the taxpayer to pay an excessive amount should any refunds covered by the waiver provisions arise. If this waiver provision has not been deleted rom the offer before it reaches the reviewing officials, the deletion should be made before the acceptance recommendation is approved.

57(10)7

STATUTORY WAIVER

57(10)7.1
SUSPENSION OF STATUTE OF LIMITATIONS

1) The compromise agreement on Form 656, Offer in Compromise, provides that the taxpayer agrees to the suspension of the running of the statutory period of limitations on both assessment and collection for the period that the offer is pending, or the period that any installment remains unpaid, and for one year thereafter. This includes the period of time in which the offer is being considered by Appeals. For the suspension provisions to be effective, both the taxpayer and the authorized Service employee must sign the data before the expiration of the statutory period, and the date the employee signs the waiver must be filled in.

2) Where multiple offers are filed by one taxpayer, the effect of the waivers on the offers is cumulative. It should be noted however, that when an offer is filed within one year after rejection or withdrawal of a pervious offer, the overlapping period should not be counted once in determining the suspension of the statutory period of limitations. While there are various methods to determine the new expiration date, only the method shown in Exhibits 5700-21 will be used for uniformity in these calculations.

3) Where an offer is submitted by a proponent other than the taxpayer, who is not authorized to act for the taxpayer, the statutory period for assessment and collection are not suspended unless the taxpayer's signature is secured. The service center or district office, whichever discovers this fact first, will flag the offer in order to alert the examining officer of the possible need to protect both statutory periods.

4) Unless a significant error or omission exists which requires return of the offer to the proponent, to ensure that the waiver provisions are effective, the waiver acceptance in the lower left corner of Form 656 will be signed at the earliest possible time after receipt. If possible, waiver acceptance will be signed on the date a processable offer is received by a delegated employee (in accordance with Delegation Order 42) in the district office or at the service center. The offer is considered pending from the date the delegated Service employee signs and dates the acceptance of the waiver of the statutory period of limitations on Form 656, until it is accepted, rejected or withdrawn. The same procedure will be followed for collateral agreements. (See IRC 6501 and 6502.) The

Service employee authorized to sign the receipt of the waiver in IMF cases only will place the appropriate alpha collection statute expiration code "P" (primary), "S" (secondary) or "B" (both) in red in the far right of the date box at the bottom of Form 656 to identify which taxpayer the extension applies to.

57(10)7.2
COLLECTION WAIVERS–FORM 656, OFFER IN COMPROMISE VIS-A-VIS FORM 900, TAX COLLECTION WAIVER

1)   The service takes the position that in any case where the taxpayer and the Service have agreed, by the execution of Form 900, Tax Collection Waiver, to extend the collection statute to a specific date, the acceptance of the waiver of the statute of limitations by an authorized Service employee when an offer is submitted will sus

pend the running of the statute of limitations. This will effectively extend the date specified on Form 900 by the number of days that the offer and any related collateral agreements are pending or by the number of days that any installments under the offer remain unpaid or that any other provisions of the offer are not carried out and for one year thereafter.

2)   This position is not governing in the Fifth Circuit (covering Texas, Louisiana and Mississippi) or the Eleventh Circuit (covering Georgia, Florida and Alabama) where the decision in United States v. Newman, 405 F. 2d 189 (5th Cir. 1968), is controlling law. It should be noted that the rule established in United States v. Newman, 405 F.2d 189 (5th Cir. 1968) states that a Form 900 waiver replaces the statutory period of limitation with a date certain beyond which the Government's cause of action is barred. The Form 900 waiver now provides that the date certain specified therein is to be further extended by any Offer in Compromise.

57(10)8
PREPARING THE FINANCIAL STATEMENT

A taxpayer seeking to compromise a liability based on doubt as to collectibility must submit a Form 433-A, Financial Statement for Individuals, Form 433-B, Collection Information Statement for Business, and/or any other financial statement prepared by the taxpayer as long as it conforms with the information provided in the Form 433A/B and is signed under penalties of perjury. The taxpayer's financial statement must reflect "N/A" (not applicable) in those blocks that do not affect the taxpayer.

57(10)9
RECEIPT AND PROCESSING

57(10)9.1
GENERAL

1) When an Offer in Compromise is received from the taxpayer, a determination will be made whether the offer is processable. This determination should be made by the personnel designated under local procedures.

2) If an offer is not processable the waiver acceptance should not be executed and the Form 656 will be returned to the taxpayer within 14 days from receipt. The offer will be returned to the taxpayer specifying what must be corrected or added before offer processing can begin. The taxpayer may correct an unprocessable offer by either:

   1. Entering and initialling the change on the Form 656 submitted or

   2. Filing a new Form 656.

3) An offer is unprocessable if:

   a) The taxpayer is not identified.

   b) The liabilities to be compromised are not identified.

   c) No amount is offered.

   d) Appropriate signatures are not present.

   e) Financial statement is not provided.

   f) The amount offered does not equal or exceed the amount shown in item 27 column (d) on Form 433-B or line 37 titled "equity in assets" on Form 433-A.

   g) An obsolete Form 656 has been used.

   h) Under no circumstances will an offer be returned solely on the basis that the cost of investigation does not justify consideration of the offer.

4) One copy of the offer will be retained in the district so that the assignment, initial processing, consideration and investigation of the offer is not delayed. The other two copies of the processable offer will be forwarded to the appropriate service center for processing.

5)   The service center will return the processed offer to the appropriate function along with two copies of Form 2515 (Record of Offer in Compromise). One copy of Form 2515 will be used for control purposes.

57(10)9.2
WITHHOLDING COLLECTION ON ACCOUNTS SOUGHT TO BE COMPROMISED

1)   Collection activity will be withheld on any open accounts if it is determined that the offer merits consideration and there is no reason to believe that collection of the tax liability will be jeopardized. If there is any indication that the filing of an Offer in Compromise was solely for the purpose of delaying collection of the liability or that the delay would jeopardize the government's interest, immediate steps should be taken to collect the unpaid liability. (See Treasury Regulation 301.7122-1(d)(2) and Policy Statement P-5-97.)

2)   If the taxpayer is currently paying under the term of an installment agreement, the taxpayer should be told to continue those payments.

3)   Where the grounds for the offer are strictly doubt as to liability and there is no evidence that filing the offer was solely for the purpose of delaying collection or that the delay would jeopardize the government's interest, collection will be withheld.

4)   If the accounts are assigned to a revenue officer disposition of the accounts will be held in abeyance until notice of the TC 480 is received.

5)   Accounts will be updated to status 71 upon receipt of notification of the TC 480 if a decision has been made to withhold collection.

6)   A status 71 should not be input if one of the co-obligors has not submitted an offer on a joint liability.

7)   Form 657 (Revenue Officer Report), which requires managerial approval, will be used by the revenue officer assigned the accounts to document the decision to continue or suspend collection activity.

8)   When collection is to be withheld the TDAs covering accounts sought to be compromised will not be placed in the closed TDA files so that all case documentation will be available. Local management will determine where the TDA case file will be retained. The Form 657 will be completed and associated with the

revenue officer history documentation and the related TDAs. The Form 657 will include information on collection potential and all investigative steps that have already been taken and the dates of those actions. The Form 657 is to be used by the offer examiner to determine what investigative steps still need to be taken.

57(10)9.3
TAXPAYER CONTACT

1) Within 30 calendar days from receipt of the offer, the examining officer should contact the taxpayer. The taxpayer should be notified of any information that the examiner needs to make a decision. The request should be reasonable and the taxpayer should be given a reasonable time to comply. However, a specified date must be given. The taxpayer will be notified that the offer will be rejected if the information is not supplied.

2) If the taxpayer does not comply, the offer should be rejected absent unusual circumstances. As outlined in Policy Statement P-5-100, the offer process cannot work if the taxpayer does not cooperate.

3) If personal contact cannot be made, Letter 1027(DO) may be used, setting out in as much detail as possible the information needed. Again, the taxpayer will be given a specific deadline and advised of the consequences of noncompliance.

57(10)10

ADEQUATE OFFER

57(10)10.1
DETERMINATION OF ADEQUATE OFFER

1) An offer is adequate if it reasonably reflects collection potential. This will include amounts that can be collected from other parties through suit, assertion of transferee liability, 100 percent penalty and other actions. Additional consideration will be given to assets and income that are available to the taxpayer but beyond the reach of the government.

2) The starting point in the consideration of an offer submitted based on doubt as to collectibility is the value of the taxpayer's assets less encumbrances which have priority over the federal tax lien. Ordinarily, the liquidating or quick sale value of assets should be used. Quick sale or liquidating value is the amount which would

be realized from the sale of an asset in a situation where financial pressures cause the taxpayer to sell in a short period of time. It should be recognized, however, that the acceptance of an offer serves the best interest of the government. Therefore, it would not be unreasonable in a given case to use forced sale value in determining collection potential. Additionally, since valuations of property, except cash or cash equivalents, are not scientifically exact, care should be exercised to avoid inflexible, non-negotiable values.

3) The Service also takes into consideration the amount that can be collected form the taxpayer's future income. In evaluating those future prospects, the taxpayer's education, profession or trade, age and experience, health, past and present income will be considered. In evaluating future income potential an evaluation must be made of the likelihood that any increase in real income will be available to pay the delinquent taxes. The Service needs to take into consideration the increasing cost of living as a factor in determining amounts potentially collectible form future incomes.

4) Rejection of an offer solely based on narrow asset and income evaluations should be avoided. The Service should attempt to negotiate offer agreements which are in the best interest of all parties. Included in determining the government's interests are the cost of collection. If an offer is rejected because more can be collected than is offered, it is generally expected that the amount determined to be collectible will actually be collected.

57(10)10.2
NEGOTIATING AN ACCEPTABLE OFFER

1) The examining officer should determine what would be an acceptable offer. The taxpayer will be given an opportunity to increase the offer. Because asset values are generally not carved in stone, offer examiners should remain flexible toward negotiating an offer that, considering all factors, would be in the Government's best interests.

a) If for any reason the offer cannot be given favorable consideration, the taxpayer should be provided the opportunity to withdraw the offer. If the taxpayer withdraws the offer, he/she should be informed that this action forfeits any appeal rights and also resumes the running of the statutory period for collection. Managers should ensure that the withdrawal is not utilized to eliminate the proper investigation of offers that have legitimate collection potential.

b) If the offer is to be rejected, the taxpayer should be advised of the available appeal procedures. If discussions with the taxpayer reflect an understanding of the basis for the planned rejection, the taxpayer should be provided an opportunity to withdraw the offer. Under these circumstances the withdrawal letter should contain the same information as if the offer were actually rejected. The information in these cases will be used to assist in further collection. These offers will be processed in the same manner as rejected.

c) In rejection or withdrawal situations where the taxpayer has made a deposit, the offer examiner should ask the taxpayer to compete Form 3040, Authorization to Apply Offer in Compromise Deposit to Liability, or include a similar authorization in withdrawal letter.

d) In situations where an offer is acceptable and a collateral agreement(s) is warranted, the taxpayer will be informed of such agreement as soon as possible in the negotiation period.

2) If after all attempts to negotiate have failed, the taxpayer should be advised that the offer will be rejected. Every effort should be made to issue the rejection memorandum as soon as possible after the decision to reject has been made.

57(10)10.3
AMDISA CHECK

Although no examination of open, unaudited returns is required when an offer is recommended for acceptance, AMDISA will be checked to determine if any tax years are being examined, such as TEFRA cases etc. If there is a return being examined, the Examination function will be contacted and advised that an offer has been submitted. Action deemed appropriate can then be coordinated between the functions.

57(10)11

AMENDED OFFERS

57(10)11.1
GENERAL

1) Changes in the amount or terms of the offer may be amended by

a) The taxpayer submitting a new Form 656, which is the preferred method;

b) The taxpayer making and initialing a change on the original offer.

2) In those rare instances where an amended offer reflects additional periods and/or class of tax, a new form must be secured.

57(10)11.2
RECEIPT OF AMENDED OFFERS IN THE DISTRICT

1) When an amended offer is received by an office within a district, a copy of the amendment and any payment received will be sent promptly to the Service Center Collection Branch (SCCB). SCCB will forward the amended Form 656 and the required copies of amended Form 2515 to the office of jurisdiction of the original offer. Field investigation should not be delayed during this process.

2) If the amendment is submitted on a new Form 656, the waiver acceptance on the face of the amended offer must be signed with the name and title by the delegated employee before sending a coy to the Service Center Collection Branch.

57(10)11.3
RECEIPT IN THE SERVICE CENTER

Amended offers received in the service center will be forwarded to the office of jurisdiction with a new form 2515, Record of Offer in Compromise, identified by the suffix "A" in the serial number block. The amount of payment received with the amended offer will be entered in item 5 of Form 2515.

_57(10)12_
OFFER INVESTIGATION

57(10)12.1
GENERAL

1) The purpose of the investigation is to determine whether the amount offered reasonably reflects collection potential. All available internal sources will be used to aid in making a determination regarding the offer. These would include, but are not limited to, the following: financial statements, previous records checks, currently not collectible accounts, 100 percent penalty files, open and closed bankruptcy files and contact with other collection personnel when prior activity is known. The expectation is that

collection issues previously addressed by field personnel will not be reexamined. Reinvestigation of issues already investigated will not be done unless there is convincing evidence that such reinvestigation is absolutely necessary. Offer examiners are not expected to conduct independent investigations. It is expected that the results of previous investigations will be used and only supplemented when necessary. For example, if a Revenue Officer has completed all the investigative requirements as outlined in IRM 5375, Currently Not Collectible Conditions, an offer submitted by the taxpayer can be considered without further investigation. Additionally, investigative actions less than 12 months may be used by the offer examiner.

2) The extent of the investigation should be practically governed by such issues as the amount of the liability, the amount of investigation previously completed and the information included on the taxpayer's financial statement. The amount of investigation will be limited to the amount normally required in a TDA case. Unless unusual circumstances exist, the examination should not extend beyond that required to report a TDA as currently not collectible. Management should take steps to ensure that investigations are not excessive. The fact that an offer has been submitted does not require extraordinary investigative actions. Additionally, officials delegated acceptance authority should not expect the investigative efforts to be beyond what is normally required in a TDA case. Extraordinary actions should not be taken solely because of the existence of an offer. The acceptance, rejection and withdrawal memorandums will include the reasons why personal inspection of assets was warranted.

3) The IDRS Command Code RTVUE will be requested for the taxpayer's last filed return to review for any assets or sources of income not listed on the financial statement. The taxpayer return only need be secured when RTVUE indicates a need.

57(10)12.2
DISTRICT OFFICE TRANSFER OF OFFERS

1) When an offer is received in a district office and the taxpayer is not located within the receiving district, region or service center area, the offer will forwarded through normal channels to the service center serving the district where the taxpayer resides. The appropriate function will prepare a memorandum specifying assignment to the correct district.

2) In situations where the taxpayer's authorized representative is located in a district other than where the taxpayer resides, the offer should normally be assigned to the district where the taxpayer is located.

57(10)12.3
COURTESY INVESTIGATION

If the taxpayer moves or relocates during the course of the offer investigation, the examining officer may decide to request a courtesy investigation rather than transferring the offer. However, if the investigation would be time consuming or complex, the offer and related accounts should be transferred.

57(10)12.4
INDICATIONS OF FRAUD

1) If the examining officer discovers indications of fraud in connection with an Offer in Compromise, the case should be referred to the Criminal Investigation function, in the same manner as any other fraud referral.

2) Action on the offer and contact with the taxpayer should be held in abeyance until the Criminal Investigation function determines a course of action. If the referral is rejected, investigation of the offer can resume. If the case is accepted, the examining officer will not contact the taxpayer regarding the status of the offer until after Criminal Investigation has informed the taxpayer of the fraud investigation. After this has been done, the taxpayer should be informed.

57(10)13

EVALUATION OF SPECIFIC ASSETS

57(10)13.1
CASH

1) The amount of cash on hand, as well as that in savings accounts and on deposit with the offer, should be considered. In analyzing a taxpayer's checking accounts and fluctuating savings accounts, the average balance over a reasonable period (generally 3 months) should be used rather than the amount on hand at a specific date in order to avoid a distorted picture of the taxpayer's cash position. Deposits in escrow accounts should not be overlooked and all special and trust accounts should be fully explored.

2) Cash deposited with the offer is an asset. However, if any portion of the deposit is borrowed with the provision that the sum must be repaid if the offer is unsuccessful, this amount should be treated as an encumbrance and the balance as the taxpayer's equity. If any portion of the amount borrowed has been repaid during consideration of the offer, this amount should be treated as the taxpayer's equity in deposit. Avoid allowing double exemptions for encumbrances. This most often occurs when the taxpayer borrows money to deposit on the offer and pledges some asset, such as a bank passbook, as collateral. When that happens, the bank deposit is encumbered, but the offer deposit is not.

3) The Examining officer should determine the taxpayer's interest in the bank accounts by ascertaining the manner in which they are held and by applying the legal principles in the legal Reference Guide for Revenue Officers.

4) The Examining officer should exercise judgment in determining whether the contents of the taxpayer's safe deposit box warrants personal inspection.

5) Some term accounts at banks or savings and loan associations may be subject to a penalty for early withdrawal. If it is anticipated that the taxpayer will incur such a penalty by withdrawing funds for payment of the amount offered, the amount of the penalty should be considered an encumbrance.

57(10)13.2
SECURITIES

1) Listed Stocks – The current value of stocks listed on an exchange or traded daily over the counter can usually be determined by reviewing stock quotations in the daily newspaper. The quick sale value is normally the same as the market value less the cost of sale.

2) Unlisted Stocks – This type of security is traded by not listed on an exchange or quoted over the counter. Valuation should be determined by taking an average of "bona fide" bid and asking prices over a reasonable period, again allowing for the costs of sale.

3) Closely Held Stock – A closely held corporation may be defined as one in which the shares of stock are owned by a relatively limited number of stockholders. Frequently, the entire stock is held by members of one family. As a result, little or no trading is found in the stock and there is no established market for the shares. In such circumstances, it will be necessary to rely upon any financial data and relevant information that is available. The sources of such information may include:

a) The taxpayer or his/her designated representative.

b) Financial publications and periodicals.

c) Corporate income tax returns.

d) Appraisals prepared by qualified, impartial experts.

e) Credit reports.

4) The value of such stock, for compromise purposes, should reflect the net worth of the assets of the closely held corporation, its earnings record, dividend policy, current financial condition, anticipated future prospects and its value as a going concern. However, when the taxpayer holds a minimal interest in a closely held corporation, has no control over its affairs, and his/her interest cannot be liquidated, such interest will be considered to have no value for compromise purposes.

57(10)13.3
LIFE INSURANCE

1) Where the insured has reserved the right to change the beneficiary or to borrow against the policy without the beneficiary's consent, the unsecured interest in the policy, including the cash surrender value, is property within the meaning of IRC 6321.

2) The cash loan value, plus all accumulated dividends and interest left with the company, is considered an asset.

3) For purposes of the offer, cash loan value is the amount the taxpayer can borrow on the policy from the insurance company, minus any automatic premium loans required to keep the contract in force.

4) Information needed to value a taxpayer's cash loan value should include the dates and amounts of any policy loans or automatic premium payments.

57(10)13.4
PENSION AND PROFIT SHARING PLANS

1) If a taxpayer is required, under terms of employment, to contribute a percentage of his/her gross earnings to a retirement plan and the amount contributed, plus any increments, cannot be withdrawn until separation, retirement, demise, etc., this asset will be considered as having no equity.

2) Where the taxpayer is not required as a condition of employment to participate in a pension plan, but voluntarily elects to do so, the equity for compromise purposes shall be the gross amount in the taxpayer's plan reduced by the employer's contributions.

3) If the taxpayer is permitted to borrow up to the full amount of his/her equity in a plan, this should be taken into consideration in determining the taxpayer's collection potential.

4) The current value of property deposited in an Individual Retirement Account (IRA), 401(k), or Keogh Act Plan Account should be considered in determining collection potential. Cash deposits should be included at full value. If assets other than cash are invested (e.g., stock, mutual funds), the current value of the investment should be used to determine collection potential. The penalty for early withdrawal and the additional tax that must be paid should be subtracted to determine this value.

57(10)13.5
FURNITURE, FIXTURES AND PERSONAL EFFECTS

1) In determining the adequacy of an offer, the taxpayer's valuation of furniture, fixtures, and personal effects listed on the financial statement is generally sufficient. The examining officer should exercise judgment in determining whether the taxpayer's assets warrant personal inspection. It is important to note that assets of substantial artistic or intrinsic value, such as jewelry, paintings or etchings, silverware, oriental rugs, antique furniture, coin, stamp, or gun collections, statuary and the like, should not be overlooked.

2) If the assets consist of business property, the examining officer should take into account any value of the fixtures the taxpayer owns.

3) The statutory exemption from levy applies to the taxpayer's furniture and personal effects and should be taken into consideration in the value of the taxpayer's interest in the property. (See IRC 6334.)

4) In any case where the taxpayer has evidence which proves that the furniture, fixtures and personal effects in his/her house are jointly owned and the assessment is made against only one of the owners the taxpayer proportionate share of the equity should be determined. This should not be less than 50% in the case of husband and wife. The value of the asset after this determination has been made should then be reduced by the statutory exemption.

57(10)13.6
MACHINERY AND EQUIPMENT

1) The value of machinery and equipment is to be determined on the basis of all relevant facts and evidence. Some assets may have value only to the taxpayer or someone in the same business as the taxpayer, while other assets will have a ready market and value easily determined from guides prepared by the industry. The value of some unusual assets, such as farm machinery and specialized equipment, can be ascertained by contacting dealers, or manufacturers of these assets.

2) Factors which should be considered in arriving at quick sale value include the difficulty of dismantling and removing machinery and equipment, the availability and size of the market for such assets, and the adaptability of such assets to other uses.

3) The examining officer may wish to request appraisals or use the services of a valuation engineer where a difficult valuation problem is involved.

4) Generally, the examining officer will use the same techniques as would be used to determine equity in potential seizure situations.

57(10)13.7
TRUCKS, AUTOMOBILES, AND DELIVERY EQUIPMENT

Assets such as trucks, delivery equipment, and automobiles usually have a ready market value which is easily determined from guides prepared by national associations and from information secured from dealers and agencies. The examining officer should exercise judgement in determining whether the taxpayer's vehicle(s) warrant personal inspection. Inspection is generally not necessary.

57(10)13.8
RECEIVABLES

1) Accounts should generally be grouped according to age such as under 90 days old and 90 days and over. However, aging of receivables should be determined on an individual case basis. In addition, a reserve for bad debts should be considered when determining net accounts receivable. Substantial accounts receivable either not pressed for payment or where the debtor is a relative, officer, or stockholder of the taxpayer should be closely examined.

2) In determining the value of the receivables where they have been discounted or pledged, the provisions of IRC 6323(c), dealing with certain commercial transactions and financing agreements, should be reviewed.

3) Notes receivable are acknowledged debts and generally not discounted as drastically as accounts receivable. Each should be examined carefully for underlying collateral and for the ability of the maker to satisfy the debt.

4) Consideration should also be given to what action would be taken on the receivable if the offer was rejected and what the potential recovery would be if levy action was taken.

57(10)13.9

REAL ESTATE

**57(10)13.91
GENERAL**

1) In determining the value of real estate, the highest and best use of the property must be considered. If the property being evaluated represents a recent purchase by the taxpayer, or if similar property in the vicinity has changed hands recently, such sales are relevant evidence of the value of the property in question. The fluctuation of property values in the area should be considered in determining how current an existing appraisal needs to be.

2) If the taxpayer's valuation was based on an appraisal by a qualified and disinterested appraiser, the taxpayer should provide a copy of each appraisal.

3) Where the property being evaluated was not purchased recently or there have been no recent sales of similar property in the area, the taxpayer may be requested to engage the services of a disinterested, qualified appraiser to appraise the property. However, such a request should be limited to situations where the value cannot be determined through some less costly methods. Normally the same methods used to determine the taxpayer's equity before seizure will be used. (See IRM 56(12)2.1.)

4) The value of any leasehold interest should be ascertained. In many cases, a property interest is retained through the lease contract (see Chapter 300 of IRM 57(16)0, Legal Reference Guide for Revenue Officers.)

5) The assessed valuation of real estate may be taken into consideration in determining the value of real estate when it reasonably reflects the quick or forced sale value or when it can be adjusted by a generally accepted percentage to achieve those values.

57(10)13.92
JOINTLY OWNED REAL PROPERTY

1) When real property is held jointly with another person, or another has some interest in the property, state law determines the extent of the taxpayer's ownership or interest therein. The legal distinction applicable to the terms "tenancy by the entirety," "joint tenancy" and "tenancy in common" will not be discussed here. (See Chapter 300 of IRM 57(16)0, Legal Reference Guide for Revenue Officers.) This subsection deals with Service practice as it relates to the adequacy of an offer where assets are jointly owned. It is reasonable to expect that if a taxpayer wishes to compromise a tax liability, the taxpayer should be asked to include in the amount offered at least a portion of the amount accessible to the taxpayer but unavailable to the Service for collection action.

2) In the consideration of real estate and other related property held by tenancy by the entirety, where the assessment for the liability is made against only one spouse, not less than 20 percent of the net equity in the property based on its quick sale value, should generally be included in the total assets available in arriving at an acceptable Offer in Compromise. (See (4) below.)

3) In the consideration of real estate and other property held by tenancy in common, or joint tenants, where the assessment is made against only one of the owners, the taxpayer's proportionate share of the quick sale value should be included in the total assets. Normally, if husband and wife own real estate as tenants in common, each is deemed to have a 50 percent share in the property. (See (4) below.)

4) These practices are considered equitable, but they are flexible and may be adjusted up or down as circumstances warrant, especially in cases where the other party has made little, if any contribution to the property. There is always the possibility that the character of the property may be changed by death, abandonment or alienation. The overall goal is to determine whether the amount offered reasonably reflects what can be collected in any other manner and is in the overall best interest of the government. Therefore, the criteria in (2) and (3) above may be ignored in appropriate cases.

5) If the liability is due from both taxpayers jointly, the total quick sale value of the property should be reflected in their offer. If an offer covers the joint liability of husband and wife, as well as the husband's or wife's individual liability, the suggested method of determining the realizable equity would be to apply it first to the joint liability, and if any equity remains, the 20% or 50% computation may be applied to the remainder. (See (2) and (3) above.)

57(10)13.10
USE OF VALUATION ENGINEERS

If dissatisfied with the taxpayer's appraisal or, where necessary, to complete the investigation, the examining officer may require the services of a valuation engineer. The valuation engineer's services should be requested by memorandum to the Examination function, according to regional and district instructions. Recommendations of the engineer will be adopted as the position of the Service unless there are clear and compelling reasons for not doing so. Use of valuation engineers should be limited to cases where no other reasonable alternatives are available.

57(10)13.11
EVALUATION OF INCOME

1) There is no fixed percentage of a taxpayer's present or future earned and unearned income that must be accounted for in deciding the acceptability of an offer. The issue is how much of the taxpayer's income is or will be realistically available to pay the delinquent taxes. In evaluating future prospects the taxpayer's education, profession or trade, age and experience, health, past and present income will be considered. An evaluation must be made of the likelihood that any increase in real income will be available to pay the delinquent taxes. Consideration should not be given to increases in income solely based on an increase in the cost of living. In cases where it is determined that the taxpayer can make installment payments, the Service normally considers that any agreement that requires more than five years to complete has a high probability of not being completed. The Service must then decide the "present value" of those five years of payment. To determine the present value of those payments use chart in Exhibit 5700-19.

2) Generally, if the taxpayer can now pay us "present value," we will give serious consideration to accepting the offer. The present value also may be a considering factor when less than five years remain on the collection statute in determining the acceptability of an offer.

57(10)13.12
POTENTIAL VALUE OF ASSETS AND EARNING POWER

The likelihood of an increase in the value of assets in the near future and any data that might affect the taxpayer's future income and earning power should be considered. An analysis of current income, profit and loss statements, sales records, and orders in hand should be made.

57(10)13.13
BANKRUPTCY, RECEIVERSHIP AND ESTATE CASES

1) In compromise cases of decedents, estates in process of administration and in bankruptcy and receivership cases, offers must show that the executor, administrator, receiver, trustee or other person making the offer is properly authorized to do so. A copy of the order of the court, or other evidence of authorization, should accompany Form 656.

2) A general statement of the circumstances which resulted in the bankruptcy or receivership, and the purpose of the receivership; that is, whether the object is liquidation of assets, conservation of assets, foreclosure of a mortgage, reorganization, etc. A copy of the petition in bankruptcy or for the appointment of a receiver, and a copy of the court order appointing the receiver or trustee can be used in lieu of a general statement. Copies of all pertinent schedules field with the court should be furnished.

3) Generally it is not the practice of the Service to consider acceptance of an offer submitted by a taxpayer in a Chapter 11, Chapter 12 or Chapter 13 proceeding, since the reorganization plan must provide for the payment of the liability in full.

4) In investigating an offer from a decedent's estate, consideration must be given to the amount which may be collectible from the enforcement of any liability for the tax by a beneficiary or transferee.

57(10)13.14
LIABILITY OF HUSBAND AND WIFE

1) An "innocent spouse" may be relieved of liability in certain cases under IRC 6013(e) and IRC 6653(b). In the event that one of the jointly liable taxpayers claims to be an "innocent spouse," the questions should be referred to the district Examination function for determination.

   a) Should the offer be acceptable, the report should not be prepared until after the district Examination function has made its determination.

   b) If the offer is to be recommended for rejection or withdrawal, the report should be prepared without delay. The report should briefly state that the question was raised and referred to the district Examination function.

57(10)13.15
EFFECT OF TRANSFEREE LIABILITY ON ADEQUACY OF OFFER

1) If transferee liability exists, an acceptable Offer in Compromise of the transferor's liability would necessarily include a sum substantially equal to the amount the Government might reasonably expect to collect from the transferee. In concluding what amount should be due, consideration must be given to all of the evidence available. One important element is the fact that the burden of proof of transferee liability rests with the government.

2) In borderline cases where there is serious question whether transferee liability may be established and sustained, it has occasionally been possible to compromise by accepting offers which include additional sums in consideration of the transferred assets(s). In other words, the amount acceptable should be based in part on the degree of doubt regarding the sustaining of any transferee liability. The offer examiner and/or the revenue officer who is considering the viability of an offer should obtain as much information as possible about the circumstances surrounding the transfer.

3) In those compromise cases in which the examining officer believes that a transferee assessment should be made, he/she should prepare, in addition to the rejection memorandum, a separate report recommending assertion of the transferee liability. See Chapter 800 of IRM 57(16)0, Legal Reference Guide for Revenue Officers, for a detailed discussion of transferee liability.

57(10)14

COMPROMISE OF EMPLOYMENT AND COLLECTED EXCISE TAX LIABILITIES

57(10)14.1
GENERAL

1) When the same business is operating, we would normally not accept an offer for an amount less than the tax, exclusive of penalties and interest. However, if considering all factors, including the taxpayer's demonstrated ability to stay current, it is obvious that accepting an offer would be in the total best interest of all parties, an offer can be accepted for an amount less than the tax as long as the amount offered reasonably reflects collection potential.

2) Where taxpayers are no longer in the same business as when the liability was incurred, the amount of the offer should reasonably reflect collection potential.

57(10)14.2

COMPROMISING CORPORATE EMPLOYMENT TAX

57(10)14.21
WITHHOLDING AND EMPLOYMENT TAXES

1) When an offer is submitted by a corporation to compromise outstanding employment taxes and such offer does not equal the trust fund portion of the tax, the assertion of the 100 percent penalty need not be held in abeyance pending final disposition of the Offer in Compromise.

2) The statutory waiver on an offer submitted by or on behalf of a corporation to compromise its tax liability will not extend the time for assessing the 100 percent penalty against a responsible person. It has been held that a 100 percent penalty provided by IRC 6672 is a liability separate and distinct from the corporate tax. In view of the distinct and separate character of the two liabilities, action extending the period of limitations as to one liable party does not automatically have a like effect on the other party.

3) An acceptable offer would be one which represents an amount which could reasonably be collected in any other manner either from the corporation or the responsible persons.

57(10)14.22
100 PERCENT PENALTY CONSIDERATIONS

1)   In order to protect the interest of the government when the 100 percent penalty can be asserted, one of the three alternatives below should be used whenever an offer has been submitted by or on behalf of a corporation to compromise a "trust fund" liability.

   a)   Assess the 100 percent penalty against the responsible persons.

   b)   Secure Form 2750, Waiver Extending Statutory Period for Assessment of 100 Percent Penalty, from each responsible person. Other protective measures can also be taken; e.g., securing a collateral agreement, a mortgage, an escrow arrangement, or a bond from the corporation's principal officer or stockholder.

   c)   Require the corporation and its responsible persons to make a joint offer covering the taxes assessed against the corporation and the 100 percent penalty not yet assessed. Secure appropriate waivers, etc., from responsible parties (See IRM 5633.21). If the joint offer is accepted, it is not necessary to assess the 100 percent penalty, since payment(s) on the offer will be credited to the corporate liability. Should the offer be defaulted and thereafter terminated, the 100 percent penalty can then be assessed, since the responsible parties will have executed the appropriate waiver(s).

2)   The method selected will be governed by the specific facts of each case. Should the joint offer in (1)(c) above be used, it must be clearly stated on the offer that it has been submitted to compromise the individual's liability for the 100 percent penalty as well as the total liability of the corporation.

3)   None of these protective steps need be taken if:

   a)   The corporation files a cash offer equaling the proposed trust fund portion of its liability; and

   b)   There is enough time left, before the statutory period expires for assessing the penalty, in which to complete action on the corporation's offer.

4)   In 100 percent penalty Offer in Compromise cases, a determination will be made on whether the taxpayer was a stockholder in the company form which the liability arose, and whether the taxpayer has, or will have a capital loss on any stock. Consideration should be given to securing a collateral agreement on Form 2261-C waiving the loss.

57(10)15

COLLATERAL AGREEMENTS

57(10)15.1
PURPOSE AND DEFINITION OF COLLATERAL AGREEMENT

1)   A collateral agreement enables the government to collect funds in addition to the amount actually secured via the offer; thereby recouping part or all of the difference between the amount of the offer and the liability compromised.

2)   Collateral agreements are not used to enable a taxpayer to submit an offer in a lesser amount than his/her financial condition dictates. Neither should they be used to collect amounts which should have been included with the offer itself.

3)   Collateral agreements should not be routinely secured but secured only when a significant recovery can reasonably be expected. For example, a future income collateral would be appropriate where it is reasonably expected that the taxpayer will be receiving a substantial increase in real income. A collateral agreement would not be entered merely on unfounded speculation about real increase in income. Additionally, a collateral agreement should not be secured to cover statistically improbable events such as lottery winnings. Securing of a collateral agreement should be the expectation is that all collateral agreements, except those designed solely to amend and clarify an offer, will be monitored for compliance. Therefore, agreements which require monitoring and which contain terms not in conformance with those outlined in the IRM will not be entered into unless approval is secured form the National Office. The request should be sent by memorandum to the Director of Operations in the office of the Assistant Commissioner (Collection).

4)   A collateral agreement can also be used to amend and clarify and offer.

5)   In cases where a taxpayer is compromising his/her portion of a joint assessment, a collateral agreement should be secured from the taxpayer submitting the offer as a means of protecting the government's right to collect the liability of the co-obligor.

57(10)15.2
GUIDELINES FOR SECURING COLLATERAL AGREEMENTS AS ADDITIONAL CONDITIONS

1) Future income collateral agreements for both individuals and corporations usually run for a period of five years. The beginning year of the collateral agreement should be the year following the year in which the offer is accepted.

2) When a taxpayer submits more than one offer to compromise different tax liabilities, a separate agreement should not be secured for each offer. It is not necessary to reference the collateral agreement on the Form 656, but the collateral agreement should accurately describe the offer or offers to which it relates, describing the date and amount of each offer, the types of tax and the periods covered. If an amended offer is filed after a collateral agreement has been secured, the agreement should be changed to conform with the amended offer.

3) When more than one agreement is required from a taxpayer, it is generally advisable to incorporate the terms of the agreements into one collateral agreement document. When one agreement is secured, special care should be taken to ensure technical and legal accuracy and consistency of the terms, and to avoid any provisions which would nullify the government's chances of recoupment. When a future income agreement is one of the agreements secured, other provisions, such as those providing for adjustment in the basis of assets or waiver of net operating losses, frequently can be incorporated into paragraph 10 on Forms 2261 and 2261-A, as shown in the following examples:

   a) Where an agreement to adjust the basis of assets is incorporated in Form 2261 or 2261-A, item 10, "for the purpose of computing income taxes of taxpayer for all years beginning after 19XX, the basis for certain assets, under existing law for computing depreciation and the gain or loss upon sales, exchange or other disposition shall be as follows:

      Name of assets_____$_____

      That in no event shall the basis set forth above be excess of the basis that would otherwise be allowable for tax purposes, except for this agreement. The limitations and provisions set forth in paragraphs numbered 5, 6, and 7 of this agreement also are applicable to this paragraph, together with those relating to the release of liens in paragraph numbered 9, subject to payment of any additional amounts of taxes which may become due and payable under the provisions of this paragraph."

b) Where an agreement waiving a net operating loss is incorporated in Form 2261 item 10, "any net operating loss deductions, under the provisions of Section 172 of the Internal Revenue Code."

4) Other agreements, such as a waiver of bad debt loss or other deductions, may also be incorporated as an additional paragraph on the future income agreement, Form 2261 and 2261-A. When another collateral agreement is incorporated in the Form 2261 or 2261-A, care should be taken to see that the provisions of the printed form relating to the amount which can be recouped, the waiver of the statue of limitations default, and release of liens are applicable to the added paragraph. Where there is insufficient space on the Form 2261 or 2261-A to insert such paragraph, simply type the paragraph numbers followed by "See Attached" and fasten a separate sheet containing the added provisions.

5) In lieu of submitting a future income collateral agreement, a taxpayer may increase the amount of his/her offer. The offer should be increased by at least an amount equivalent to what the Government could reasonably expect to recover via the future income agreement.

57(10)15.3
TERMS AND CONDITIONS

1) Under the terms of a future income agreement, each year the agreement is in force, the taxpayer is required to submit Form 3439, Statement of Annual Income (Individual), or Form 3439-A statement of Annual Income (Corporation), and a copy of his/her Federal Income Tax Return, with the payment computed to be due. Individual taxpayer's agreement generally provide for payments ranging from 20 to 50 percent of "annual income" (less Federal Income Tax) in excess of an amount which represents the taxpayers's ordinary and necessary living expenses. "Annual income " as computed under the terms of the agreement is intended to represent all income available to the taxpayer for payment under the collateral agreement in any given year. A figure is excluded for ordinary and necessary living expenses and the payment required represents only graduated percentages of income available to the taxpayer which exceeds ordinary and necessary expenses.

2) In arriving at the amount of annual income to be excluded for ordinary and necessary living expenses, each individual taxpayer's case is unique. The terms should be the result of negotiations between the taxpayer and the Service. The government cannot tell the taxpayer what his/her cost living should be. On the other

hand, the Government is not required to consider every expenditure claimed by the taxpayer as being ordinary and necessary. In working out a mutually acceptable exclusion figure, many factors must be weighed. The Government should consider the anticipated rate of inflation, excepted changes in the size of the family, state and local taxes, FICA taxes withheld and unusual expenses such as alimony, child support and high medical and dental costs. This should be projected over the life of the agreement.

3) The memorandum recommending acceptance should explain the basis for the agreement. Form 433-A and 433-B (if applicable) or Form 4822, Statement of Annual Estimated Personal and Family Expenses, (Examination form), may be used to determine the taxpayer's living expenses. The figures shown thereon should be as accurate as possible.

4) In corporate cases, a similar analysis should be made.

57(10)15.4
DEFINITION OF "ANNUAL INCOME"

1) If the examining officer and the taxpayer decide that some of the deductions taken in arriving at the adjusted gross income of individuals or the taxable income of corporations should not be allowed in computing, "annual income", the standard definition on the forms 2261 and 2261-A should be changed before the agreement is signed. However, such changes should extremely rare because it will increase the cost on monitoring.

2) Both the individual and corporate taxpayer are permitted to exclude from "annual income" the Federal income tax paid for the year for which annual income is being computed, and a payment made under the terms of the Offer in Compromise itself (Form 656) for the year in which such payment is made. However, taxpayers may not exclude payments on future income agreements form "annual income." A provision limiting deductions for net operating losses is also included on the Forms 2261 and 2261-A. Waiver overpayments made under the terms of an Offer in Compromise do not constitute "payments made under the terms of an Offer in Compromise" which can be used as a deduction when computing annual income for the purpose of this section.

3) It is usually advisable to use the standard definition on the agreement forms. However, in certain cases, to assure maximum recoupment, it is sometimes essential to refine the definition of "annual income" and include features pertinent to a specific

situation. Changes should not be made which might nullify the government's chance of recoupment and thereby make the agreement ineffective, or give any taxpayer a special or added advantage. For example, the definition of "annual income" would not ordinary be changed to include a deduction for state income or sales taxes paid, which are includible under necessary living expenses.

4) In certain Offers in Compromise cases it is in the best interest of the government to include contributions made by the taxpayer to a Keogh plan or an Individual Retirement Account (IRA), in computing "annual income" under the terms of a Form 2261. Additional paragraph should be added to the form and numbered "10" or the next ascending number. The paragraph must specifically provide for the contributions to be added back to adjusted gross income, as defined in IRC 62, in computing "annual income."

   a) The paragraph to be used to included contributions to a Koegh plan is as follows:

   "That in computing annual income, the deductions allowed by Code Section 404 for contributions on behalf of self-employed individual will be added back adjusted gross income as defined in Code Section 62."

   b) The paragraph to be used to include contributions to an individual Retirement Account as follows:

   "That in computing annual income, the deduction allowed by Code Section 219 for contributions to an individual retirement account described in Code Section 408(a) or for an individual retirement annuity described in Code Section 408(b), will be added back to adjusted gross income as defined in Code Section 62."

57(10)15.5
COMPUTATION OF "ANNUAL INCOME"

1) The term, "annual income" must be interpreted strictly in accordance with the definition set forth in the collateral agreement accepted as a part of the taxpayer's offer. The definitions on Form 2261 and 2261-A pinpoint the deductions which must be added back to adjusted gross income (individuals) and taxable income

(corporations), the addition of nontaxable income and deduction permitted for income tax paid and the payments made on the Offer in Compromise in computing "annual income." Experience has shown, however, that misunderstanding arise over which deductions and additions are proper under the "annual income definition-particularly with regards to the definition of Form 2261.

2) To clarify the computations of "annual income" for individuals, the usual deductions and additions are outlined below. The starting point in arriving at the "annual income" figure is adjusted gross income as defined in IRC Section 62 with the following deductions and additions:

    a) Add to adjusted gross income:

        1. Losses from sale or exchange of property; these includes losses from sale or disposition of capital assets of the taxpayer, bad debt loss, worthless stock, etc., which were taken as a deduction in arriving at adjusted gross income on the taxpayer's return. "Sale or exchange" is intended to include dispositions through foreclosures repossession, etc.

        2. All nontaxable income and profits, or gains from any source whatsoever (including the fair market value of gifts, bequests, devises, or inheritances)-this is intended to be all-inclusive and covers all income, earning, gifts, etc., not includible on taxpayer's return but which were actually or constructively received. These include items such as sick pay, insurance proceeds, and nontaxable gains realized form a condemnation award or involuntary conversion under IRC Section 1033. As an example of what might be considered a gift, it was held that a taxpayer's interest in a home, which was purchased with the wife's funds after his offer was accepted and titled in the names of the taxpayer and wife, was considered a gift to the taxpayer and the fair market value of his interest included in "annual income."

3) Also IRC Section 86 provides that gross income will include a certain portion of Social Security and Railroad Retirement benefits over a base income amount. (It should be noted that in the case of a married taxpayer filing a separate return, the base amount is zero). Since the law now provides for inclusion of these benefits in gross income, they also comprise a portion of the taxpayer's annual income for purposes of computing the amount due on the collateral agreement.

b) Subtract from adjusted gross income:

1. Federal income tax actually paid for the year in question at the time the "annual income" statement is submitted. Appropriate adjustments may be in the Statement of Annual Income at a later date, it and when additional taxes are paid or refund is made, even though occurring in a subsequent year. Self- employment tax is considered a part of income tax and, therefore, deductible but Federal Insurance Contributions tax withheld from wages may not be deducted. When a joint return is filed and only one spouse is liable under the collateral agreement, it is reasonable to require the taxpayer to compute his/her deduction for current Federal income tax paid on the basis of the ratio of his/her adjusted gross income to the total joint adjusted gross income.

2. Payment made on the Offer in Compromise itself for the year in which such payment is made, 1.2 payment made on the principal amount of the offer, together with any interest paid. Amounts deposited with the offer is accepted, since prior to the date the offer is accepted, such deposits are funds of the taxpayer and maybe withdrawn at any time. Payment made under the collateral agreement may not included as a deduction under "payments made under the terms of an Offer in Compromise" which can be used as a deduction when computing annual income for the purpose of this section.

c) Taxpayer is a stockholder in closely held corporation in cases where there is a possibility that the taxpayer could incorporate his/her business, manipulate earning from a corporation in which he/she is stockholder, or in a similar manner attempt to defeat the purpose of the collateral agreement, the definition of "annual income" of Form 2261 embraces provisions which require the taxpayer to include his/her proportionate share of the :corporate annual income" in excess of $10,000 using a basis the corporate net income determined for federal income tax purposes subject to limitations set forth in the paragraph numbered 3 of Form 2261. If the corporation's taxable year does not coincide with the taxpayer's taxable year, the taxpayer should include his/her proportionate share of the net corporate income for the corporation year ended during the year for which the annual income is being computed.

57(10)15.6
ENFORCEABLE CONTRACT

The election by the taxpayer to be taxed as a corporation does not change status of the income from such business for the purpose of computing "annual income" as an individual under the collateral agreement. Nor does it affect the individual's basis for certain assets. The courts have not hesitated to penetrated the corporate veil and look beyond the juristic entity at the actual and substantial beneficiaries. Therefore, in computing the amount due and payable by the Individual under the collateral agreement, the income earned while electing to be taxed as a corporation under IRC 1361, and the pro rata share of the corporation's earning to be re-computed in accordance with the terms and conditions of the collateral agreement – should be included in the amount "annual income" figure. Failure to pay the amount due shall constitute a default within the meaning and intent of the default paragraph contained in the collateral agreement.

57(10)15.7
AGREEMENTS REDUCING THE BASIS OF ASSETS

1) In cases where the basis of assets owned by the taxpayer is substantial, a collateral agreement reducing the basis of assets may be considered. Negotiations with the taxpayer could result in an adjusted basis downward as low as zero. For 2261-B, collateral Agreement-Adjusted Basis of Specific Assets, is used to reduce the basis of assets. It should provide for the reduced basis as of the beginning of the taxpayer's tax year in the year offer is accepted or the following year.

2) Assets which are adaptable to reduced basis include land, buildings, expensive items of machinery and equipment, stocks, bonds, interest in a partnership, certain noted, accounts receivable, etc. Assets not adaptable to a reduced basis are those of negligible value, accounts and notes receivable if they consist of numerous small items, inventories and other items which are depleted rapidly or are difficult to trace.

3) It is obvious that an agreement reducing the basis of assets is not appropriate in every case. For example, where the difficulty of determining compliance and the creation of tax problems would offset or nullify the benefit of the reduction, or where the liability involved is small, an agreement of this type would be of no value.

57(10)15.8 AGREEMENTS WAIVING LOSSES

1) Where net operating losses and capital losses were incurred before, during or after the periods covered by the offer, particularly if such losses may be carried over two years ending after the date of acceptance, a collateral agreement waiving any carryback or carryover benefits may be considered, thus increasing the taxpayer's tax liabilities for the affected periods. Form 2261-C, Collateral Agreement—Waiver of Net Operating Losses and Capital Losses, is designed to cover all net operating losses, capital losses, and unused investment credits, sustained for the year indicated, subject to the limitation contained in the form. In corporation cases, if a future income collateral agreement has been secured on Form 2261-A, it is not necessary to secure a separate agreement waiving operating losses incurred prior to the calendar year in which the offer is accepted, since such a waiver is incorporated in Form 2261-A.

2) When an individual or other non-corporate taxpayer has a net capital loss carryover, consideration should be given to securing a collateral agreement waiving any carryover benefits. Under IRC 1212(b), individuals and other noncorporate taxpayers may carry over a net capital loss for an unlimited period until the loss is exhausted. Use Form 2261-C in this situation.

3) A collateral agreement waiving capital losses, is effective until the full amount of the liability which was compromised, plus interest and penalty that would have been due in the absence of the compromise, is recouped by payments on the offer and related collateral agreement. To arrive at the amount of the loss carryover which may be available after full payment of the liability, the original loss would be reduced by the amount of capital loss which would have been taken in the absence of compromise.

57(10)15.9 AGREEMENT FOR ONE OBLIGOR INVOLVED IN JOINT ASSESSMENT

1) An individual may submit an offer to compromise his/her portion of a joint liability. The situation may arise in the case of husband and wife, or any other individual jointly and severally liable for the tax. The question then is whether such a compromise would in effect compromise the liability of both and prevent the collection of any additional sum from the other party. Very little has been written on the subject in a tax situation except in the case of United States v. Wainer (C.A. 7th 1954) 211F.2d 669. In that case, the Court

reserved the government's right to collect the balance of the tax from the possessor of interest in the property, after crediting the assessment with the amount paid under the terms of the compromise made with the co-obligor. Chief Counsel's opinion regarding these situation is outlined as follows:

a) In general under the provisions of the Code the liability for the tax on a joint return is expressly made "joint and several." These words have an established and definite common law meaning. Congress did not specifically provide that the release of one of the obligors should discharge the other. We must, therefore, look to the common law, or to the statues of the various states, to determine the effect of the release. The state statues on this subject are not uniform.

b) Effect of State Legislation—Many states have enacted legislation d eclaring that a release of a joint or several obligor shall not effect the other obligors. An express reservation of the right to proceed against a co-obligor who is not a party to the release is held by many courts to prevent the release from discharging the other party. However, there is no uniformity as to the amount for which the other obligor may be held. In some States, the balance can be collected from the other obligor(s) whereas in others, only the proportionate share of the total liability can be collected from them. Other courts follow the common law rule which requires the execution of an agreement (between the Service and the taxpayer) known as a "covenant not to sue" the "released" obligor. In this type of case, the balance of the unpaid liability can be collected from the remaining obligor or obligors.

c) Conclusion in light of the case of United States vs. Wainer: It is reasonably clear that the same rule regarding the legal effect of the release of a co-obligor in cases involving contracts and judgments will be applied in cases involving federal taxes. State statutes and decisions on the subject will be considered and followed, although no husband-wife joint tax assessment case involving the release or compromise of tax liability of one them appears as yet to have reached the courts. It would not seem to be safe to proceed on any other principle.

2) To protect the interest of the government insofar as collection from the other parties to a joint assessment (husband and wife or other joint obligors) is concerned, a co-obligor agreement should be secured from the maker of the offer. If both parties have submitted separate offers which are going to be recommended for acceptance, co-obligor agreements will be secured from each taxpayer. Every attempt should be made to secure a joint offer thus, eliminating the

need for a co-obligor agreement. If this attempt is unsuccessful, the execution of a collateral agreement such as Pattern Letter P-229, exhibit 5700-24, reserves the right of the Government to proceed against joint obligors of the taxpayer. In common law jurisdiction where taxpayers are jointly liable for the payment of an assessed tax, the acceptance of an Offer in Compromise from one of the taxpayers will release not only that taxpayer from further liability for the remaining tax, but will also release the other taxpayer from liability as well, unless, the acceptance reserves the right to proceed against the other obligor. Pattern Letter P-229 is a collateral agreement secured from the taxpayer (or the maker of the offer) and used in common law jurisdictions as a means of reserving the government's right to proceed against co-obligors of the taxpayer. The agreement does not release the taxpayer from the liability for the difference between the amount of the Offer in Compromise and the total amount of the outstanding tax liability, but it does prohibit the government from taking any collection action (by suit, levy and seizure or any other means) against the taxpayer for recovery of that difference. By utilizing this agreement, the government has preserved its right to proceed against the co-obligors of the taxpayer for the remaining liability.

3)   In states in which the statutes provide that the remaining obligor can be pursued for any unpaid balance of the tax liability, the agreement (Pattern Letter P-230, Exhibit 5700-25) should be used. It states that the offer is submitted to compromise the individual's liability only and shall not be constructed as proposing to release any co-obligors.

4)   In the following instances, a co-obligor agreement would not be warranted.

a)   The offer is equal to or in excess of the taxpayer's proportionate share of the liability.

b)   No possibility exists for collecting any amount from the other joint obligor(s).

c)   The proportionate share of the liability which remain outstanding is in excess of the amount collectible from the other joint obligor(s).

1.   While the situations above outline practical considerations which could justify a deviation from the general rule, no action should be taken which would jeopardize the government's interest. The amount of the liability involved and other particulars have to be considered before deciding which procedure to use.

57(10)16
ACCEPTANCE RECOMMENDATION

57(10)16.1
GENERAL

1) When it is determined that the offer should be recommended for acceptance, the following documents will be prepared:

   a) Form 7249, Offer Acceptance Report (Exhibit 5700-20)

   b) A memorandum, which fully supports the acceptance recommendation.

   c) A supplemental information report, if required, and

   d) The acceptance letter P-673 (exhibit 5700-29), with all enclosures, (a copy of Form 656 and all collateral agreements).

2) The work papers and/or history sheets, maintained as part of the case file, should reflect the scope of the examination and contain all the documentation of facts and information which formed the basis for the recommendation.

57(10)16.2
PREPARATION OF FORM 7249,
OFFER ACCEPTANCE REPORT

57(10)16.21
GENERAL

1) All items of Form 7249 should be completed. The "date assessed" column should reflect only the earliest unpaid assessment for each module. Compute accrued interest and penalties to a date approximating the date of actual acceptance, taking into consideration the time usually required to complete all processing actions on the case. Lien fees and other collection costs may be combined with "Assesses Penalties" and separate assessment dates need not be shown for them.

2) When the liability covered by the offer is spread over more years or periods that can be shown on the lines provided in the Schedule of Liability, the remaining years and/or periods will be carried over to a second sheet rather than crammed into one tabulation. For the sake of uniformity, the first page of the report showing the liability should be cut off along the line just below the word "Total." The statement "Unpaid liabilities continued on next page" should be inserted in the space provided for the totals.

57(10)16.22
SEPARATE FORM 7249 FOR EACH OFFER

When one taxpayer, or related taxpayers, such as a husband and wife, partners or a group of consolidated corporations, files several offers to compromise separate assessments, and the collectibility of the liabilities arises from the principal source, a separate Form 7249 should be prepared for each offer, with one memorandum, setting forth reasons for acceptance. When more than one offer is involved, acceptance authority will determined by the total of all unpaid liabilities and statutory additions.

57(10)16.23
SIGNATURE AND INITIALS OF FORM 7249

Form 7249 should be signed by the examining officer and by all reviewers. Management should ensure that reviews are kept to the absolute minimum. When the offer involves an unpaid liability, including interest, additions amount, addition to the tax, assessable penalty or $500 or more, Form 7249 must not be signed by the delegated official until the required legal opinion is obtained from the district counsel. In cases involving liabilities under $500, Form 7249 may be signed as soon as it is concluded that the offer is acceptable.

57(10)16.24
LEGAL OPINION OF COUNSEL

1) The primary role of Counsel in reviewing offers is to determine whether or not the offer is legally sufficient to meet the standard of doubt as to liability or doubt as to collectibility.

   a) Factual determinations by the Service will not be re-examined by counsel unless patently erroneous. Asset valuations are largely matters of administrative discretion and judgment and they should rarely be questioned by Counsel.

   b) When a file is lacking information sufficient for Counsel to render a reliable legal opinion, it should be brought informally to the attention of the forwarding office.

   c) When considering a case based on doubt as to collectibility, the amount should be considered legally sufficient if it is within a reasonable range of the predicted results in litigation.

   d) An offer based on doubt as to collectibility should be considered legally sufficient if it closely approximates the taxpayer's collection potential considering what would be legally and practically obtainable through available enforced collection procedures, either administrative or judicial. All sources subject to enforced collection should be considered, including fraudulently conveyed assets and other sources of collection form third parties. Forced sale values can be considered legally sufficient.

e) Counsel's signature on the Form 7249 constitutes the legal opinion required by I.R.C. 7122. If Counsel determines that the offer is not legally sufficient, the Form 7249 will not be signed and the offer may not be accepted by the authorized official. In such cases, a memorandum will be prepares explaining why the offer is not legally sufficient.

f) Occasionally, although an offer may be legally sufficient, Counsel may have reservations as to whether it should be accepted, based on policy or other non-legal concerns. Such concerns will be promptly discussed with the responsible Service officials. Is these reservations are not successfully resolved, Counsel will nevertheless issue the necessary legal opinion. Issues not related to the legal sufficiency of the offer are not grounds to decline to issue the opinion. If Counsel wishes to comment on its concerns or to recommend that the offer be rejected, this will be done in a separate memorandum.

57(10)16.3
ACCEPTANCE MEMORANDUM

The examining officer will prepare a memorandum which fully supports the acceptance recommendation. Management should ensure that this memorandum contains only the information needed to allow the delegated official to make a decision.

57(10)16.4
SUPPLEMENTAL INFORMATION REPORT

A supplemental information report should only be prepared when the examining officer wants to discuss issues about the taxpayer's private affairs which would be pertinent to the delegated official's overall understanding of the case. Information previously discussed in the acceptance memorandum need not be reiterated in the supplemental report.

57(10)16.5
ACCEPTANCE LETTER

Pattern Letter P-673 should be used when accepting the offer. Enclosed with this letter will be a copy of the Form 656 and all collateral agreements.

_57(10)16.6_

FINAL PROCESSING OF COMPLETED OFFER

57(10)16.61
ACCEPTANCES

1) After the delegated official, see Delegation Order No. 11, as revised, accepts an offer by signing the appropriate Form 7249 and acceptance letter and having his/her signature fixed to at least one copy of these documents, the case will be returned to the function designation responsibility to process offers and will complete the following:

   a) Date the signed original and all copies of the acceptance letter.

   b) Make a sufficient number of photocopies of the letter as may be required and any documents outlining the terms and condition of the agreement.

   c) Mail the original acceptance letter to the taxpayer as of day the letter is dated. If the liability has not yet been assessed, the letter will not be sent before the tax is assessed.

   d) Make a sufficient number of photocopies of the Form 7249.

   e) Post Form 2515 in the compromise case file and a copy of Form 2515 offer control file with the date of acceptance.

   f) Place the signed original and one copy of the Form 7249 and a copy of the acceptance letter in the offer case file.

   g) Transmit the offer file to the Service Center Collection Branch.

   h) Place a copy of Form 7249 in the file designated by the district director for public inspection.

   i) If the amount of the offer is full paid at the time of acceptance of the offer, whether or not there is a collateral agreement involved:

   1. TDAs covering accounts compromised are to be placed in the closed TDA file.

   2. Federal tax liens, covering only those accounts compromised, will be released, provided nothing is due at that time under a collateral agreement.

   j) If the offer is a deferred payment offer, whether or not there is a collateral agreement involved:

1. TDAs covering accounts compromised are to be places in the closed files.

2. Federal tax liens covering the accounts compromised cannot be released until the amount of the offer, including accrued interest, has been paid in full, provided nothing is due at that time under collateral agreement.

2) Upon acceptance of an offer involving a co-obligor situation on a joint income tax liability, the service center will establish a NMF TDA against the co-obligor for the full amount of the remaining liability, unless otherwise directed.

57(10)16.7
IMPLEMENTATION OF OFFER AGREEMENT AFTER ACCEPTANCE

The district and service centers, each with certain fixed responsibilities, are jointly charged with coordination and follow-up on accepted Offers in Compromise. Enforcement safeguards are provided to ensure compliance with the terms of installment offers and collateral agreements.

57(10)16.8
RELEASE OF LIENS

57(10)16.81
DISTRICT OFFICE RESPONSIBILITIES

1) When all the terms and conditions of the offer have been met, the Federal Tax lien(s) relating to the liability will be released. Failure to issue a prompt release could have a serious adverse affect on the taxpayer who could seek redress from the Service. If a future income collateral agreement is involved, the taxpayer must be current with its terms and conditions:

a) If it is not clear whether the taxpayer has complied with all the terms of the offer, the advice of District Counsel should be sought.

b) The taxpayer who submitted the offer to compromise his/her liability only (and such offer having been accepted) is entitled to a release of the Government's lien unless the issuance of the release is prohibited by the lien provisions of any related collateral agreement. To protect the Government's rights under its lien against any remaining parties liable for the unpaid assessment, parts of Forms 668-Y, Certificate of Release of Federal Tax Lien, should be modified accordingly. (See Exhibit 5700-40).

57(10)16.9

PUBLIC INSPECTION OF ACCEPTED OFFERS IN COMPROMISE

57(10)16.91
AUTHORITY

Public inspection of certain information regarding all Offers in Compromise accepted under Section 7122 of the Code is authorized by Section 6103(k)(1) of the Internal Revenue Code.

57(10)16.92
PUBLIC INSPECTION PROCEDURES

For a period of one year, a copy of the appropriate Form 7249, Offer Acceptance Report, for each accepted offer (including those accepted by the service center director) will be made available for examination in the office of the district director, having jurisdiction of the taxpayer. The inspection file will be maintained so that it is readily available for examination by the public.

57(10)17

REJECTION AND WITHDRAWAL REPORT

57(10)17.1
GENERAL INFORMATION

1) When an Offer in Compromise is not acceptable or has been withdrawn, the following documents will be prepared:

    a) Form 1271, Rejection or Withdrawal Memorandum

    b) Rejection or withdrawal letter to the taxpayer, and

    c) A memorandum outlining the reasons for rejections.

57(10)17.2
PREPARATION OF FORM 1271 FOR REJECTION OFFERS

All items of Form 1271 should be completed by the examining officer except the sate of rejection letter. This block will be completed by the function designated to complete final processing of the offer and will reflect the date the rejection letter is mailed. The Description of Liability section will reflect the current balance tax, penalty and interest, for periods identified on Form 656. The figures should reflect the most recently identifiable balance due. The delegated official will sign all rejection reports. The person preparing Form 1271 as well as all reviewers should also sign.

57(10)17.3
REJECTION MEMORANDUM

A memorandum outlining the reasons for rejection must accompany Form 1271. The memorandum should be as brief as possible. If the offer was based on doubt as to collectibility, the fact as to collectibility must be set out in sufficient detail including the amounts and terms determined to be acceptable, so that the information can be used both for further collection action and as a basis for discussion of the case in the event the rejection is appealed. Additionally, if any account was currently not collectible or in installment status, the memorandum should contain a recommendation whether the account should be reactivated.

57(10)17.4
PREPARATION OF FORM 1271 FOR WITHDRAWN OFFERS

1)   All items of Form 1271 should be completed by the examining officer except for the date if the withdrawal letter. This block will be completed by the function designated to completed the final processing of the offer and will reflect the date withdrawal letter is mailed to the taxpayer.

2)   The delegated official will sign all withdrawal reports. The person preparing For 1271 and all reviewers should also sign.

57(10)17.5
WITHDRAWAL MEMORANDUM

Generally, the memorandum withdrawal accompanying Form 1271 will not require as much detail as a rejection case. However, any other information which the examining officer determined useful for further collection action or reference purposes should be included in the memorandum. If appropriate a recommendation as to whether accounts in currently not collectible status should be reactivated should be made.

57(10)17.6
REJECTION AND WITHDRAWAL LETTERS

1) When it is determined that the offer is unacceptable or has been withdrawn, a letter will be addressed to the taxpayer advising that the offer is rejected or that it is considered as withdrawn. The opening paragraph should show the nature of the offer (cash or deferred payment), the amount of the offer, the class of tax or penalty to be compromised, the years of periods covered by the offer, and the reason for the rejection of the offer. The amount of the liability should not be mentioned in this letter. In withdrawal cases where the offer is signed by the taxpayer, by specifically authorized representative or by an officer in corporation cases, the withdrawal letter should be addressed to the taxpayer. A copy of the letter will be sent to the authorized representative if requested in the power of attorney. The portion of the taxpayer's letter withdrawing the offer should be quoted and not paraphrased.

2) The following pattern letters are used to advised a taxpayer that the offer is rejected or considered withdrawn:

   a) Pattern Letter P-238 (Exhibit 5700-36)-Rejections letter for all classes of tax.

   b) Pattern Letter P-241 (Exhibit 5700-38)-Withdrawal letter.

3) These pattern letters are not intended to be all-inclusive, but will be applicable in most cases. When the reasons of rejection given in the pattern letter do not apply or when the quoting of the taxpayer's letter withdrawing the offer will confuse the issue, the pattern letters should be adjusted to suit the particular case involved.

4) The rejection letter will explain the written appeal procedure and give him/her 30 days in which to respond with an appeal. The rejection letter will contain the specific reasons for the rejection.

5) The delegated official will sign all rejection letters.

57(10)17.7
REJECTION BECAUSE OF THE DEATH OF THE TAXPAYER

1) The death of the taxpayer or other proponent while an offer is under consideration makes the offer legally unacceptable. To clear Service records a pro forma rejection letter will be issued. (Exhibit 5700-37)

2) In the case of an individual offer, the letter should be sent to "Estate of (taxpayer's name)." In the case of a joint, it should be sent to the surviving spouse, who also should be advised that the offer may be re-submitted showing one party as deceased.

57(10)17.8
TAXPAYER RESPONSE TO REJECTION LETTER

1) A taxpayer may appeal an examining officer's determination orally or in writing if the total liability does not exceed $2,500 for any taxable year or taxable period. In any such case the taxpayer may submit, if desired, a written statement outlining the facts, law or arguments on which the taxpayer relies. When any case is to be forwarded to Appeals based on an oral request, the Form 2873 should so state and name the Service employee to whom the request was made.

2) If the total liability exceeds $2,500 for any taxable year or period, the taxpayer must file a written protest to receive Appeals consideration.

3) If a taxpayer responds timely to an appeal, and the information in the protest letter is insufficient to adequately process the appeal, the taxpayer or proponent will be advised of the required information and provided 15 days to perfect the protest.

4) The taxpayer's protest will be evaluated. If new information is submitted, this should be evaluated. If the reevaluation leads to a different conclusion, the taxpayer will be notified and the case will not be forward to Appeals.

5) If it is determined that the case file should be forwarded on to Appeals office, the case file should contain the amount and terms determined to be acceptable or the reasons why the offer was inappropriate.

57(10)17.9
REJECTED AND WITHDRAWN OFFER PROCESSING

1) After the official delegated to reject offers or acknowledge withdrawal of offers has signed Form 1271 and the rejection or withdrawal letter, the case will be returned to the appropriate function which will:

a) Date the rejection or withdrawal letter.

b) Make a sufficient number of photocopies of the letter as may be required.

c) Mail the original rejection or withdrawal letter to the taxpayer, including instructions for preparing a written appeal. (See Exhibit 5700-36.)

d) Make a sufficient number of copies of Form 1271, as many as be required.

e) Post the Forms 2515 in the compromise case file and in the offer control file with the date of rejection or withdrawal.

f) When a recommendation has been made on Form 1271 to reactivate accounts in currently not collectible status, note the copies of the rejection or withdrawal letter with instructions to SCCB (Service Center Collection Branch) as follows: "input TC 531 simultaneously with TC 481 or TC 482, as applicable."

g) If there is no appeal or the offer is withdrawn, place the original and one copy of Form 1271 and two copies of the rejection or withdrawal letter in the Offer in Compromise case file. Transmit the Offer in Compromise case file to Service Center Collection Branch.

h) Any accounts in status 71 should be reversed by the district office and a determination made as to whether further collection action should be initiated or allowed the case to proceed through normal processing. Reversal of status 71 on accounts which were previously in status 26 will generate hard copy TDAs and go directly to the new T-sign. A copy of Form 1271, the memorandum outlining the basis for rejection and withdrawal, and other information that will aid collection of the liability will be forward to the revenue officer to be associated with the reissued TDAs. If the accounts were in a status other than 26, and the decision has been made to enforce collection input 22, "0 DOAO-6401 and send the file to the responsible unit. Hard copy TDAs will be generated.

i) If the offer is rejected or withdrawn, the amount deposited will be refunded unless the taxpayer authorizes that the payment be applied to the liability. If an executed Form 3040, Authorization to Apply Offer in Compromise Deposit to Liability, is not included in the case file of the rejected offer or if the taxpayer's withdrawal letter does not specify the disposition to be made of the offer deposit, issue a Form 2209, Courtesy Investigation, requesting that a Form 3040 be secured. The offer deposit will be applied to the liability as of the date of the offer is rejected or withdrawn.

57(10)18
OFFERS INVOLVING PROPOSALS TO DISCHARGE PROPERTY FROM THE EFFECT OF TAX LIENS

Whether a proposal for subordination or discharge of specific property from the effect of a Federal tax lien will be processed on its merits will depend upon the acceptability of the Offer in Compromise. If not acceptable, the offer should be rejected and the proposal for discharged should be processed to a conclusion. If acceptable, the offer should be processed, since the acceptance and payment of the offer full would permit the release of all property from the Federal tax lien, including the property covered by the application to discharge from the effects of Federal tax lien. After a deferred payment offer has been accepted, a proposal to discharge certain property may be considered and approved provided the proposal represents the full value of the taxpayer's interest in the property and the total proceeds (to the extent of the value of the government's interest in such property under its lien) are applied on the unpaid balance of the accepted offer.

57(10)19
CASES INVOLVING ASSIGNMENTS FOR THE BENEFITS OF CREDITORS

In these cases the consideration of an Offer in Compromise frequently presents questions concerning the right of the government to priority in the collection of the tax claims over the claims of other creditors of the taxpayer. The right of these other creditors are based on liens which may be recognized by state law, but because of the taxpayer's assignment his/her assets for the benefit of creditors, the provisions of 31 USC 3717 apply. In evaluating the rights of all creditors, all fact and circumstances relating to the carious claims must be made. This includes all pertinent dates, such as the origin and filing of all claims and liens and the steps which have been taken toward the enforcement of the claimants and liens and the steps which have been taken toward the enforcement of the claimant's alleged rights. An assignee for the benefit of creditors, as well as an executor or administrator of a decedent's estate, may become personally liable if the priority rights of the United States are disregarded when the funds of the estate are disbursed. In assignment cases, particularly those where a corporation is the assignor and the tax liability sought to be compromised consists of withholding of Federal Insurance Contributions taxes or any of the taxes which the assignor might be required to withhold or collect from others and pay over to the government, the possibility of enforcing the 100 percent penalty provisions of the code should be considered. For a discussion of the liability under 31 USC 3713 (formerly 31 USC 191), see the Legal Reference Guide for Revenue Officers.

57(10)20

RESCISSION OF ACCEPTED OFFERS

57(10)20.1
GENERAL

1) A compromise is a contract which is binding and conclusive on both the government and the proponent and precludes further inquiry into the matters to which it relates. In the absence of fraud or mutual mistake, the courts have consistently denied either party recovery of any part of the consideration given with a settlement when it was properly rendered under a compromise agreement. However, an Offer in Compromise, which has been accepted under a mutual mistake as to a material fact, or because of the false representations made by one party about a material fact, may be rescinded or set aside. The meaning, validity and consideration of such contract is subject to interpretation by a court.

2) If has been held that unconscious ignorance by both parties of a fact material to the contract, or belief by both parties in the present existence of something material to the contract, constitute a mutual mistake of fact. In certain court cases it has been decided that any compromise settlement entered into under a mutual mistake was in effect without consideration and therefore, was not a bar to the taxpayer's right to recover. Ordinarily, the fact that both parties have misconstrued the law does not rendered the compromise subject to rescission-a compromise is rescindable because of a mutual mistake of fact but not because of a mutual mistake of law.

3) To constitute fraud which will nullify a compromise, it must appear that the representations as to material facts were false; that the maker knew them to be false; that they were made for the purpose of including, and did induce the other party to make the contract; and that the latter had the right to rely on them and did rely of them thereby sustaining injury. When revoking such an accepted offer, the possibility of actually being able to collect an amount larger that realize under the accepted offer is an important factor.

57(10)20.2
RESCISSION PROCEDURE

1) An offer may be rescinded, if legally justifiable, in the following manner:

    a) The appropriate function will prepare a letter to the taxpayer identifying the Offer in Compromise and advising that the acceptance of the offer is rescinded and the acceptance letter revoked. The letter should state the grounds for rescission in general terms and contain a demand for payment of the unpaid tax liability. The letter will be signed by the appropriate approving official.

b) If the liability was $500 or more, the rescission letter must be approved by district counsel. If the liability was under $500, approval is not required.

c) If the offer had been accepted by an Appeals Office, the case should be sent to the appropriate Appeals office for final determination that offer be rescinded.

57(10)21
COMPROMISE OF AN ACCEPTED OFFER

57(10)21.1
GENERAL

There are cases in which the taxpayer is unable to pay the balance of an accepted offer and/or the balance of the contingent liability under the terms of collateral agreement. In this situation the Service has the option of temporarily adjusting the terms of the offer, formally compromising the existing compromise, or exercising the default provisions of the offer.

57(10)21.2
AUTHORITY TO COMPROMISE BALANCE DUE UNDER A COMPROMISE CONTRACT

1) IRC Section 7122 authorizes the Commissioner to accept an Offer in Compromise of an accepted Offer in Compromise.

2) A proposal to compromise the balance of an accepted offer must rest on doubt as to collectibility, or doubt as to liability and collectibility. doubt as to liability will arise only where there is doubt as to the meaning and interpretation of Form 656 and/or the collateral agreement.

57(10)21.3
RECEIPT AND PROCESSING

Proposals received in district offices will be immediately transmitted to SCCB for processing, together with any payment received. The office of jurisdiction which initially accepted the offer will consider that taxpayers proposal.

57(10)21.4
FORM AND AMOUNT OF OFFER

1) No offer form (such as Form 656) is prescribed for use in submitting such a proposal. The proposal should be made in letter form, addressed to the Commissioner of Internal Revenue and mailed to the Service Center Collection branch monitoring the offer.

2) The total amount offered to satisfy the balance due under a compromise contract must be paid in full on or before notice of acceptance of the proposal.

3) The proposal letter should contain the following information:

   a) The amount proposed and the terms of payment within limitations discussed in (2) above.

   b) The date of acceptance of the original offer.

   c) The waiver of any and all claims to amounts due from the United States up to the time of acceptance, to the extent of the difference between the amount offered and the amount of the c,aim covered by the offer. Pattern letters included as Exhibit 5700-42 to 5700-44 are furnished to cover the usual situations encountered.

4) When the proposal is based on doubt as to collectibility, the taxpayer must submit a financial statement. In addition, the following information should be obtained, where applicable:

   a) copy of taxpayer's most recent income tax returns

   b) latest profit and loss statement

   c) appraisal of work in process at present time to determine its value

   d) estimate of the remaining liability under the terms of the future income collateral agreement

   e) reasons why request is being made to compromise the existing agreement

57(10)21.41
CONSIDERATION OF PROPOSAL

1) The consideration of such a proposal will be made by the office of jurisdiction which originally accepted the taxpayer's offer. Acceptance of the taxpayer's proposal will depend on whether it is in the best interest of the government. The factors to be considered

for accepting the proposal are the same utilized when considering the merits of an offer submitted on a form 656.

2)   The information required to support the proposal should fit the case. The taxpayer's statement of his/her current financial condition should be accompanied by a description of future prospect and any other information which might have a bearing upon the acceptability of the offer, The taxpayer's income for the past three years should be ascertained, and when all information is available, the amount of his/her future income should be estimated and projected over the period covered by the remaining terms of the original Offer in Compromise agreement. Comparison should then be made between the amount of the taxpayer's offer and the amount which is anticipated to be recouped under the remaining terms of the original Offer in Compromise agreement.

57(10)21.42
PROCESSING COMPLETED INVESTIGATIONS

1)   After the investigation, the examining officer will forward the proposal, investigative report, memorandum containing a complete statement of the facts in the case and his/her recommendation to the appropriate function for review. The appropriate function will prepared or review the acceptance or rejection letter. (See Pattern Letters included as Exhibit 5700-45, 5700-46 and 5700-48).

2)   If the taxpayer's proposal is acceptable, the procedures for acceptance of original offers will be followed.

3)   If the proposal is not acceptable, the examiner's memorandum and the rejection letter, together with the case file, will be forwarded to the official with delegated authority to reject offers, for approval and signature.

4)   Final processing of accepted or rejected proposals will be conducted by the appropriate function, following the guidelines for acceptance or rejection of original offers.

57(10)21.5

COLLECTION FUNCTION PROCESSING OF POTENTIAL DEFAULTED CASES

57(10)21.51
GENERAL

1) Upon receipt in the district, the case will be assigned in a manner determined by district management.

2) An attempt will be made to secure compliance. Any remittance received will be attached to the case file and forwarded through the appropriate function to the service center for deposit. Cash remittances will be converted to bank draft or money orders.

3) If compliance is not immediately secured, the case will be evaluated in light of all the information submitted by the service center and a decision will be made whether to recommend termination of the offer or consider temporary adjustment of its terms. The offer should not be terminated unless the evidence indicates that termination is in the government's best interest.

4) Before termination of an offer, the taxpayer may be allowed to reduce his/her payments temporarily, providing there is evidence that the taxpayer is acting in good faith and not attempting to place assets beyond the reach of the government. This does not require a formal revision of the terms of the conditionally accepted offer. The following courses of action should be considered before terminating an offer:

   a) Where a deferred payment offer has not been paid full and there is the possibility the taxpayer may be able to pay the balance within six months or less, the taxpayer can be granted an extension of time for payment. Taxpayers in default should be advised of the serious consequences of defaulting on an offer and the actions the Service can pursue. Any request for extension of time for payment by the taxpayer should be in writing.

   b) If a taxpayer requests an extension of time for payment exceeding six months, or permission to make payments different than those specified in the offer or the collateral agreement, the request will be analyzed and a decision will be made based on the taxpayer's financial condition. This decision cannot, however, result in the taxpayer paying less than the amount accepted. If the request is granted, a letter signed by an appropriate delegated official should be sent to the taxpayer. The letter should inform the taxpayer that action to terminate the offer will be held in abeyance. It should be specific to the temporary terms of repayment or other provisions agreed upon. The letter should specify that this action is not to be construed as an amendment to the offer or as a waiver of the government's right under the default provisions. The case file and a copy of letter should be returned to the service center with memorandum summarizing the changes authorized.

c)   If a bond has been filed or other security obtained for payment of the offer, consideration should be given to collection from such source. It may be necessary to refer the case to the District Counsel for review and decision.

d)   If the payment default has been caused by the death of the taxpayer, the examining officer should determine whether the estate of the taxpayer can and will pay the balance due on the offer. If it appears that sufficient funds are available but there will be a delay before funds are dispersed, a moratorium may be recommended. If authorized by the appropriate approving official, as described in (b) above, a letter as described in (c) above will be issued.

5)   When the investigation is completed, all cases, along with reports and recommendations, will be returned to the appropriate function for final action. If the offer is to be terminated, a letter should be prepared for the signature of a delegated official. (See Delegation Order No. 11 as revised.)

6)   If the offer was originally accepted by the Appeals Office or by regional counsel, the termination recommendation will be referred to the appropriate office for preparation of the termination letter and signature by the appropriate delegated official, (See Delegation Order No. 11).

57(10)21.52
PROCESSING TERMINATION CASES

1)   When an Offer in Compromise is in default, the delegated official, (See Delegation Order No. 11, as revised), has the following options under the specific terms of the offer:

a)   Proceed immediately by suit to collect the entire unpaid balance of the offer; or

b)   Proceed immediately by suit to collect as liquidated damage, an amount equal to the compromised liability, minus any deposits already received under the terms of the Offer in Compromise, with interest on the unpaid balance from the date of default at the annual rate as established by section 662 of the Code; or *c)* Disregard the amount of such offer and apply all amounts previously deposited thereunder against the amount of the compromised liability, and without further notice of any kind, asses and/or collect by levy or suit the balance of such liability. A recommendation for suit should be referred to Counsel for consideration and proper action.

 2) Except in cases coming within the jurisdiction of the Appeals Office, the appropriate Collection function will prepare the termination letter for the delegated official's signature, (See Delegation Order No. 11, as revised), and return the case file and a copy of the termination letter to the service center under a separate Form 3210, Document Transmittal, which should be highlighted as a "terminated offer." Where appropriate, SPF will follow normal procedures to revoke the lien release and reinstate the tax lien against the taxpayer.

 3) Pattern Letters P-242, P-243 and P-244 (Exhibits 5700-101 through 103) are used in cases where taxpayer has not complied with the terms of the offer and/or related collateral agreement. The termination letter should refer to the applicable terms of the offer and/or collateral agreement and to the taxpayer's failure to comply with these terms.

 4) The Service Center Examination function should be advised of the termination of all Offers in Compromise involving collateral agreements, other than those agreements pertaining only t future income and those Form, 2261-D.

57(10)22
PENALTY OFFERS

57(10)22.1
JURISDICTION OF PENALTY OFFERS

 1) The service center has authority to consider penalty offers based upon doubt as to liability. District office action or investigation is not necessary unless the offer is based upon doubt as to collectibility or there are unusual circumstances or complex questions involved. In the latter case, the Service Center Collection function will first consult the district office liaison in an effort to settle questions over the telephone rather than transferring the case. The necessity for an actual transfer will be jointly decided by the appropriate district manager and the manager of the Service Center Collection function.

2)   Fraud, penalties, including interest, and negligence penalties, including interest, require district office consideration.

3)   Penalties that are not subject to reasonable cause determination are not subject to compromise based on doubt as to liability. These offers can only be based on doubt as to collectibility and these offers will be assigned to the district office.

57(10)22.2

PRELIMINARY REQUIREMENTS

57(10)22.21
ADMINISTRATIVE APPEAL PROCEDURE

The Service has an administrative procedure whereby a taxpayer may appeal the validity of a penalty assessment either before or after paying it. In addition, the Appeals officer may be delegated authority to settle penalty assessments. Therefore, before informing the taxpayer about the option of submitting an offer to compromise a disputed penalty, the administrative appeal procedure should be explained and taxpayers should be encourages to use it.

57(10)22.3
PROCESSING OF PENALTY OFFERS

1)   A penalty offer will not be favorably considered if the penalty itself is already paid. Since there is no outstanding liability subject to subject to compromise, the offer should be rejected immediately. Normal rejection procedures will be followed.

2)   If a penalty is full paid in error (such as an offset from another module) the offer may still be considered. If the offer is accepted, the excess of payment over the amount of the offer would be refunded to the taxpayer.

57(10)22.4
TAX, INTEREST AND PENALTIES MUST BE PAID

1)   A penalty cannot be compromised before the tax, if any, interest on the tax and any other penalties are paid. When an offer to compromise a penalty is filed and if these items have not been paid, action on the offer will generally be held in abeyance until payment is made. The taxpayer will be notified and given a reasonable time to pay the liability.

2)   If the outstanding tax, interest on the tax and other penalties are not paid within a reasonable time, the offer should be rejected.

IRS TAX COLLECTION GUIDELINES

COLLECTION ACTIVITY

5223

Analysis of Taxpayer's Financial Condition

(1) The analysis of the taxpayer's financial condition provides the interviewer with a basis to make one or more of the following decisions:

    (a) require payment from available assets;

    (b) secure a short-term agreement or a longer installment agreement;

    (c) report the account currently not collectible;

    (d) recommend or initiate enforcement action (this would also be based on the results of the interview);

    (e) file a Notice of Federal Tax Lien; and/or

    (f) explain the offer in compromise provisions of the Code to the taxpayer.

(2) In all steps that follow, information on the financial statement will be compared with other financial information provided by the taxpayer, particularly the copy of the taxpayer's latest Form 1040. If there are significant discrepancies, they should be discussed with the taxpayer. In the event further documentation is needed, it will be the taxpayer's responsibility to provide it. Discrepancies and their resolution will be noted in the case file history.

(3) Analyze assets to determine ways of liquidating the account:

    (a) if the taxpayer has cash equal to the tax liability, demand immediate payment;

    (b) otherwise, review other assets which may be pledged or readily converted to cash (such as stocks and bonds, loan value of life insurance policies, etc.);

    (c) if necessary, review any unencumbered assets, equity in encumbered assets, interests in estates and trusts, lines of credit (including available credit on bank charge cards), etc., from which money may be secured to make payment. In addition, consider the taxpayer's ability to make an unsecured loan. If the taxpayer belongs to a credit union, the taxpayer will be asked to borrow from that source. Upon identification of potential sources of loans, establish a date that the taxpayer is expected to make payments; and

    (d) if there appears to be no borrowing ability, attempt to get the taxpayer to defer payment of other debts in order to pay the tax first.

(4) When analysis of the taxpayer's assets has given no obvious solution for liquidating the liability, the income and expenses should be analyzed.

    (a) When deciding what is an allowable expense item, the employee may allow:

        1. expenses which are necessary for the taxpayer's production of income (for example, dues for a trade union or professional organization; child care payments which allow a taxpayer to work);

        2. expenses which provide for the health and welfare of the taxpayer and family. The expense must be reasonable for the size of the family and the geographic location, as well as any unique individual circumstances. An expense will not be allowed if it serves to provide an elevated standard of living, as opposed to basic necessities. Also, an expense will not be allowed if the taxpayer has a proven record of not making the payment. Expenses allowable under this category are:

           a. rent or mortgage for place of residence;

           b. food;

           c. clothing;

           d. necessary transportation expense (auto insurance, car payment, bus fare, etc.);

           e. home maintenance expense (utilities, home-owner insurance, home-owner dues, etc.);

           f. medical expenses; health insurance;

           g. current tax payments (including federal, state and local);

           h. life insurance, but not if it is excessive to the point of being construed as an investment;

           i. alimony, child support or other court-ordered payment.

        3. Minimum payments on secured or legally perfected debts (car payments, judgments, etc.) will normally be allowed. However, if the encumbered asset represents an item which would not be considered a necessary living expense (e.g., a boat, recreational vehicle, etc.), the taxpayer should be advised that the debt payment will not be included as an allowable expense.

        4. Payments on unsecured debts (credit cards, personal loans, etc.) may not be allowed if omitting them would permit the taxpayer to pay in full within 90 days. However, if the taxpayer cannot fully pay within that time, minimum payments may be allowed if failure to make them would

ultimately impair the taxpayer's ability to pay the tax. The taxpayer should be advised that since all necessary living expenses have been allowed, no additional charge debts should be incurred. Generally, payments to friends or relatives will not be allowed. Dates for final payments on loans or installment purchases, as well as final payments on revolving credit arrangements after allowing minimum required payments, will be noted so the additional funds will be applied to the liability when they become available. If permitting the taxpayer to pay unsecured debts results in inability to pay or in only having a small amount left for payment of the tax, the taxpayer should be advised that a portion of the money available for payment of debts will be used for payment of the taxes and that arrangements must be made with other creditors accordingly.

(b)   As a general rule, expenses not specified in (a) above will be disallowed. However, an otherwise disallowable expense may be included if the employee believes an exception should be made based on the circumstances of the individual case. For instance, if the taxpayer advises that an educational expense or church contribution is a necessity, the individual circumstances must be considered. If an exception is made, document the case history to explain the basis for the exception.

(c)   The taxpayer will be required to verify and support any expense which appears excessive based on the income and circumstances of that taxpayer. However, proof of payment does not automatically make an item allowable. The criteria in (4)(a) apply.

(d)   In some cases, expense items or payments will not be due in even monthly increments. For instance, personal property tax may be due once a year. Unless the taxpayer substantiates that money is being set aside on a monthly basis, the expense will be allowed in total in the month due and the payment agreement adjusted accordingly for that month. Expense items with varying monthly payments should be averaged over a twelve-month period unless the variation will be excessive. In such instances, exclude the irregular months from the average. For example, if a utility bill will be excessive during the three winter months, average the other nine months.

(e)   In arriving at available net income, analyze the taxpayer's deductions to ensure that they are reasonable and allowable. The only automatically allowable deductions from gross pay or income are federal, state and local taxes (including FICA or other mandatory retirement program).

1.   Other deductions from gross pay or income will be treated and listed as expenses, but only to the extent they meet the criteria in (4)(a) above.

2.   To avoid affording the taxpayer a double deduction for one expense, ensure that such amounts remain in the total net pay figure and are also entered on the expense side of the income and expense analysis.

3.   If the exemptions on the W-4 are going to be decreased, make the appropriate adjustments in the net income figures.

(f)   To reach an average monthly take-home pay for taxpayers paid on a weekly basis, multiply the weekly pay times 52 weeks divided by 12 months (or multiply amount times 4.3 weeks). If the taxpayer is paid biweekly, multiply pay times 26 weeks divided by 12 months (or multiply amount times $2\,^1/6$). If the taxpayer is paid semimonthly, multiply pay times 2.

(g)   The amount to be paid monthly on an installment agreement payment will be at least the difference between the taxpayer's net income and allowable expenses. If the taxpayer will not consent to the proposed installment agreement, he/she should be advised that enforced collection action may be taken. The taxpayer should also be advised that an appeal of the matter may be made to the immediate manager.

(5)   When an analysis of the taxpayer's financial condition shows that liquidation of assets and payments from present and future income will not result in full payment, consider the collection potential of an offer in compromise.

5225

Verification of Taxpayer's Financial Condition

(1)   In some cases it will be necessary or desirable to obtain additional information about the taxpayer's financial condition. The extent of the investigation will depend upon the circumstances in each case.

(2)   If items appear to be over- or understated, or out of the ordinary, the taxpayer should be asked to explain and substantiate if necessary. The explanation will be documented in the case history. If the explanation is unsatisfactory or cannot be substantiated, the amount should be revised appropriate to the documentation available.

5231.1

General Installment Agreement Guidelines

(1) When taxpayers state inability to pay the full amount of their taxes, installment agreements are to be considered.

(2) Future compliance with the tax laws will be addressed and any returns and/or tax due within the period of the agreement must be filed and paid timely.

(3) Levy source information, including complete addresses and ZIP codes, will be secured.

(4) Equal monthly installment payments should be requested. Payment amounts may be increased or decreased as necessary.

(5) Once the determination is made that the taxpayer has the capability to make a regular installment payment, that agreement will be monitored through routine provisions unless the payment amount is less than $10 (in which case the account should be reported currently not collectible). The major benefits of this approach are issuance of reminder and default notices (if the account is system-monitored) and enforcement action if the agreement is not kept.

(6) The taxpayer should be allowed to select the payment due date(s). But if there is no preference, the date when the taxpayer would generally be in the best financial position to make the payment(s) should be chosen.

(7) If the interviewer and the taxpayer cannot agree on the amount of installments, the taxpayer should be advised that an appeal may be made to the immediate manager.

(8) An installment agreement which lasts more than two years must be reviewed at the mid-point of the agreement, but in no event less than every two years.

Levy and Sale

5311

Introduction and General Concepts

(1)   Under the Internal Revenue Code, levy is defined as the power to collect taxes by distraint or seizure of the taxpayer's assets. Through levy, we can attach property in the possession of third parties or the taxpayer. Generally, a notice of levy is used to attach funds due the taxpayer from third parties. Levy on property in possession of the taxpayer is accomplished by seizure and public sale of the property. There is no statutory requirement as to the sequence to be followed in levying, but it is generally less burdensome and time consuming to levy on funds in possession of third parties.

(2)   Levy authority is far reaching. It permits a continuous attachment of the non-exempt portion of the wage or salary payments due the taxpayer, and the seizure and sale of all the taxpayer's assets except certain property that is specifically exempt by law. Prior to levying on any property belonging to a taxpayer, the Service must notify the taxpayer in writing of the Service's intention to levy. The statute does not require a judgment or other court order before levy action is taken. The Supreme Court decision in the matter of *G.M. Leasing Corporation v. United States*, 429 U.S. 338 (1977), held that an entry without a warrant and search of private areas of both residential and business premises for the purpose of seizing and inventorying property pursuant to Internal Revenue Code section 6331 is in violation of the Fourth Amendment. Prior to seizure of property on private premises, a consent to enter for the purpose of seizing or writ of entry from the local courts must be secured.

(3)   Procedures are designed (except in jeopardy cases) to give taxpayers a reasonable chance to settle their tax liabilities voluntarily before the more drastic enforcement actions are started. At least one final notice must be issued before service of a notice of levy.

(4)   Under the self-assessment system, a taxpayer is entitled to a reasonable opportunity to voluntarily comply with the revenue laws. This concept should also be followed in connection with levy action. This does not mean that there should be a reluctance to levy if the circumstances justify that action. However, before levy or seizure is taken on an account, the taxpayer must be informed, except in jeopardy situations, that levy

or seizure will be the next action taken and given a reasonable opportunity to pay voluntarily. Once the taxpayer has been advised and neglects to make satisfactory arrangements, levy action should be taken expeditiously, but not less than 10 days after notice.

(5) Notification prior to levy must be given in accordance with (2) above. It should be specific that levy action will be the next action taken. In the event the service center has not sent the taxpayer the 4th notice which includes notice of intention to levy at least 10 days before the levy, the revenue officer must provide the notice to the taxpayer as indicated in (2) above.

(6) A notice of levy should be served only when there is evidence or reasonable expectation that the third party has property or rights to property of the taxpayer. This concept is of particular significance, since processing of notices of levy is time consuming and often becomes a sensitive matter if it appears the levy action was merely a "fishing expedition."

5312

Statutory Authority to Levy

(1) IRC 6331 provides that if any person liable to pay any tax neglects or refuses to pay the tax within 10 days after notice and demand, the tax may be collected by levy upon any property or rights to property belonging to the taxpayer or on which there is a lien.

(2) IRC 6331 also provides that if the Secretary determines that the collection of tax is in jeopardy, immediate notice and demand for payment may be made and, upon the taxpayer's failure to pay the tax, collection may be made by levy without regard to the 10-day period. However, if a sale is required, a public notice of sale may not be issued within the 10-day period unless IRC 6336 (relating to sale of perishable goods) is applicable.

(3) Under the IRC, the term "property" includes all property or rights to property, whether real or personal, tangible or intangible. The term "tax" includes any interest, additional amount, addition to tax, or assessable penalty, together with any cost that may accrue.

(4) Generally, property subject to a Federal tax lien which has been sold or otherwise transferred by the taxpayer, may be levied upon in the hands of the transferee or any subsequent transferee. However, there are exceptions for securities, motor vehicles and certain retail and casual sales.

(5) Levy may be made on any person in possession of, or obligated with respect to, property or rights to property subject to levy. These include, but are not necessarily limited to, receivables, bank accounts, evidences of debt, securities and accrued salaries, wages, commissions, and other compensation.

(6) The IRC does not require that property be seized in any particular sequence. Therefore, property may be levied upon regardless of whether it is real or personal, tangible or intangible, and regardless of which type of property is levied upon first.

(7) Whenever the proceeds from the levy on any property or rights to property are not sufficient to satisfy the tax liability, additional levies may be made upon the same property, or source of income or any other property or rights to property subject to levy, until the account is fully paid. However, further levies should be timed to avoid hardship to the taxpayer or his/her family.

5314.1

Property Exempt From Levy

(1) IRC 6334 enumerates the categories of property exempt from levy as follows.

    (a) *Wearing apparel and school books necessary for the taxpayer or for members of his family*—No specific value limitation is placed on these items since the intent is to prevent seizing the ordinary clothing of the taxpayer or members of the family. Expensive items of wearing apparel, such as furs, are luxuries and are not exempt from levy.

    (b) *Fuel, provisions and personal effects*—This exemption is applicable only in the case of the head of a family and applies only to so much of the fuel, provisions, furniture, and personal effects of the household and of arms for personal use, livestock, and poultry as does not exceed $1,500 in value.

    (c) *Books and tools of a trade, business or profession*—This exemption is for so many of the books and tools necessary for the trade, business, or profession of the taxpayer as do not exceed in the aggregate $1,000 in value.

(d) *Unemployment benefits*—This applies to any amount payable to an individual for unemployment (including any portion payable to dependents) under an unemployment compensation law of the United States, any state, the District of Columbia or the Commonwealth of Puerto Rico.

(e) *Undelivered mail*—Addressed mail which has not been delivered to the addressee.

(f) *Certain annuity and pension payments.*

(g) *Workmen's compensation*—Any amount payable to an individual as workmen's compensation (including any portion payable to dependents) under a workmen's compensation law of the United States, any state, the District of Columbia, or the Commonwealth of Puerto Rico.

(h) *Judgment for support of minor children*—If the taxpayer is required by judgment of a court of competent jurisdiction, entered prior to the date of levy, to contribute to the support of his/her minor children, so much of his/her salary, wages, or other income as is necessary to comply with such judgment.

(i) *Minimum Exemption from Levy on Wages, Salary and Other Income*—IRC 6334(a)(9) limits the effect of levy on wages, salary and other income, by an amount of $75 per week for the taxpayer and an additional $25 a week for the spouse and each dependent claimed by the taxpayer. Income not paid or received on a weekly basis will, for the purpose of computing exemptions, be apportioned as if received on a weekly basis.

(2) In addition, Public Law 89-538 exempts deposits to the special Treasury fund made by servicemen and servicewomen (including officers) and Public Health Service employees on permanent duty assignment outside the United States or its possessions.

(3) Except for the exemptions in (1) and (2) above, no other property or rights to property are exempt from levy. No provision of state law can exempt property or rights to property from levy for the collection of federal taxes. The fact that property is exempt from execution under state personal or homestead exemption laws does not exempt the property from federal levy.

(4) The revenue officer seizing property of the type described in (1)(a), (b), and (c) above should appraise and set aside to the owner the amount of property to be exempted.

538(10)

Records of Attorneys, Physicians, and Accountants

(1) Records maintained by attorneys, physicians, and accountants concerning professional services performed for clients are usually of little intrinsic value and possess minimum sale value. Questions of confidential or privileged information contained in these records may cause complications if the records are seized. Additionally, the case files of the professional person frequently either are, or contain, property of the client, and therefore to this extent are not subject to seizure. Accordingly, it is not believed desirable to seize case files or records for payment of the taxpayer's tax liabilities.

(2) When office facilities or office equipment of attorneys, physicians, or public accountants are seized for payment of taxes, case files and related files in seized office facilities or office equipment of such persons will not be personally examined by the revenue officer even though information concerning accounts receivable may be contained in the files. When storage facilities (filing cabinets, etc.) are seized, the taxpayer should be requested to remove all case files promptly.

583(11)

Safe Deposit Boxes

538(11).1

General

(1) The procedures outlined below should be followed in an attempt to secure the opening of a taxpayer's safe deposit box in instances in which the taxpayer's consent to or cooperation in opening the box cannot be obtained.

(2) Ordinarily two keys are used to open a safe deposit box: a master key held by the bank or trust company which owns the box and an individual key in the possession of the person who rents the box.

(3) Irrespective of the possession of the necessary equipment to do so, it is not to be expected that a bank or trust company will open a safe deposit box without the consent of the lessee of the box unless protected by a court order. Under these

circumstances the government must prevent the taxpayer from having access to the box, or obtain a court order directing that the box be opened, by force if necessary.

(4) At the time that a safety deposit is secured, Publication 787, Seal for Securing Safety Deposit Boxes, will be signed by the revenue officer and affixed over the locks for security while the box remains under seizure. When the box is eventually opened, all residue from the seal should be removed by the revenue officer, or the bank official in the revenue officer's presence, with isopropyl alcohol or a similar solvent. To avoid damage to the safety deposit box, no sharp implement or abrasive substance should be used. The seal will dissolve when saturated with alcohol and rubbed with a cloth.

583(11).2

Preventing Access to Safe Deposit Box

(1) A notice of lien should be filed prior to seizure since assets other than cash may be in the safe deposit box.

(2) A notice of levy, Form 668-A, with a copy of the notice of lien attached, should be served on an officer of the bank or trust company and request made for surrender of the contents of the box.

(3) The official may advise that the institution does not have the necessary key to open the safe deposit box or that the institution does not have the authority to open it. He/she may also suggest that the lessee's (taxpayer's) consent be secured, or that a court order be obtained to open the box.

(4) Under these circumstances, the revenue officer should not insist that the box be opened and no attempt should be made to have the box opened by force. The box should be sealed by affixing a seizure notice, Publication 787, Seal for Securing Safety Deposit Boxes. It should be placed over the locks in such a manner so that the box cannot be opened without removing, tearing or destroying the affixed seal. The bank or trust company should then be advised not to permit the box to be opened except in the presence of a revenue officer.

(5) Usually, taxpayers who have been reluctant to cooperate will eventually find it necessary to open their boxes, and will only be able to do so in the presence of a

revenue officer. At that time, the revenue officer, with Form 668-B in his/her possession, will be in a position to seize any property in the box.

(6)   When the rental period of the safe deposit box expires and is not renewed, a bank or trust company usually has the right and power to open the box. The revenue officer should attempt to ascertain the true situation in any given case, and if the right and power exists, should try to take advantage of this opportunity to seize the contents of the box.

538(11).3

Obtaining Court Order To Open

(1)   Occasionally, the procedure outlined in IRM 538(11).2 will not be satisfactory and immediate action may be desirable or necessary. For instance, the statute of limitations may be about to expire, the taxpayer may have disappeared or be in concealment, or the taxpayer or bank officials may refuse cooperation and deny access to a safe deposit box.

(2)   Under these circumstances a Summons should be prepared and served on the taxpayer-boxholder in an attempt to secure information as to the contents of the box and to gain access. If this action does not accomplish the desired results, a writ of entry should be sought or a suit requested to open the safe deposit box.

Currently Not Collectible Accounts

5610

Determination of Currently Not Collectible Taxes

5611

General

(1) A Collection employee may determine that the accounts are currently not collectible.

(2) Reporting an account currently not collectible does not abate the assessment. It only stops current efforts to collect it. Collection can start again any time before the statutory period for collection expires.

5632

Unable-To-Pay Cases—Hardship

5632.1

General

(1) If collection of the liability would prevent the taxpayer from meeting necessary living expenses, it may be reported currently not collectible under a hardship closing code. Sometimes accounts should be reported currently not collectible even though the Collection Information Statement (CIS) shows assets or sources of income subject to levy.

   (a) [The Manual] provides guidelines for analyzing the taxpayer's financial condition.
   (b) Since each taxpayer's circumstances are unique, other factors such as age and health must be considered as appropriate.
   (c) Document and verify the taxpayer's financial condition.
   (d) Consider the collection potential of an offer in compromise.

(2) Consider an installment agreement before reporting an account currently not collectible as hardship.

5712

Grounds for Compromise

5712.1

General Guidelines

The compromise of a tax liability can only rest upon doubt as to liability, doubt as to collectibility, or doubt as to both liability and collectibility. IRC 7122 does not confer authority to compromise tax, interest, or penalty where the liability is clear and there is no doubt as to the ability of the Government to collect. To compromise there must be room for mutual concessions involving either or both doubt as to liability or doubt as to ability to pay. This rules out, as ground for compromise, equity or public policy considerations peculiar to a particular case, individual hardships, and similar matters which do not have a direct bearing on liability or ability to pay.

5713.2

Advising Taxpayers of Offer Provisions

(1) When criminal proceedings are not contemplated and an analysis of taxpayer's assets, liabilities, income and expenses shows that a liability cannot realistically be paid in full in the foreseeable future, the collection potential of an offer in compromise should be considered. While it is difficult to outline the exact circumstances when an offer would be the appropriate collection tool, the existence of any of the following should govern offer consideration.

   (a) Liquidation of assets and payments from present and future income will not result in full payment of tax liability.

   (b) A non-liable spouse has property which he/she may be interested in utilizing to secure a compromise of spouse's tax debt.

   (c) The taxpayer has an interest in assets against which collection action cannot be taken. For example, the taxpayer who owes a separate liability, has an interest in property held in "tenancy by the entirety" which cannot be reached or subjected to the Notice of Federal Tax Lien because of the provisions of state law. Under the compromise procedures, the taxpayer's interest is included in the total assets available in arriving at an acceptable offer in compromise.

(d) The taxpayer has relatives or friends who may be willing to lend or give the taxpayer funds for the sole purpose of reaching a compromise with the Service.

5721

General

The offer in compromise is the taxpayer's written proposal to the Government and, if accepted, is an agreement enforceable by either party under the law of contracts. Therefore, it must be definite.in its terms and conditions, since it directly affects the satisfaction of the tax liability.

5723.1

Prescribed Form

A taxpayer seeking to compromise a tax liability based on doubt as to collectibility must submit Form 433, Statement of Financial Condition and Other Information. This form includes questions geared to develop a full and complete description of the taxpayer's financial situation.

5723.3

Refusal To Submit Financial Statement

If a taxpayer professing inability to pay refuses to submit the required Form 433, the offer will be immediately rejected since the Service cannot determine whether the amount offered is also the maximum amount collectible.

5725.1

Liability of Husband and Wife

(1) Under IRC 6013(d)(3), the liability for income tax on a joint return by husband and wife is expressly made "joint and several." Either or both of the spouses are liable for the entire amount of the tax shown on a joint return. When the liability of both parties is sought to be compromised, the offer should be submitted in the names of

and signed by both spouses in order to make the waiver and other provisions of the offer form effective against both parties.

(2) An "innocent spouse" may be relieved of liability in certain cases under IRC 6013(e) and IRC 6653(b). In the event that one of the jointly liable taxpayers claims to be an "innocent spouse," the question should be referred to the district Examination function for determination.

   (a) Should the offer be acceptable, the report should not be prepared until after the district Examination function has made its determination. Since a favorable decision for the party claiming "innocent spouse" will change the amount of the liability sought to be compromised, any recommendation for acceptance must reflect the redetermined liability.

5740

Investigation of Offers

5741.1

General

(1) Once an offer in compromise is received in Special Procedures function, a determination whether the offer merits further consideration must be made. SPf should use all information contained in the offer file and may consult with the revenue officer assigned the TDAs [tax deficiency assessments] to obtain additional financial information or verify existing information.

(2) Summary rejection in SPf can be made on the grounds that the offer is frivolous, was filed merely to delay collection, or where there is no basis for compromise. A desk review of the offer can result in this determination. Although not all-inclusive, the following list provides guidelines on the criteria for summary rejection most often encountered:

   (a) Taxpayer has equity in assets subject to the Federal tax lien clearly in excess of the total liability sought to be compromised,

   (b) The total liability is extremely large and the taxpayer has offered only a minimum sum well below his/her equity and earning potential (e.g., offering $100 to compromise a $50,000 tax liability). Although the taxpayer could be persuaded to raise the offer, the fact that this initial amount offered was so low indicates bad faith and the desire to delay collection,

(c)   The taxpayer is not current in his/her filing or payment requirements for periods not included in the offer,

(d)   The taxpayer refuses to submit a complete financial statement (Form 433),

(e)   Acceptance of the offer would adversely affect the image of the government,

(f)   Taxpayer has submitted a subsequent offer which is not significantly different from a previously rejected offer and the taxpayer's financial condition has not changed,

(g)   In cases involving doubt as to liability for the 100-percent penalty, the liability is clearly established and the taxpayer has offered no new evidence to cast doubt on its validity.

5741.2

Public Policy

(1)   An accepted offer, like any contract, is an agreement between two parties resulting from a "meeting of the minds." It is incumbent upon each party to negotiate the best terms possible. Normally, the offer and subsequent negotiations are of a private nature. However, when accepting an offer, the Service is in a unique position since it represents the government's interest in the negotiations and the accepted offer becomes part of public record. Therefore, public policy dictates that an offer can be rejected if public knowledge of the agreement is detrimental to the government's interest. The offer may be rejected even though it can be shown conclusively that the amounts offered are greater than could reasonably be collected in any other manner. Because the Government would be in the position of foregoing revenue, the circumstances in which public policy considerations could be used to reject the offer must be construed very strictly. The following may be used as a guideline for instances where public policy issues are most often encountered:

(a)   Taxpayer's notoriety is such that acceptance of an offer will hamper future Service collection and/or compliance efforts. However, simply because the taxpayer is famous or well-known is not a basis in and of itself for rejecting the offer on public policy grounds.

(b)   There is a possibility of establishing a precedent which might lead to numerous offers being submitted on liabilities incurred as a result of occupational drives to enforce tax compliance.

(c)   Taxpayer has been recently convicted of tax related crimes. Again, the notoriety of the individual should be considered when making a public policy determination. The publicity surrounding the case, taxpayer's compliance since the case was concluded, or the taxpayer's position in the community should all be considered prior to rejecting an otherwise acceptable offer.

(d)   Situations where it is suspected that the financial benefits of criminal activity are concealed or the criminal activity is continuing would normally preclude acceptance of the offer for public policy reasons. Criminal Investigation function should be contacted to coordinate the Government's action in these cases.

Your Rights

AS A TAXPAYER

As a taxpayer, you have the right to be treated fairly, professionally, promptly, and courteously by Internal Revenue Service employees. Our goal at the IRS is to protect your rights so that you will have the highest confidence in the integrity, efficiency, and fairness of our tax system. To ensure that you always receive such treatment, you should know about the many rights you have at each step of the tax process.

Free Information and Help in Preparing Returns

You have the right to information and help in complying with the tax laws. In addition to the basic instructions we provide with the tax forms, we make available a great deal of other information.

Taxpayer publications. We publish over 100 free taxpayer information publications on various subjects. One of these, Publication 910, *Guide to Free Tax Services*, is a catalog of the free services and publications we offer. You can order all publications and any tax forms or instructions you need by calling us toll-free at 1-800-TAX-FORM (829-3676).

Other assistance. We provide walk-in tax help at many IRS offices and recorded telephone information on many topics through our *Tele-Tax* system. The telephone numbers for *Tele-Tax*, and the topics covered, are in certain tax forms' instructions and publications. Many of our materials are available in Braille (at regional libraries for the handicapped) and in Spanish. We provide help for the hearing-impaired via special telephone equipment.

We have informational videotapes that you can borrow. In addition, you may want to attend our education programs for specific groups of taxpayers, such as farmers and those with small businesses.

In cooperation with local volunteers, we offer free help in preparing tax returns for low-income and elderly taxpayers through the Volunteer Income Tax Assistance (VITA) and Tax Counseling for the Elderly (TCE) Programs. You can get information on these programs by calling the toll-free telephone number for your area.

Copies of tax returns. If you need a copy of your tax return for an earlier year, you can get one by filling out Form 4506, *Request for Copy of Tax Form*, and paying a small fee. However, you often only need certain information, such as the amount of your reported income, the number of your exemptions, and the tax shown on the return. You can get this information free if you write or visit an IRS office or call the toll-free number for your area.

Privacy and Confidentiality

You have the right to have your personal and financial information kept confidential. People who prepare your return or represent you *must* keep your information confidential.

You also have the right to know why we are asking you for information, exactly how we will use any information you give, and what might happen if you do not give the information.

Information sharing. Under the law, we can share your tax information with State tax agencies and, under strict legal guidelines, the Department of Justice and other federal agencies. We can also share it with certain foreign governments under tax treaty provisions.

Courtesy and Consideration

You are always entitled to courteous and considerate treatment from IRS employees. If you ever feel that you are not being treated with fairness, courtesy, and consideration by an IRS employee, you should tell the employee's supervisor.

Protection of Your Rights

The employees of the Internal Revenue Service will explain and protect your rights as a taxpayer at all times. If you feel that this is not the case, you should discuss the problem with the employee's supervisor.

Complaints

If for any reason you have a complaint about the IRS, you may write to the District Director or Service Center Director for your area. We will give you the name and address if you call our toll-free phone number listed later.

Representation and Recordings

Throughout your dealings with us, you can represent yourself, or, generally with proper written authorization, have someone represent you in your absence. During an interview, you can have someone accompany you.

Department of the Treasury
Internal Revenue Service
Publication 1 (Rev. 10-90)

Cat. No. 64731W

If you want to consult an attorney, a certified public accountant, an enrolled agent, or any other person permitted to represent a taxpayer during an interview for examining a tax return or collecting tax, we will stop and reschedule the interview. We cannot suspend the interview if you are there because of an administrative summons.

You can generally make an audio recording of an interview with an IRS Collection or Examination officer. Your request to record the interview should be made in writing, and must be received 10 days before the interview. You must bring your own recording equipment. We also can record an interview. If we do so, we will notify you 10 days before the meeting and you can get a copy of the recording at your expense.

Payment of Only the Required Tax

You have the right to plan your business and personal finances so that you will pay the least tax that is due under the law. You are liable only for the correct amount of tax. Our purpose is to apply the law consistently and fairly to all taxpayers.

If Your Return is Questioned

We accept most taxpayers' returns as filed. If we inquire about your return or select it for examination, it does not suggest that you are dishonest. The inquiry or examination may or may not result in more tax. We may close your case without change. Or, you may receive a refund.

Examination and inquiries by mail. We handle many examinations and inquiries entirely by mail. We will send you a letter with either a request for more information

or a reason why we believe a change needs to be made to your return. If you give us the requested information or provide an explanation, we may or may not agree with you and we will explain the reasons for any changes. You should not hesitate to write to us about anything you do not understand. If you cannot resolve any questions through the mail, you can request a personal interview. You can appeal through the IRS and the courts. You will find instructions with each inquiry or in Publication 1383, *Correspondence Process.*

Examination by interview. If we notify you that we will conduct your examination through a personal interview, or you request such an interview, you have the right to ask that the examination take place at a reasonable time and place that is convenient for both you and the IRS. If the time or place we suggest is not convenient, the examiner will try to work out something more suitable. However, the IRS makes the final determination of how, when, and where the examination will take place. You will receive an explanation of your rights and of the examination process either before or at the interview.

If you do not agree with the examiner's report, you may meet with the examiner's supervisor to discuss your case further.

Repeat examinations. We try to avoid repeat examinations of the same items, but this sometimes happens. If we examined your tax return for the same items in either of the 2 previous years and proposed no change to your tax liability, please contact us as soon as possible so we can see if we should discontinue the repeat examination.

Explanation of changes. If we propose any changes to your return, we will explain the reasons for the changes. It is

important that you understand these reasons. You should not hesitate to ask about anything that is unclear to you.

Interest. You must pay interest on additional tax that you owe. The interest is generally figured from the due date of the return. But if our error caused a delay in your case, and this was grossly unfair, we may reduce the interest. Only delays caused by procedural or mechanical acts not involving the exercise of judgment or discretion qualify. If you think we caused such a delay, please discuss it with the examiner and file a claim for refund.

Business taxpayers. If you are in an individual business, the rights covered in this publication generally apply to you. If you are a member of a partnership or a shareholder in a small business corporation, special rules may apply to the examination of your partnership or corporation items. The examination of partnership items is discussed in Publication 556, *Examination of Returns, Appeal Rights, and Claims for Refund.* The rights covered in this publication generally apply to exempt organizations and sponsors of employee plans.

An Appeal of the Examination Findings

If you don't agree with the examiner's findings, you have the right to appeal them. During the examination process, you will be given information about your appeal rights. Publication 5, *Appeal Rights and Preparation of Protests for Unagreed Cases*, explains your appeal rights in detail and tells you exactly what to do if you want to appeal.

Appeals Office. You can appeal the findings of an examination within the IRS through our Appeals Office. Most

Income Tax Appeal Procedure

At any stage
☐ You can agree and arrange to pay.
☐ You can ask for a notice of deficiency so you can file a petition with the Tax Court.
☐ You can pay the tax and file a claim for refund.

*Further appeals to the courts may be possible, except there is no appeal under the Tax Court's small tax case procedure.

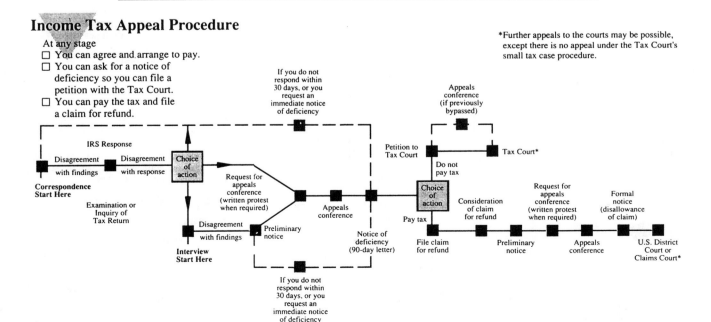

differences can be settled through this appeals system without expensive and time-consuming court trials. If the matter cannot be settled to your satisfaction in Appeals, you can take your case to court.

Appeals to the courts. Depending on whether you first pay the disputed tax, you can take your case to the U.S. Tax Court, the U.S. Claims Court, or your U.S. District Court. These courts are entirely independent of the IRS. As always, you can represent yourself or have someone admitted to practice before the court represent you.

If you disagree about whether you owe additional tax, you generally have the right to take your case to the U.S. Tax Court if you have not yet paid the tax. Ordinarily, you have 90 days from the time we mail you a formal notice (called a "notice of deficiency") telling you that you owe additional tax, to file a petition with the U.S. Tax Court. You can request simplified small tax case procedures if your case is $10,000 or less for any period or year. A case settled under these procedures cannot be appealed.

If you have already paid the disputed tax in full, you may file a claim for refund. If we disallow the claim, you can appeal the findings through our Appeals Office. If you do not accept their decision or we have not acted on your claim within 6 months, then you may take your case to the U.S. Claims Court or your U.S. District Court.

Recovering litigation expenses. If the court agrees with you on most issues in your case, and finds that our position was largely unjustified, you may be able to recover some of your administrative and litigation costs. To do this, you must have used all the administrative remedies available to you within the IRS. This includes going through our Appeals system and giving us all the information necessary to resolve the case.

Publication 556, *Examination of Returns, Appeal Rights, and Claims for Refund*, will help you more fully understand your appeal rights.

Fair Collection of Tax

Whenever you owe tax, we will send you a bill describing the tax and stating the amounts you owe in tax, interest, and penalties. Be sure to check any bill you receive to make sure it is correct. You have the right to have your bill adjusted if it is incorrect, so you should let us know about an incorrect bill right away.

If we tell you that you owe tax because of a math or clerical error on your return, you have the right to ask us to send you a formal notice (a "notice of deficiency") so that you can dispute the tax, as discussed earlier. You do not have to pay the additional tax at the same time that you ask us for the formal notice, if you ask for it within 60 days of the time we tell you of the error.

If the tax is correct, we will give you a specific period of time to pay the bill in full. If you pay the bill within the time allowed, we will not have to take any further action.

We may request that you attend an interview for the collection of tax. You will receive an explanation of your rights and of the collection process either before or at the interview.

Your rights are further protected because we are not allowed to use tax enforcement results to evaluate our employees.

Payment arrangements. You should make every effort to pay your bill in full. If you can't, you should pay as much as you can and contact us right away. We may ask you for a complete financial statement to determine how you can pay the amount due. Based on your financial condition, you may qualify for an installment agreement. We can arrange for these payments to be made through payroll deduction. We will give you copies of all agreements you make with us.

If we approve a payment agreement, the agreement will stay in effect only if:

You give correct and complete financial information,

You pay each installment on time,

You satisfy other tax liabilities on time,

You provide current financial information when asked, and

We determine that collecting the tax is not at risk.

Following a review of your current finances, we may change your payment agreement. We will notify you 30 days before any change to your payment agreement and tell you why we are making the change.

We will not take any enforcement action (such as recording a tax lien or levying on or seizing property), until after we have tried to contact you and given you the chance to voluntarily pay any tax due. Therefore, it is very important for you to respond right away to our attempts to contact you (by mail, telephone, or personal visit). If you do not respond, we may have no choice but to begin enforcement action.

Release of liens. If we have to place a lien on your property (to secure the amount of tax due), we must release the lien no later than 30 days after finding that you have paid the entire tax and certain charges, the assessment has become legally unenforceable, or we have accepted a bond to cover the tax and certain charges.

Recovery of damages. If we knowingly or negligently fail to release a lien under the circumstances described above, and you suffer economic damages because of our failure, you can recover your actual economic damages and certain costs.

If we recklessly or intentionally fail to follow the laws and regulations

for the collection of tax, you can recover actual economic damages and certain costs.

In each of the two situations above, damages and costs will be allowed within the following limits. You must exhaust all administrative remedies available to you. The damages will be reduced by the amount which you could have reasonably prevented. You must bring suit within 2 years of the action.

Incorrect lien. You have the right to appeal our filing of a Notice of Federal Tax Lien if you believe we filed the lien in error. If we agree, we will issue a certificate of release, including a statement that we filed the lien in error.

A lien is incorrect if:

You paid the entire amount due before we filed the lien,

The time to collect the tax expired before we filed the lien,

We made a procedural error in a deficiency assessment, or

We assessed a tax in violation of the automatic stay provisions in a bankruptcy case.

Levy. We will generally give you 30 days notice before we levy on any property. The notice may be given to you in person, mailed to you, or left at your home or workplace. On the day you attend a collection interview because of a summons, we cannot levy your property unless the collection of tax is in jeopardy.

Property that is exempt from levy. If we must seize your property, you have the legal right to keep:

Necessary clothing and schoolbooks,

A limited amount of personal belongings, furniture, and business or professional books and tools,

Unemployment and job training benefits, workers' compensation, welfare, certain disability payments, and certain pension benefits,

The income you need to pay court-ordered child support,

Mail,

An amount of weekly income equal to your standard deduction and allowable personal exemptions, divided by 52, and

Your main home, unless collection of tax is in jeopardy or the district director (or assistant) approves the levy in writing.

If your bank account is levied after June 30, 1989, the bank will hold your account up to the amount of the levy for 21 days. This gives you time to settle any disputes concerning ownership of the funds in the account.

We generally must release a levy issued after June 30, 1989, if:

You pay the tax, penalty, and interest for which the levy was made,

The IRS determines the release will help collect the tax,

You have an approved installment agreement for the tax on the levy,

The IRS determines the levy is creating an economic hardship, or

The fair market value of the property exceeds the amount of the levy and release would not hinder the collection of tax.

If at any time during the collection process you do not agree with the collection officer, you can discuss your case with his or her supervisor.

If we seize your property, you have the right to request that it be sold within 60 days after your request. You can request a time period greater than 60 days. We will comply with your request unless it is not in the best interest of the government.

Access to your private premises. A court order is not generally needed for a collection officer to seize your property. However, you don't have to allow the employee access to your private premises, such as your home or the non-public areas of your business, if the employee does not have court authorization to be there.

Withheld taxes. If we believe that you were responsible for seeing that a corporation paid us income and social security taxes withheld from its employees, and the taxes were not paid, we may look to you to pay an amount based on the unpaid taxes. If you feel that you don't owe this, you have the right to discuss the case with the collection officer's supervisor. You may also request an appeals hearing within 30 days of our proposed assessment of employment taxes. You generally have the same IRS appeal rights as other taxpayers. Because the U.S. Tax Court has no jurisdiction in this situation, you must pay at least part of the withheld taxes and file a claim for refund in order to take the matter to the U.S. District Court or U.S. Claims Court.

The amount of tax withheld from your wages is determined by the W-4, *Employees Withholding Allowance Certficate*, you give your employer. If your certificate is incorrect, the IRS may instruct your employer to increase the amount. We may also assess a penalty. You have the right to appeal the decision. Or, you can file a claim for refund and go to the U.S. Claims Court or U.S. District Court.

Publications 586A, *The Collection Process (Income Tax Accounts)*, and 594, *The Collection Process (Employment Tax Accounts)*, will help you understand your rights during the collection process.

The Collection Process

To stop the process at any stage, you should pay the tax in full. If you cannot pay the tax in full, contact us right away to discuss possible ways to pay the tax.

Start here

First notice and demand for unpaid tax

10 days later

Enforcement authority arises (a notice of a lien may be filed)

Up to 3 more notices sent over a period of time asking for payment

Notice of intent to levy is sent by certified mail (final notice)

30 days later

Enforcement action to collect the tax begins (levy, seizure, etc.)

Refund of Overpaid Tax

Once you have paid all your tax, you have the right to file a claim for a refund if you think the tax is incorrect. Generally, you have 3 years from the date you filed the return or 2 years from the date you paid the tax (whichever is later) to file a claim. If we examine your claim for any reason, you have the same rights that you would have during an examination of your return.

Interest on refunds. You will receive interest on any income tax refund delayed more than 45 days after the **later** of either the date you filed your return or the date your return was due.

Checking on your refund. Normally, you will receive your refund about 6 weeks after you file your return. If you have not received your refund within 8 weeks after mailing your return, you may check on it by calling the toll-free Tele-Tax number in the tax forms' instructions.

If we reduce your refund because you owe a debt to another Federal agency or because you owe child support, we must notify you of this action. However, if you have a question about the debt that caused the reduction, you should contact the other agency.

Cancellation of Penalties

You have the right to ask that certain penalties (but not interest) be cancelled (abated) if you can show reasonable cause for the failure that led to the penalty (or can show that you exercised due diligence, if that is the applicable standard for that penalty).

If you relied on wrong advice you received from IRS employees on the toll-free telephone system, we will cancel certain penalties that may result. But you have to show that your reliance on the advice was reasonable.

If you relied on incorrect written advice from the IRS in response to a written request you made after January 1,

1989, we will cancel any penalties that may result. You must show that you gave sufficient and correct information and filed your return after you received the advice.

Special Help to Resolve Your Problems

We have a Problem Resolution Program for taxpayers who have been unable to resolve their problems with the IRS. If you have a tax problem that you cannot clear up through normal channels, write to the Problem Resolution Office in the district or Service Center with which you have the problem. You may also reach the Problem Resolution Office by calling the IRS taxpayer assistance number for your area. If you are hearing-impaired with TV/Telephone (TTY) access, you may call 1-800-829-4059.

If your tax problem causes (or will cause) you to suffer a significant hardship, additional assistance is available. A significant hardship may occur if you cannot maintain necessities such as food, clothing, shelter, transportation, and medical treatment.

There are two ways you can apply for relief. You can submit Form 911, *Application for Taxpayer Assistance Order to Relieve Hardship*, which you can order by calling 1-800-TAX-FORM (829-3676). You can choose instead to call 1-800-829-1040, to request relief from your hardship. The Taxpayer Ombudsman, Problem Resolution Officer, or other official will then review your case and may issue a Taxpayer Assistance Order (TAO), to suspend IRS action.

Taxpayer Assistance Numbers

You should use the telephone number shown in the white pages of your local telephone directory under U.S. Government, Internal Revenue Service, Federal Tax Assistance. If there is not a specific number listed, call toll-free 1-800-829-1040.

You can also find these phone numbers in the instructions for Form 1040. You may also use these numbers to reach the Problem Resolution Office. Ask for the Problem Resolution Office when you call.

U.S. taxpayers abroad may write for information to:

Internal Revenue Service
Attn: IN:C:TPS
950 L'Enfant Plaza South, S.W.
Washington, D.C. 20024

You can also contact your nearest U.S. Embassy for information about what services and forms are available in your location.

Service Center
Problem Resolution Offices

Correspondence should be addressed to:

Problem Resolution Office
Internal Revenue Service Center

with the appropriate address from the following list.

Andover Service Center
310 Lowell Street (Stop 122)
Andover, MA 05501

Atlanta Service Center
P. O. Box 48-549 (Stop 29-A)
Doraville, GA 30362

Austin Service Center
P. O. Box 934
(Stop 1005 AUSC)
Austin, TX 78767

Austin Compliance Center
P. O. Box 2986
(Stop 1005 AUCC)
Austin, TX 78768

Brookhaven Service Center
P. O. Box 960 (Stop 102)
Holtsville, NY 11742

Cincinnati Service Center
P. O. Box 267 (Stop 11)
Covington, KY 41019

Fresno Service Center
P. O. Box 12161
Fresno, CA 93776

Kansas City Service Center
P. O. Box 24551
Kansas City, MO 64131

Memphis Service Center
P. O. Box 30309 AMF
(Stop 77)
Memphis, TN 38130

Ogden Service Center
P. O. Box 9941
(Stop 1005)
Ogden, UT 84409

Philadelphia Service Center
P. O. Box 16053
Philadelphia, PA 19114

District
Problem Resolution Offices

Correspondence and facsimile transmissions should be addressed to:

Problem Resolution Office
Internal Revenue Service

with the appropriate address from the following list.

Aberdeen District
115 4th Ave. S.E.
Aberdeen, SD 57401
(605) 226-7278
FAX: (605) 226-7270

Albany District
Leo O'Brien Federal Building
Clinton Ave. & N. Pearl Street
Albany, NY 12207
(518) 472-4482
FAX: (518) 472-3626

Albuquerque District
P. O. Box 1040 (Stop 1005)
Albuquerque, NM 87103
(505) 766-3760
FAX: (505) 766-1317

Anchorage District
P. O. Box 101500
Anchorage, AK 99510
(907) 261-4228 or 4230
FAX: (907) 261-4413

Atlanta District
P. O. Box 1065
Room 1520 (Stop 202-D)
Atlanta, GA 30370
(404) 331-5232
FAX: (404) 730-3438

Augusta District
220 Main Mall Road
South Portland, ME 04106
(207) 780-3309
FAX: (207) 780-3515

Austin District
P. O. Box 1863 (Stop 1005)
Austin, TX 78767
(512) 499-5875
FAX: (512) 499-5687

Baltimore District
P. O. Box 1553 Room 620A
Baltimore, MD 21203
(301) 962-2082
FAX: (301) 962-9572

Birmingham District
500 22nd Street South
Stop 316
Birmingham, AL 35233
(205) 731-1177
FAX: (205) 731-0017

Boise District
550 West Fort Street
Box 041
Boise, ID 83724
(208) 334-1324
FAX: (208) 334-9663

Boston District
JFK P. O. Box 9103
Boston, MA 02203
(617) 565-1857
FAX: (617) 565-4959

Brooklyn District
G. P. O. Box R
Brooklyn, NY 11202
(718) 780-6511
FAX: (718) 780-6045

Buffalo District
P. O. Box 500
Niagara Square Station
Buffalo, NY 14201
(716) 846-4574
FAX: (716) 846-5473

Burlington District
Courthouse Plaza
199 Main Street
Burlington, VT 05401
(802) 860-2008
FAX: (802) 860-2006

Cheyenne District
308 West 21st Street
(Stop 1005)
Cheyenne, WY 82001
(307) 772-2489
FAX: (307) 772-2488

Chicago District
230 S. Dearborn Street
Room 3214
Chicago, IL 60604
(312) 886-4396
FAX: (312) 886-1564

Cincinnati District
P. O. Box 1818
Cincinnati, OH 45201
(513) 684-3094
FAX: (513) 684-2445

Cleveland District
P. O. Box 99709
Cleveland, OH 44199
(216) 522-7134
FAX: (216) 522-2992

Columbia District
P. O. Box 386, MDP-03
Columbia, SC 29202-0386
(803) 765-5939
FAX: (803) 253-3910

Dallas District
P. O. Box 50008 (Stop 1005)
Dallas, TX 75250
(214) 767-1289
FAX: (214) 767-2178

Denver District
P. O. Box 1302 (Stop 1005)
Denver, CO 80201
(303) 844-3178
FAX: (303) 844-4900

Des Moines District
P. O. Box 1337 (Stop 2)
Des Moines, IA 50305
(515) 284-4780
FAX: (515) 284-4299

Detroit District
P. O. Box 330500 (Stop 7)
Detroit, MI 48232-6500
(313) 226-7899
FAX: (313) 226-3502

Fargo District
P. O. Box 8
Fargo, ND 58107
(701) 239-5141
FAX: (701) 239-5644

Ft. Lauderdale District
P. O. Box 17167
Plantation, FL 33318
(305) 424-2385
FAX: (305) 424-2483

Greensboro District
320 Federal Place
Room 214B
Greensboro, NC 27401
(919) 333-5061
FAX: (919) 333-5630

Hartford District
135 High Street (Stop 219)
Hartford, CT 06103
(203) 240-4179
FAX: (203) 240-4023

Helena District
Federal Building
301 S. Park Avenue
Helena, MT 59626-0016
(406) 449-5244
FAX: (406) 449-5342

Honolulu District
P. O. Box 50089
Honolulu, HI 96850
(808) 541-3300
FAX: (808) 541-1117

Houston District
1919 Smith Street (Stop 1005)
Houston, TX 77002
(713) 653-3660
FAX: (713) 653-3708

Indianapolis District
P. O. Box 44687 (Stop 11)
Indianapolis, IN 46244
(317) 226-6332
FAX: (317) 226-6110

**Assistant Commissioner
(International)**
950 L'Enfant Plaza
Washington, DC 20024
(202) 447-1020
FAX: (202) 287-4466

Jackson District
100 West Capitol Street
Suite 504, Stop 31
Jackson, MS 39269
(601) 965-4800
FAX: (601) 965-5796

Jacksonville District
P. O. Box 35045
(Stop D:PRO)
Jacksonville, FL 32202
(904) 791-3440
FAX: (904) 791-2266

Laguna Niguel District
P. O. Box 30207
Laguna Niguel, CA
92607-0207
(714) 643-4182
FAX: (714) 643-4436

Las Vegas District
4750 West Oakey Blvd.
Las Vegas, NV 89102
(702) 455-1099
FAX: (702) 455-1009

Little Rock District
P. O. Box 3778 (Stop 3)
Little Rock, AR 72203
(501) 324-6260
FAX: (501) 324-5109

Los Angeles District
P. O. Box 1791
Los Angeles, CA 90053
(213) 894-6111
FAX: (213) 894-6365

Louisville District
P. O. Box 1735
(Stop 120)
Louisville, KY 40201
(502) 582-6030
FAX: (502) 582-5580

Manhattan District
P. O. Box 408
Church Street Station
New York, NY 10008
(212) 264-2850
FAX: (212) 264-6949

Milwaukee District
P. O. Box 386 Room M-28
Milwaukee, WI 53201
(414) 297-3046
FAX: (414) 297-1640

Nashville District
P. O. Box 1107 (MDP 22)
Nashville, TN 37202
(615) 736-5219
FAX: (615) 736-7489

New Orleans District
600 S. Maestri Place
(Stop 12)
New Orleans, LA 70130
(504) 589-3001
FAX: (504) 589-3112

Newark District
Problem Resolution Unit
P. O. Box 1143
Newark, NJ 07101
(201) 645-6698
FAX: (201) 645-3323

Oklahoma City District
P. O. Box 1040 (Stop 1005)
Oklahoma City, OK 73101
(405) 231-5125
FAX: (405) 231-4929

Omaha District
106 S. 15th Street (Stop 2)
Omaha, NE 68102
(402) 221-4181
FAX: (402) 221-4030

Parkersburg District
P. O. Box 1388
Parkersburg, WV 26102
(304) 420-6616
FAX: (304) 420-6699

Philadelphia District
P. O. Box 12010
Philadelphia, PA 19106
(215) 597-3377
FAX: (215) 440-1456

Phoenix District
2120 N. Central Avenue
(Stop 1005)
Phoenix, AZ 85004
(602) 379-3604
FAX: (602) 379-3530

Pittsburgh District
P. O. Box 705
Pittsburgh, PA 15230
(412) 644-5987
FAX: (412) 644-2769

Portland District
P. O. Box 3341
Portland, OR 97208
(503) 326-4166
FAX: (503) 326-5453

Portsmouth District
P. O. Box 720
Portsmouth, NH 03802
(603) 433-0571
FAX: (603) 433-0739

Providence District
380 Westminster Mall
Providence, RI 02903
(401) 528-4034
FAX: (401) 528-4646

Richmond District
P. O. Box 10113, Room 5502
Richmond, VA 23240
(804) 771-2643
FAX: (804) 771-2008

Sacramento District
P. O. Box 2900 (Stop SA 5043)
Sacramento, CA 95812
(916) 978-4079
FAX: (916) 978-5052

St. Louis District
P. O. Box 1548 (Stop 002)
St. Louis, MO 63188
(314) 539-6770
FAX: (314) 539-3990

St. Paul District
P. O. Box 64599
St. Paul, MN 55164
(612) 290-3077
FAX: (612) 290-4236

Salt Lake City District
P. O. Box 2069 (Stop 1005)
Salt Lake City, UT 84110
(801) 524-6287
FAX: (801) 524-6080

San Francisco District
P. O. Box 36136 (Stop 4004)
450 Golden Gate Avenue
San Francisco, CA 94102
(415) 556-5046
FAX: (415) 556-4456

San Jose District
P. O. Box 100
San Jose, CA 95103
(408) 291-7132
FAX: (408) 291-7109

Seattle District
P. O. Box 2207 (Stop 405)
Seattle, WA 98111
(206) 442-7393
FAX: (206) 442-1176

Springfield District
P. O. Box 19201 (Stop 22)
Springfield, IL 62794-9201
(217) 492-4517
FAX: (217) 492-4073

Wichita District
P. O. Box 2907 (Stop 1005)
Wichita, KS 67201
(316) 291-6506
FAX: (316) 291-6557

Wilmington District
844 King Street, Room 3402
Wilmington, DE 19801
(302) 573-6052
FAX: (302) 573-6309

National Office
1111 Constitution Ave., N.W.
Room 3003 C:PRP
Washington, DC 20224
(202) 566-6475
FAX: (202) 377-6154

Free Tax Publications

The Internal Revenue Service publishes many free publications to help you "make your taxes less taxing." The publications listed on this page give general information about taxes for individuals, small businesses, farming, fishing, and recent tax law changes. (Forms and schedules related to the subject matter of each publication are indicated after each listing.) You may want to order one of these publications, and then, if you need more detailed information on any subject, order the specific publication about it.

Publications and forms listed in this booklet can be ordered by calling IRS toll-free at:

1-800-829-3676

or by using the order blank on page 29 of this publication.

1 Your Rights as a Taxpayer

To ensure that you always receive fair treatment in tax matters, you should know what your rights are. This publication clarifies your rights at each step in the tax process.

1S Derechos del Contribuyente (Your Rights as a Taxpayer) Spanish version of Publication 1.

3 Tax Information for Military Personnel

This publication gives information about the special tax situations of active members of the Armed Forces. It includes information on items that are includible in and excludable from gross income, alien status, dependency exemptions, sale of residence, itemized deductions, tax liability, and filing returns.

Forms 1040, 1040A, 1040EZ, 1040NR, 1040X, 1310, 2106, 2688, 2848, 3903, 3903F, 4868 and W-2.

4 Student's Guide to Federal Income Tax

This publication explains the federal tax laws that apply to high school and college students. It describes the student's responsibilities to file and pay taxes, how to file, and how to get help.

Examples illustrate typical situations. Filled-in forms and schedules show how to report income and deductions.

Forms 104EZ, W-2 and W-4.

17 Your Federal Income Tax

This publication can help you prepare your individual tax return. It takes you through the individual tax return and explains the tax laws that cover salaries and wages, interest and dividends, rental income, gains and losses, adjustments to income (such as alimony and IRA contributions), and itemized deductions. Also, it covers the new earned income credit rules.

Examples illustrate typical situations. Filled-in forms and schedules show how to report income and deductions.

The tax table, tax rate schedules, and earned income credit tables are included in this publication.

Forms 1040, 1040A, 1040EZ, Schedules A, B, D, E, R, SE, Forms W-2, 2106, 2119, 2441, 3903.

225 Farmer's Tax Guide

This publication explains the federal tax laws that apply to farming. It gives examples of typical farming situations and discusses the kind of farm income you must report and the different deductions you can take.

Schedules A, D, F, SE (Form 1040), and Forms 1040, 4136, 4562, 4684, 4797, 6251.

334 Tax Guide for Small Business

This book explains some federal tax laws that apply to businesses. It describes the four major forms of business organizations—sole proprietorship, partnership, corporation, and S corporation—and explains the tax responsibilities of each.

This publication is divided into eight parts. Part I contains general information on business organization and accounting practices. Part II discusses the tax aspects for the assets used in a business.

Parts III and IV explain how to figure your business income for tax purposes. They describe the kinds of income you must report and the different types of business deductions you can take.

Part V discusses the rules that apply when you sell or exchange business assets or investment property. It includes chapters on the treatment of capital gains and losses, and on involuntary conversions, such as theft and casualty losses. The chapters in Part VI bring together some specific tax considerations for each of the four major forms of business organizations.

Part VII explains some of the credits that can reduce your income tax and some of the other taxes you may have to pay in addition to income tax. It also discusses information returns that you may have to file. Part VIII shows how to fill out the main income tax forms businesses use.

Schedule C (Form 1040), Schedule K-1 (Forms 1065 and 1120S), Forms 1065, 1120, 1120-A, 1120S, 4562.

595 Tax Guide for Commercial Fishermen

This publication will familiarize you with the federal tax laws as they apply to the fishing industry. It is intended for sole proprietors who use Schedule C (Form 1040) to report profit or loss from fishing. It does not cover corporations or partnerships.

The last chapter includes a sample fisherman's recordkeeping system and illustrates filled-in tax forms.

Schedule C (Form 1040), Forms 1099-MISC, 4562, 4797.

More Free Tax Publications

Beginning on this page is a list of most often used free tax publications in numerical order.

15 Circular E, Employer's Tax Guide

Every employer automatically receives this publication on its revision and every person who applies for an employer identification number receives a copy.
Forms 940, 941, and 941E.

51 Circular A, Agricultural Employer's Tax Guide

Form 943

54 Tax Guide for U.S. Citizens and Resident Aliens Abroad

This publication discusses the tax situations of U.S. citizens and resident aliens who live and work abroad. In particular, it explains the rules for excluding income and excluding or deducting certain housing costs. Answers are provided to questions that taxpayers abroad most often ask.
Forms 2555, 1116, and 1040, Schedule SE (Form 1040).

80 Circular SS, Federal Tax Guide for Employers in the Virgin Islands, Guam, American Samoa, and the Commonwealth of the Northern Mariana Islands

Forms 940, 941SS and 943.

179 Circular PR, Guía Contributiva Federal Para Patronos Puertorriqueños (Federal Tax Guide for Employers in Puerto Rico)

Forms W-3PR, 940PR, 941PR, 942PR, and 943PR.

349 Federal Highway Use Tax on Heavy Vehicles

This publication explains which trucks, truck-tractors, and buses are subject to the federal highway use tax on heavy motor vehicles, which is one source of funds for the national highway construction program. You may be liable for this tax if a taxable highway motor vehicle is either registered or required to be registered in your name. The publication tells you how to figure and pay any tax due on your taxable vehicle.
Form 2290.

378 Fuel Tax Credits and Refunds

This publication explains the credit or refund allowable for the federal excise taxes paid on certain fuels, and the income tax credit available for alcohol used as a fuel.
Forms 843, 4136 and 6478.

448 Federal Estate and Gift Taxes

This publication explains federal estate and gift taxes.
Forms 706 and 709.

463 Travel, Entertainment, and Gift Expenses

This publication explains what expenses you may deduct for business-related travel, entertainment, local transportation, and gifts and it discusses the reporting and recordkeeping requirements for these expenses.

The publication also summarizes the reimbursement and accounting rules for employees and self-employed persons (including independent contractors).
Form 2106.

501 Exemptions, Standard Deduction, and Filing Information

This publication provides answers to some basic tax questions: who must file; who should file; what filing status to choose; how many exemptions to claim; and how to figure the amount of the standard deduction. It also covers the social security number requirement for dependents and rules for foster care providers.
Forms 2120 and 8332.

502 Medical and Dental Expenses

This publication tells you how to figure your deduction for medical and dental expenses. You may take this deduction only if you itemize your deductions on Schedule A (Form 1040).

It explains which specific expenses can be deducted and which cannot.
Schedule A (Form 1040).

503 Child and Dependent Care Expenses

This publication explains the credit you may be able to take if you pay someone to care for your dependent who is under age 13, your disabled dependent, or your disabled spouse. For purposes of the credit, "disabled" refers to a person physically or mentally not capable of self-care.

This publication also explains the tax rules covering benefits paid under an employer-provided dependent care assistance plan.

Publication 926 (listed below) explains the employment taxes you may have to pay if you are a household employer.
Schedule 2 (Form 1040A), and Form 2441.

504 Tax Information for Divorced or Separated Individuals

This publication explains tax rules of interest to divorced or separated individuals. It covers filing status, dependency exemptions, and the treatment of alimony and property settlements.

505 Tax Withholding and Estimated Tax

This publication explains the two methods of paying tax under our pay-as-you-go system.

They are:

1. Withholding. Your employer will withhold income tax from your pay. Tax is also withheld from certain other types of income. You can have more or less withheld, depending on your circumstances.

2. Estimated tax. If you do not pay your tax through withholding, or do not pay enough tax that way, you might have to pay estimated tax.

This publication also explains how to take credit on your 1991 return for your tax withholding and estimated tax payments, and how to figure the penalty for underpayment of estimated tax.
Forms W-4, W-4P, W-4S, 1040-ES, 2210, and 2210F.

508 Educational Expenses

This publication explains what work-related educational expenses qualify for deduction, how to report your expenses and any reimbursement you receive, and which forms and schedules to use.
Form 2106 and Schedule A (Form 1040).

509 Tax Calendars for 1992

510 Excise Taxes for 1992

This publication covers in detail the various federal excise taxes reported on Form 720. These include the following groupings: environmental taxes; facilities and service taxes on communications and air transportation; fuel taxes; manufacturers' taxes; vaccines; tax on heavy trucks, trailers, and tractors; luxury taxes; and tax on ship passengers. In addition, it briefly describes other excise taxes and tells which forms to use in reporting and paying the taxes.
Forms 637, 720, 6197, 6627, 8743, and 8807.

513 Tax Information for Visitors to the United States

This publication briefly reviews the general requirements of U.S. income tax laws for foreign visitors. You may have to file a U.S. income tax return during your visit. Most visitors who come to the United States are not allowed to work in this country. Please check with the Immigration and Naturalization Service before you take a job.
Forms 1040C, 1040NR, 2063, and 1040-ES (NR).

514 Foreign Tax Credit for Individuals

This publication may help you if you paid foreign income tax. You may be able to take a foreign tax credit or deduction to avoid the burden of double taxation. The publication explains which foreign taxes qualify and how to figure your credit or deduction.
Form 1116.

515 Withholding of Tax on Nonresident Aliens and Foreign Corporations

This publication provides information for withholding agents who are required to withhold and report tax on payments to nonresident aliens and foreign corporations. Included are three tables listing U.S. tax treaties and some of the treaty provisions that provide for reduction of or exemption from withholding for certain types of income.

Forms 1042 and 1042S, 1001, 4224, 8233, 1078, 8288, 8288-A, 8288-B, 8804, 8805, and W-8, 8813, and 8709.

516 Tax Information for U.S. Government Civilian Employees Stationed Abroad

This publication covers the tax treatment of allowances, reimbursements, and business expenses that U.S. government employees, including foreign service employees, are likely to receive or incur.

517 Social Security for Members of the Clergy and Religious Workers

This publication discusses social security coverage and the self-employment tax for the clergy. It also tells you how, as a member of the clergy (minister, member of a religious order, or Christian Science practitioner), you may apply for an exemption from the self-employment tax that would otherwise be due for the services you perform in the exercise of your ministry. Net earnings from self-employment are explained and sample forms are shown.

Form 2106, Form 1040, Schedule SE (Form 1040), and Schedule C (Form 1040).

519 U.S. Tax Guide for Aliens

This comprehensive publication gives guidelines on how to determine your U.S. tax status and figure your U.S. tax.

Resident aliens, like U.S. citizens, generally are taxed by the United States on income from all sources. Nonresident aliens generally are taxed only on income from sources in the United States. The income may be from investments or from business activities such as performing personal services in the United States. An income tax treaty may reduce the standard 30% tax rate on nonresident aliens' investment income. Their business income is taxed at the same graduated rates that apply to U.S. citizens or residents.

Aliens admitted to the United States with permanent immigrant visas are resident aliens, while temporary visitors generally are nonresident aliens. Aliens with other types of visas may be resident aliens or nonresident aliens, depending on the length and nature of their stay.

Forms 1040, 1040C, 1040NR, 2063, and Schedule A (Form 1040).

520 Scholarships and Fellowships

This publication explains the tax laws that apply to U.S. citizens and resident aliens who study, teach, or conduct research in the United States or abroad under scholarships and fellowship grants.

Form 1040A, 1040EZ.

521 Moving Expenses

This publication explains how, if you changed job locations last year or started a new job, you may be able to deduct your moving expenses. You may qualify for a deduction whether you are self-employed or an employee. The expenses must be closely related to the start of work at your new job location. You must meet a distance test and a time test. You also may be able to deduct expenses of moving to the United States if you retire while living and working overseas or if you are a survivor or dependent of a person who died while living and working overseas.

To deduct your allowable moving expenses, you must itemize your deductions. You should use Form 3903, Moving Expenses, if your move is within or to the United States or its possessions. You should use Form 3903F, Foreign Moving Expenses, if your move is outside the United States or its possessions.

Forms 3903, 3903F, and 4782.

523 Tax Information on Selling Your Home

This publication explains how to treat any gain from selling your main home, how to postpone the tax on part or all of the gain on the sale of your home, and how to exclude part or all of the gain from your gross income if you are 55 or older.

Form 2119.

524 Credit for the Elderly or the Disabled

This publication explains how to figure the credit for the elderly or the disabled. You may be able to claim this credit if you are 65 or older, or if you are retired on disability and were permanently and totally disabled when you retired. Figure the credit on Schedule R (Form 1040), or Schedule 3 (Form 1040A), Credit for the Elderly or the Disabled. You cannot take the credit if you file a Form 1040EZ.

Schedule R (Form 1040).

525 Taxable and Nontaxable Income

This publication discusses wages, salaries, fringe benefits, and other compensation received for services as an employee. In addition, it discusses items of miscellaneous taxable income as well as items that are exempt from tax.

526 Charitable Contributions

If you make a charitable contribution or gift to, or for the use of, a qualified organization, you may be able to claim a deduction on your tax return. This publication explains what a charitable contribution is, how the deduction is claimed, and what limits apply.

Schedule A (Form 1040).

527 Residential Rental Property

This publication discusses rental income and expenses, including depreciation, and explains how to report them on your return. It covers casualty losses on rental property and limits on rental losses. It also provides information on reporting the sale of rental property.

Schedule E (Form 1040), and Forms 4562 and 4797.

529 Miscellaneous Deductions

This publication discusses expenses you generally may take as miscellaneous deductions on Schedule A (Form 1040), such as business employee expenses and expenses of producing income. It does not discuss other itemized deductions, such as the ones for charitable contributions, moving expenses, interest, taxes, or medical and dental expenses.

Schedule A (Form 1040), Form 2106.

530 Tax Information for Homeowners (Including Owners of Condominiums and Cooperative Apartments)

This publication gives information about home ownership and federal taxes. It explains how to determine basis, how to treat settlement and closing costs, and how to treat repairs and improvements you make. The publication discusses itemized deductions for mortgage interest, real estate taxes, and casualty and theft losses. It also explains the mortgage interest credit.

531 Reporting Income From Tips

This publication gives advice about keeping track of cash and charge tips and explains that all tips received are subject to federal income tax. The publication also explains the rules about the information that employers must report to the Internal Revenue Service about their employees' tip income.

Forms 4070 and 4070A.

533 Self-Employment Tax

This publication explains the self-employment tax, which is a social security and Medicare tax for people who work for themselves. It is similar to the social security and Medicare taxes withheld from the pay of wage earners.

Social security and Medicare benefits are available to people who are self-employed just as they are to wage earners. Your payments of self-employment tax contribute to your coverage under the social security system.

Schedule SE (Form 1040).

534 Depreciation

This publication discusses the various methods of depreciation, including the modified accelerated cost recovery system (MACRS). This publication covers:
- What can be depreciated
- Section 179 deduction
- MACRS-assets placed in service after 1986
- ACRS-assets placed in service after 1980 and before 1987

- The limitations for passenger automobiles and other "listed property" placed in service after June 18, 1984
- Methods used for assets placed in service before 1981 and for assets not qualifying for ACRS and MACRS
- Example with a filled-in Form 4562. *Form 4562.*

535 Business Expenses

This publication discusses business expenses such as fringe benefits, rent, interest, taxes, insurance, and retirement plans. It also outlines the choice to capitalize certain business expenses, discusses amortization and depletion, covers some business expenses that may be deductible in some circumstances and not deductible in others, and points out some expenses that are not deductible.

536 Net Operating Losses

This publication explains how to figure a net operating loss (NOL) and when to use one. An NOL worksheet is included.
Form 1045, Schedule A.

537 Installment Sales

This publication discusses sales arrangements that provide for part or all of the selling price to be paid in a later year. These arrangements are "installment sales." If you finance the buyer's purchase of your property, instead of having the buyer get a loan or mortgage from a bank (or other lender), you probably have an installment sale.
Form 6252.

538 Accounting Periods and Methods

This publication explains which accounting periods and methods can be used for figuring federal taxes, and how to apply for approval to change from one period or method to another. Most individual taxpayers use the calendar year for their accounting period and the cash method of accounting.
Forms 1128 and 3115.

541 Tax Information on Partnerships

Form 1065, Schedules K and K-1 (Form 1065).

542 Tax Information on Corporations

Forms 1120 and 1120-A.

544 Sales and Other Dispositions of Assets

This publication explains how to figure gain and loss on various transactions, such as trading or selling an asset used in a trade or business, and it explains the tax results of different types of gains and losses. Not all transactions result in taxable gains or deductible losses, and not all gains are taxed the same way.
Schedule D (Form 1040) and Form 4797.

547 Nonbusiness Disasters, Casualties, and Thefts

This publication explains when you can deduct a disaster, casualty, or theft loss. Casualties are events such as hurricanes, earthquakes, tornadoes, fires, floods, vandalism, loss of deposits in a bankrupt or insolvent financial institution, and car accidents. The publication also explains how to treat the reimbursement you receive from insurance or other sources.
Form 4684.

550 Investment Income and Expenses

This publication explains which types of investment income are and are not taxable, when the income is taxed, and how to report it on your tax return. The publication discusses the treatment of tax shelters and investment-related expenses. The publication also explains how to figure your gain and loss when you sell or trade your investment property.
Forms 1099-INT, 1099-DIV, 6781, and 8815, Schedules B and D (Form 1040).

551 Basis of Assets

This publication explains how to determine the basis of property. The basis of property you buy is usually its cost. If you received property in some other way, such as by gift or inheritance, you normally must use a basis other than cost.

552 Recordkeeping for Individuals

This publication can help you decide what records to keep and how long to keep them for tax purposes. These records will help you prepare your income tax returns so that you will pay only your correct tax. If you keep a record of your expenses during the year, you may find that you can reduce your taxes by itemizing your deductions. Deductible expenses include medical and dental bills, interest, contributions, and taxes.

553 Highlights of 1991 Tax Changes

This publication discusses the more important changes in the tax rules brought about by recent legislation, rulings, and administrative decisions. It does not discuss all new tax rules or detail all changes. It highlights the important recent changes that taxpayers should know about when filing their 1991 tax forms and when planning for 1992.

554 Tax Information for Older Americans

This publication gives tax information of special interest to older Americans. An example takes you through completing a tax return and explains such items as the sale of a home, the credit for the elderly or the disabled, and pension and annuity income. The publication includes filled-in forms and schedules that show how these and other items are reported.
Schedules B, D, and R (Form 1040), and Forms 1040, 1040A, and 2119.

555 Federal Tax Information on Community Property

This publication may help married taxpayers who are domiciled in one of the following community property states: Arizona, California, Idaho, Louisiana, Nevada, New Mexico, Texas, Washington or Wisconsin. If you wish to file a separate tax return, you should understand how community property laws affect the way you figure your tax before completing your federal income tax return.

556 Examination of Returns, Appeal Rights, and Claims for Refund

This publication may be helpful if your return is examined by the Internal Revenue Service. It explains that returns are normally examined to verify the correctness of reported income, exemptions, or deductions, and it describes what appeal rights you have if you disagree with the results of the examination.

The publication also explains the procedures for the examination of items of partnership income, deduction, gain, loss, and credit. Information is given on how to file a claim for refund, the time for filing a claim for refund, and any limit on the amount of refund.
Forms 1040X and 1120X.

556S Revisión de las Declaraciones de Impuesto, Derecho de Apelación y Reclamaciones de Reembolsos (Examination of Returns, Appeal Rights, and Claims for Refund)

(Spanish version of Publication 556.)
Forms 1040X and 1120X.

557 Tax-Exempt Status for Your Organization

This publication discusses how organizations become recognized as exempt from federal income tax under section 501(a) of the Internal Revenue Code. (These include organizations described in Code section 501(c).) The publication explains how to get a ruling or determination letter recognizing the exemption, and it gives other information that applies generally to all exempt organizations.
Forms 990, 990EZ, 990PF, 1023, and 1024.

559 Tax Information for Survivors, Executors, and Administrators

This publication can help you report and pay the proper federal income tax if you are responsible for settling a decedent's estate. This publication also answers many questions that a spouse or other survivor faces when a person dies.

Questions answered include:

What was the decedent's tax liability for the year of death? When is the last return due? How is the income taxed from the date of the decedent's death to the distribution of the estate? Who is responsible for the decedent's tax? What are the tax problems of the heirs?

How does the survivor (or beneficiary) treat bequests or inheritances received from the estate of a decedent?

Form 1040, Form 1041, and Form 4810.

560 Retirement Plans for the Self-Employed

This publication discusses retirement plans for self-employed persons and certain partners in partnerships. These retirement plans are sometimes called Keogh plans or HR-10 plans.

If you set up a retirement plan that meets certain legal requirements, you may be able to deduct your payments to the plan. In addition, income earned by the plan will be tax-free until it is distributed.

561 Determining the Value of Donated Property

This publication can help donors and appraisers determine the value of property (other than cash) that is given to qualified organizations. It explains what kind of information you need to support a charitable deduction you claim on your return.

Form 8283.

564 Mutual Fund Distributions

This publication discusses the federal income tax treatment of distributions paid or allocated to you as an individual shareholder of a mutual fund. A comprehensive example shows distributions made by a mutual fund and an illustration of Form 1040.

Form 1040, Schedules B and D (Form 1040), and Form 1099-DIV.

570 Tax Guide for Individuals With Income From U.S. Possessions

This publication is for individuals with income from American Samoa, Guam, the Commonwealth of the Northern Mariana Islands, Puerto Rico, and the U.S. Virgin Islands.

Forms 4563, 5074, and 8689.

571 Tax-Sheltered Annuity Programs for Employees of Public Schools and Certain Tax-Exempt Organizations

This publication explains the rules concerning employers qualified to buy tax-sheltered annuities, eligible employees who may participate in the program, and the amounts that may be excluded from income.

Form 5330.

575 Pension and Annuity Income (Including Simplified General Rule)

This publication explains how to report pension and annuity income on your federal income tax return. It also explains the special tax treatment for lump-sum distributions from pension, stock bonus, or profit-sharing plans.

Forms 1040, 1040A, 1099-R and 4972.

578 Tax Information for Private Foundations and Foundation Managers

This publication covers tax matters of interest to private foundations and their managers, including the tax classification of the foundations, filing requirements, the tax on net investment income, and various excise taxes on transactions that violate the foundation rules.

Form 990-F.

579S Cómo Preparar la Declaración de Impuesto Federal (How to Prepare the Federal Income Tax Return)

Forms 1040, 1040A, 1040EZ.

583 Taxpayers Starting a Business

This publication shows sample records that a small business can use if it operates as a sole proprietorship. Records like these will help you prepare complete and accurate tax returns and make sure you pay only the tax you owe. This publication also discusses the taxpayer identification number businesses must use, information returns businesses may have to file, and the kinds of business taxes businesses may have to pay.

Schedule C (Form 1040), and Form 4562.

584 Nonbusiness Disaster, Casualty, and Theft Loss Workbook

This workbook can help you to figure your loss from a disaster, casualty or theft. It will help you most if you list your possessions before any losses occur. The workbook has schedules to help you figure the loss on your home and its contents. There is also a schedule to help you figure the loss on your car, truck, or motorcycle.

586A The Collection Process (Income Tax Accounts)

This publication explains your rights and duties as a taxpayer who owes tax. It also explains the legal obligation of the Internal Revenue Service to collect overdue taxes, and the way we fulfill this obligation. It is not intended to be a precise and technical analysis of the law in this area.

586S Proceso de Cobro (Deudas Del Impuesto Sobre Ingreso)

(Spanish version of Publication 586A)

587 Business Use of Your Home

This publication can help you decide if you qualify to deduct certain expenses for using part of your home in your business. You must meet specific tests and your deduction is limited. Deductions for the business use of a home computer are also discussed.

Schedule C (Form 1040), Form 4562, and Form 8829.

589 Tax Information on S Corporations

This publication discusses the way corporations are taxed under subchapter S of the Inter-

nal Revenue Code. In general, an S corporation does not pay tax on its income. Instead, it passes through its income and expenses to its shareholders who then report them on their own tax returns.

Forms 1120S and Schedule K-1 (Form 1120S).

590 Individual Retirement Arrangements (IRAs)

This publication explains the rules for and the tax benefits of having an individual retirement arrangement (IRA). An IRA is a personal savings plan that offers you tax advantages to set aside money for your retirement. Your contributions to an IRA may be deductible in part or in full and the earnings and gains in your IRA are generally not taxed until they are distributed to you.

Topics covered in this publication include:

– Who can set up an IRA
– Kinds of IRAs
– Deductible and nondeductible contributions
– Rollovers and other transfers
– Distributions, including required minimum distributions
– Acts that result in penalties
– Simplified Employee Pensions (SEPs)

Forms 1040, 1040A, 5329 and 8606.

593 Tax Highlights for U.S. Citizens and Residents Going Abroad

This publication briefly reviews various U.S. tax provisions that apply to U.S. citizens or resident aliens who live or work abroad and expect to receive income from foreign sources.

594 The Collection Process (Employment Tax Accounts)

This booklet explains your rights and duties as a taxpayer who owes employer's quarterly federal taxes. It also explains how we fulfill the legal obligation of the Internal Revenue Service to collect these taxes. It is not intended as a precise and technical analysis of the law.

594S Proceso de Cobro (Deudas Del Impuesto Por Razón Del Empleo)

(Spanish version of Publication 594.)

596 Earned Income Credit

This publication discusses who may receive the earned income credit, and how to figure and claim the credit. There is a discussion on the three credits that are available under the earned income credit. There is also a worksheet for persons who are eligible for the self-employed health insurance deduction and want to take the health insurance credit. Included in this publication are the new earned income credit tax tables. Also discussed is how to receive advance payments of the earned income credit.

Forms W-5, 1040, 1040A, and Schedule EIC.

597 Information on the United States-Canada Income Tax Treaty

This publication reproduces the entire text of the U.S.-Canada income tax treaty, and also gives an explanation of provisions that often apply to U.S. citizens or residents who have Canadian source income. There is also a discussion that deals with certain tax problems that may be encountered by Canadian residents who temporarily work in the United States.

598 Tax on Unrelated Business Income of Exempt Organizations

This publication explains the unrelated business income tax provisions that apply to most tax-exempt organizations. An organization that regularly operates a trade or business that is not substantially related to its exempt purpose may be taxed on the income from this business. Generally, a tax-exempt organization with gross income of $1,000 or more from an unrelated trade or business must file a return.

Form 990-T

686 Certification for Reduced Tax Rates in Tax Treaty Countries

This publication explains how U.S. citizens, residents, and domestic corporations may certify to a foreign country that they are entitled to tax treaty benefits.

721 Tax Guide to U.S. Civil Service Retirement Benefits

This publication explains how the federal income tax rules apply to the benefits that retired federal employees or their survivors receive under the U.S. Civil Service Retirement System or Federal Employees' Retirement System. There is also information on estate taxes.

Forms 1040 and 1040A.

850 English-Spanish Glossary of Words and Phrases Used in Publications Issued by the Internal Revenue Service

901 U.S. Tax Treaties

This publication provides information about the reduced tax rates and exemptions from U.S. taxes provided under U.S. tax treaties with foreign countries. This publication is intended for residents of those countries who receive income from U.S. sources. Information for foreign workers and students is emphasized.

Form 1040NR.

904 Interrelated Computations for Estate and Gift Taxes

Forms 706 and 709.

907 Tax Information for Persons with Handicaps or Disabilities

This publication explains tax rules of interest to people who are handicapped or disabled and to those who have dependents who are disabled. For example, you may be able to take a tax credit for certain disability payments, you may be able to deduct medical expenses, and you may be able to take a credit for expenses of care of persons with disabilities.

Schedule A (Form 1040), Schedule R (1040), and Form 2441.

908 Bankruptcy and Other Debt Cancellation

This publication explains the income tax aspects of bankruptcy and discharge of debt for individuals and small businesses.

Forms 982, 1040, 1041, 1120.

909 Alternative Minimum Tax for Individuals

This publication discusses the alternative minimum tax which applies to individuals. It also discusses the credit for prior year minimum tax.

Forms 6251 and 8801.

911 Tax Information for Direct Sellers

This publication may help you if you are a "direct seller," a person who sells consumer products to others on a person-to-person basis. Many direct sellers sell door-to-door, at sales parties, or by appointment in someone's home. Information on figuring your income from direct sales as well as the kinds of expenses you may be entitled to deduct is also provided.

Schedules C and SE (Form 1040).

915 Social Security Benefits and Equivalent Railroad Retirement Benefits

This publication explains when you have to include part of your social security or equivalent railroad retirement benefits in income on Form 1040 or Form 1040A. It also explains how to figure the amount to include.

Forms SSA-1099 and RRB-1099, Social Security Benefits Worksheet. Notice 703, Forms SSA-1042S and RRB-1042S.

917 Business Use of a Car

This publication explains the expenses that you may deduct for the business use of your car. Car expenses that are deductible do not include the cost of commuting from your home to your regular workplace. The publication also discusses the taxability of the use of a car provided by an employer and rules on leasing a car for business.

Form 2106.

919 Is My Withholding Correct for 1992?

This publication helps employees check their withholding. This publication has worksheets that will help them estimate both their 1992 tax and their total 1992 withholding. The employees can then compare the two amounts. The publication tells employees what to do if too much or too little tax is being withheld.

Form W-4.

924 Reporting of Real Estate Transactions to IRS

This publication informs sellers of certain real estate about the information they must provide to the real estate reporting person in order that the reporting person can complete the Form 1099-S that must be filed with IRS.

925 Passive Activity and At-Risk Rules

This publication covers the rules that limit passive activity losses and the at-risk limits.

Form 8582.

926 Employment Taxes for Household Employers

This publication shows how a household employer reports federal income tax withholding, social security and Medicare taxes (FICA taxes), and unemployment taxes (FUTA). You may be a household employer if you have a babysitter, maid, or other employee who works in your house. The publication also shows what records you must keep.

Forms W-2, W-3, 940, 940-EZ and 942.

929 Tax Rules for Children and Dependents

This publication describes the tax laws affecting dependents and certain children. It explains their filing requirement and standard deduction amount for dependents. It also explains when and how a child's parents may include their child's interest and dividend income on their return, and when and how a child's parents are required to report part of their child's investment income on their return.

Forms 8615, 8814, and 8803.

936 Home Mortgage Interest Deduction

This publication covers the rules governing the deduction of home mortgage interest, including points. It also covers the limits to your deduction if your acquisition cost exceeds $1 million ($500,000 if you are married filing separately) or your home equity debt exceeds $100,000 ($50,000 if you are married filing separately). Worksheets are provided to determine what interest expenses qualify as home mortgage interest.

Form 1040 and Schedule A (Form 1040).

937 Business Reporting

This publication explains your responsibilities, if you have employees, to withhold federal income taxes and social security and Medicare taxes (FICA taxes) from their wages, and to pay social security and Medicare taxes and federal unemployment taxes (FUTA taxes). It discusses the rules for advance payment of the earned income credit, and for reporting and allocating tips.

It also provides information on reporting non-wage payments on Form 1099-MISC, discusses backup withholding, and contains a chart listing the reporting requirements for many information returns including the Form 1099 series.

Form W-2, W-4, 940, 941, and 1099-MISC.

938 Real Estate Mortgage Investment Conduits (REMICS) Reporting Information (And Other Collateralized Debt Obligations (CDOs))

This publication discusses reporting requirements for issuers of real estate mortgage investment conduits (REMICs) and collateralized debt obligations (CDOs). This publication also contains a directory of REMICS and CDOs to assist brokers and middlemen in fulfilling their reporting requirements.

939 Pension General Rule (Nonsimplified Method)

This publication covers the nonsimplified General Rule for the taxation of pensions or annuities, which must be used if the Simplified General Rule is not applicable or is not chosen. For example, the nonsimplified method must be used for payments under commercial annuities. The publication also contains the necessary actuarial tables for this method.

945 Tax Information for Those Affected by Operation Desert Storm

This publication describes the tax benefits available to those involved in Operation Desert Shield/Storm. It includes information on combat zone compensation exclusion and when to file returns. It also has answers to questions about persons who die in a combat zone or in a terroristic or military action.

946 How to Begin Depreciating Your Property

This new publication is intended for use by individuals who are depreciating property for the first time. It discusses:
- Section 179 deduction,
- MACRS, and
- Listed property.

The publication contains worksheets to help figure the deduction in all areas and contains a comprehensive example using these worksheets and Form 4562.

947 Power of Attorney and Practice Before the IRS

This publication explains who can represent a taxpayer before the IRS and what forms or documents are used to authorize a person to represent a taxpayer. The roles of practitioners and specially authorized nonpractitioners are discussed. Examples are included to help explain some of the different uses of power of attorney. *Form 2048 and 8821.*

1004 Identification Numbers Under ERISA

1045 Information for Tax Practitioners

1212 List of Original Issue Discount Instruments

This publication explains the tax treatment of original issue discount (OID). It describes how:
- Brokers and other middlemen, including those who may hold the debt instruments as nominees for the owners, should report OID to IRS and to the owners on Forms 1099-OID or 1099-INT, and

- Owners of OID debt instruments should report OID on their income tax returns. The publication gives rules for figuring the discount amount to report each year, if required. It also gives tables showing OID amounts for certain publicly traded OID debt instruments, including short-term U.S. Government securities.

1244 Employee's Daily Record of Tips (Form 4070-A) and Employee's Report of Tips to Employer (Form 4070)

This publication explains how you must report tips if you are an employee who receives tips. Copies of the monthly tip report you must give your employer are included, as well as a daily list you can use for your own records. *Forms 4070 and 4070-A.*

1544 Reporting Cash Payments of Over $10,000 (Received in a Trade or Business)

This publication explains when and how persons in a trade or business must file a Form 8300 when they receive cash payments of more than $10,000 from one buyer. It also discusses the substantial penalties for not filing the form. *Form 8300.*

1581 Foreign Investment in U.S. Real Property

This publication explains the tax consequences of a sale of U.S. real property by a nonresident alien owner. *Form 1040NR, Schedule D (Form 1040), and Forms 4797, 6251, 8228, 8288A, 8288B.*

What Is Tele-Tax?

Recorded Tax Information includes about 140 topics of tax information that answer many Federal tax questions. You can listen to up to three topics on each call you make.

Automated Refund Information is available so you can check the status of your refund.

How Do I Use Tele-Tax?

- Touch-tone service is available Monday through Friday from 7:00 A.M. to 11:30 P.M. (Hours may vary in your area.)

- Rotary or pulse dial service is available Monday through Friday during regular office hours.

Choosing The Right Number

Use only the number listed on this page for your area. Use a local city number only if it is not a long distance call for you. **Please do not dial "1-800" when using a local city number.** However, when dialing from an area that does not have a local number, be sure to dial "1-800" before calling the toll-free number.

Recorded Tax Information

Topic numbers are effective January 1, 1992. A complete list of these topics is on the next page.

Touch-tone service is available 24 hours a day, 7 days a week.

Rotary or pulse dial service is available Monday through Friday during regular office hours.

Select, by number, the topic you want to hear. **For the directory of topics, listen to topic no. 323.**

Have paper and pencil handy to take notes.

Call the appropriate phone number listed on this page.

- If you have a touch-tone phone, immediately follow the recorded instructions, or
- If you have a rotary or pulse dial phone, wait for further recorded instructions.

Automated Refund Information

Be sure to have a copy of your tax return available since you will need to know the first social security number shown on your return, the filing status, and the **exact** amount of your refund.

Then, call the appropriate phone number listed on this page and follow the recorded instructions.

The IRS updates refund information every 7 days. If you call to find out about the status of your refund and do not receive a refund mailing date, please wait 7 days before calling back.

Toll-free Tele-Tax telephone numbers

Alabama
1-800-829-4477

Alaska
1-800-829-4477

Arizona
Phoenix, 252-4909
Elsewhere, 1-800-829-4477

Arkansas
1-800-829-4477

California
Counties of: Alpine, Amador, Butte, Calaveras, Colusa, Contra Costa, Del Norte, El Dorado, Glenn, Humboldt, Lake, Lassen, Marin, Mendocino, Modoc, Napa, Nevada, Placer, Plumas, Sacramento, San Joaquin, Shasta, Sierra, Siskiyou, Solano, Sonoma, Sutter, Tehama, Trinity, Yolo, and Yuba,
    1-800-829-4032
Los Angeles, 617-3177
Oakland, 839-4245
Elsewhere, 1-800-829-4477

Colorado
Denver, 592-1118
Elsewhere, 1-800-829-4477

Connecticut
1-800-829-4477

Delaware
1-800-829-4477

District of Columbia
882-1040

Florida
1-800-829-4477

Georgia
Atlanta, 331-6572
Elsewhere, 1-800-829-4477

Hawaii
1-800-829-4477

Idaho
1-800-829-4477

Illinois
Chicago, 886-9614
In area code 708,
    1-312-886-9614
Springfield, 789-0489
Elsewhere, 1-800-829-4477

Indiana
Indianapolis, 631-1010
Elsewhere, 1-800-829-4477

Iowa
Des Moines, 284-7454
Elsewhere, 1-800-829-4477

Kansas
1-800-829-4477

Kentucky
1-800-829-4477

Louisiana
1-800-829-4477

Maine
1-800-829-4477

Maryland
Baltimore, 466-1040
Elsewhere, 1-800-829-4477

Massachusetts
Boston, 523-8602
Elsewhere, 1-800-829-4477

Michigan
Detroit, 961-4282
Elsewhere, 1-800-829-4477

Minnesota
St. Paul, 644-7748
Elsewhere, 1-800-829-4477

Mississippi
1-800-829-4477

Missouri
St. Louis, 241-4700
Elsewhere, 1-800-829-4477

Montana
1-800-829-4477

Nebraska
Omaha, 221-3324
Elsewhere, 1-800-829-4477

Nevada
1-800-829-4477

New Hampshire
1-800-829-4477

New Jersey
1-800-829-4477

New Mexico
1-800-829-4477

New York
Bronx, 406-4080
Brooklyn, 858-4461
Buffalo, 685-5533
Manhattan, 406-4080
Queens, 858-4461
Staten Island, 858-4461
Elsewhere, 1-800-829-4477

North Carolina
1-800-829-4477

North Dakota
1-800-829-4477

Ohio
Cincinnati, 421-0329
Cleveland, 522-3037
Elsewhere, 1-800-829-4477

Oklahoma
1-800-829-4477

Oregon
Portland, 294-5363
Elsewhere, 1-800-829-4477

Pennsylvania
Philadelphia, 627-1040
Pittsburgh, 261-1040
Elsewhere, 1-800-829-4477

Puerto Rico
1-800-829-4477

Rhode Island
1-800-829-4477

South Carolina
1-800-829-4477

South Dakota
1-800-829-4477

Tennessee
Nashville, 242-1541
Elsewhere, 1-800-829-4477

Texas
Dallas, 767-1792
Houston, 850-8801
Elsewhere, 1-800-829-4477

Utah
1-800-829-4477

Vermont
1-800-829-4477

Virginia
Richmond, 783-1569
Elsewhere, 1-800-829-4477

Washington
Seattle, 343-7221
Elsewhere, 1-800-829-4477

West Virginia
1-800-829-4477

Wisconsin
Milwaukee, 273-8100
Elsewhere, 1-800-829-4477

Wyoming
1-800-829-4477

Tele-Tax Topic Numbers and Subjects

IRS Procedures and Services

Topic No.	Subject
101	IRS help available—Volunteer tax assistance programs, toll-free telephone, walk-in assistance, and outreach program
102	Tax assistance for individuals with disabilities and the hearing impaired
103	Small Business Tax Education Program (STEP)—Tax help for small businesses
104	Problem Resolution Program—Help for problem situations
105	Public libraries—Tax information tapes and reproducible tax forms
106	Examination procedures and how to prepare for an audit
107	The collection process
108	Tax fraud—How to report
109	Types of organizations that qualify for tax-exempt status
110	Organizations—How to apply for exempt status
111	Examination appeal rights
112	Electronic filing
113	Special Enrollment Examination to practice before IRS
114	Power of attorney information
115	Change of address—How to notify IRS
911	Hardship assistance applications
999	Local information

Filing Requirements, Filing Status, Exemptions

Topic No.	Subject
151	Who must file?
152	Which form—1040, 1040A, or 1040EZ?
153	When, where, and how to file
154	What is your filing status?
155	Dependents
156	Estimated tax
157	Amended returns
158	Decedents

Types of Income

Topic No.	Subject
201	Wages and salaries
202	Tips
203	Interest received
204	Dividends
205	Refund of state and local taxes
206	Alimony received
207	Business income
208	Sole proprietorship
209	Capital gains and losses
210	Pensions and annuities
211	Pensions—The general rule and the simplified general rule
212	Lump-sum distributions
213	Rental income and expenses
214	Renting vacation property/Renting to relatives
215	Royalties
216	Farming and fishing income
217	Earnings for clergy
218	Unemployment compensation
219	Gambling income and expenses
220	Bartering income
221	Scholarship and fellowship grants
222	Nontaxable income
223	Social security and equivalent railroad retirement benefits
224	401(k) plans
225	Passive activities—Losses/credits
226	Tax statements from the Railroad Retirement Board

Adjustments to Income

Topic No.	Subject
251	Individual retirement arrangements (IRAs)
252	Alimony paid
253	Bad debt deduction
254	Tax shelters

Itemized Deductions

Topic No.	Subject
301	Should I itemize?
302	Medical and dental expenses
303	Taxes
304	Moving expenses
305	Interest expense
306	Contributions
307	Casualty losses
308	Miscellaneous expenses
309	Business use of home
310	Business use of car
311	Business travel expenses
312	Business entertainment expenses
313	Educational expenses
314	Employee business expenses

Tax Computation

Topic No.	Subject
351	Tax and credits figured by IRS
352	Self-employment tax
353	Five-year averaging for lump-sum distributions
354	Alternative minimum tax
355	Gift tax
356	Estate tax
357	Standard deduction
358	Tax on a child's investment income

Tax Credits

Topic No.	Subject
401	Child and dependent care credit
402	Earned income credit
403	Credit for the elderly or the disabled

General Information

Topic No.	Subject
451	Substitute tax forms
452	Highlights of 1991 tax changes
453	Refunds—How long they should take
454	Copy of your tax return—How to get one
455	Forms/Publications—How to order
456	Tax shelter registration
457	Extension of time to file your tax return
458	Form W-2—What to do if not received
459	Penalty for underpayment of estimated tax
460	Recordkeeping
461	How to choose a tax preparer
462	Failure to pay child/spousal support and other Federal obligations
463	Withholding on interest and dividends
464	Highway use tax
465	Checklist/Common errors when preparing your tax return
466	Withholding on pensions and annuities
467	Foreign currency transactions
468	Desert Storm/Desert Shield

IRS Notices and Letters

Topic No.	Subject
501	Notices—What to do
502	Notice of underreported income—CP 2000
503	IRS notices and bills/Penalty and interest charges

Basis of Assets, Depreciation, Sale of Assets

Topic No.	Subject
551	Sale of your home—General
552	Sale of your home—How to report gain
553	Sale of your home—Exclusion of gain, age 55 and over
554	Basis of assets
555	Depreciation
556	Installment sales

Employer Tax Information

Topic No.	Subject
601	Social security and Medicare withholding rates
602	Form W-2—Where, when, and how to file
603	Form W-4—Employee's Withholding Allowance Certificate
604	Federal tax deposits—General
605	Employer identification number—How to apply
606	Form 942—Employer's Quarterly Tax Return for Household Employees
607	Form 941—Deposit requirements
608	Form 941—Employer's Quarterly Federal Tax Return
609	Form 940—Deposit requirements
610	Form 940/940-EZ—Employer's Annual Federal Unemployment Tax Return
611	Targeted jobs credit
612	Tips—Withholding and reporting

Form 1099 Series and Related Information Returns—Filing Magnetically or Electronically

Topic No.	Subject
651	Who must file—Originals and corrections
652	Acceptable media/Locating a third party to prepare your files
653	Applications, forms, and information
654	Waivers, extensions, and format deviations
655	Test files and combined Federal/state filing
656	Electronic filing of information returns
657	Information Returns Program Bulletin Board System

Tax Information for Aliens and U.S. Citizens Living Abroad

Topic No.	Subject
701	Resident and nonresident aliens
702	Dual-status alien
703	Alien tax clearance
704	Foreign earned income exclusion—General
705	Foreign earned income exclusion—Who qualifies?
706	Foreign earned income exclusion—What qualifies?
707	Foreign tax credit

The following topics are in Spanish:

Topic No.	Subject
751	Who must file?
752	Which form to use?
753	What is your filing status?
754	Earned income credit
755	Highlights of 1991 tax changes
756	Forms and publications—How to order
757	Alien tax clearance
758	Refunds—How long they should take
759	IRS help available—Volunteer tax assistance programs, toll-free telephone, walk-in assistance, and outreach program
760	Social security and equivalent railroad retirement benefits
761	Why do I have to turn in a Form W-4 to my employer?

Tax Information for Puerto Rico Residents

Topic No.	Subject
851	Who must file a U.S. income tax return in Puerto Rico
852	Deductions and credits for Puerto Rico filers
853	Federal employment taxes in Puerto Rico
854	Tax assistance for residents of Puerto Rico

Topic numbers are effective January 1, 1992.

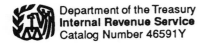

Department of the Treasury
Internal Revenue Service
Catalog Number 46591Y

Publication 586A
(Rev. April 91)

The Collection Process (Income Tax Accounts)

Existe una versión de esta publicación en español, la Publicación 586S, que puede obtener en la oficina local del Servicio de Impuestos Internos.

Introduction

This pamphlet explains your rights and duties as a taxpayer owing a bill for taxes. It also explains the legal obligation of the Internal Revenue Service to collect overdue taxes, and how we fulfill this obligation. It is not intended as a precise and technical analysis of the law.

By law, the Internal Revenue Service is empowered to collect certified child support obligations. The collection and payment of these liabilities, with certain exceptions, is the same as for unpaid taxes.

Liability for Unpaid Taxes

Notice and Demand. Each tax return filed with the Internal Revenue Service is checked for mathematical accuracy and to see if appropriate payment has been made. If all the tax has not been paid, we will send you a bill (including tax, interest and penalties), which is a *notice* of tax due and *demand* for payment. In most cases you are given 10 days from the date of the notice of tax due before we may take enforced collection action. However, if we have reason to believe that collection is endangered, we may give notice and demand immediate payment. If immediate payment is not made, enforced collection action may be taken without regard to the 10–day period normally provided. See information under **Levy** regarding Final Notice (Notice of Intent to Levy) 30–day period.

Corrective Action. If you owe taxes because not enough tax was withheld from your wages, you should file a new Form W–4, Employee's Withholding Allowance Certificate, with your employer(s) claiming a lower number of withholding allowances. For assistance in computing the correct number of withholding allowances, see Publication 919, "Is My Withholding Correct?"

Payment Procedure

Tax Bill Contains Error. If you believe your bill contains an error, you should immediately reply in writing to the office which sent the bill. You should send copies of any records with your reply which would help in correcting the error. If we determine you are correct, we will adjust your account after you pay any tax , interest, and penalty still due .

Unable to Make Full Payment. If you cannot pay your bill in full, you should pay as much as you can and write us immediately, explaining your circumstances. We may ask you to complete a Collection Information Statement so that we can review your financial condition to determine how you can pay the amount due.

If you have assets we can identify which could readily be sold, mortgaged, or used to secure funds to pay the taxes, we will ask you to do so. Or we may ask you to secure a commercial loan if we determine that you are able to do so. If you neglect or refuse to pay in full, we may take enforced collection action.

Installment Payments. If we determine that you can only pay the tax liability through installments, we will help you prepare a form itemizing your monthly income and expenses to determine the maximum amount you can pay. In certain cases we can arrange, through a payroll agreement, for your employer to withhold and regularly pay to us amounts deducted from your pay, or allow you to pay by other means such as electronic transfers from your bank account.

Once an installment agreement is granted, you must make each payment on time. If payment cannot be made timely, notify us of the circumstances. You must pay all future taxes as they become due, file all returns timely, and provide supplemental financial information when requested. During the time you are making payments, interest and penalty will accrue.

During the time you are making payments, we may file a Notice of Federal Tax Lien to secure the Government's interest until the final payment is made. We may require you to give us current information regarding your financial condition to see if your payments can be increased. If you fail to meet the terms of the agreement, or fail to provide financial information when requested, the agreement may be defaulted and we may take enforced collection action without an additional Final Notice (Notice of Intent to Levy).

You have the right, unless collection is endangered, to a 30–day notification of the termination, alteration, or modification of an agreement based on an IRS determination of change in financial condition.

Delayed Collection. If we determine that you cannot make any payment towards your liability, we may temporarily delay collection until your financial condition improves. This does not mean your debt is forgiven, or that the penalty for late payment and interest stop accruing. We may file a Notice of Federal Tax Lien to protect the Government's interest during this period.

Refund Offset. If you become entitled to a refund during the time you owe unpaid taxes, we will apply the refund to the unpaid tax liability and refund the balance, if any, to you.

Bankruptcy Proceedings. If you are a debtor in an ongoing bankruptcy, do not pay the bill without immediately contacting your IRS office. While the bankruptcy proceeding will not necessarily relieve your obligation to pay, a temporary stay of collection may be in effect.

Enforced Collection Policy

Enforced collection action includes the filing of a Notice of Federal Tax Lien, the serving of a Notice of Levy and/or the seizure and sale of your property (personal, real and/or business). We normally take these actions only after we try to contact you and give you the opportunity to pay voluntarily.

Notice of Federal Tax Lien. Once notice and demand for payment is sent and you neglect or refuse to pay the tax, a lien attaches to all your property (e.g., house, automobile) and rights to property (e.g., accounts receivable). This lien is not valid against claims of certain types of creditors until a Notice of Federal Tax Lien (lien) has been filed as a matter of public record. The filing of a notice of lien is often necessary to protect the Government's interest. It is a public notice to your creditors that the Government has a claim against all your property, including property which is acquired after the lien came into existence.

Once filed, a lien may harm your credit rating.

A Release of the Notice of Federal Tax Lien will be issued within 30 days after the tax due (including interest and other additions to the tax) if:

1) satisfied by payment or adjustment; or
2) Within 30 days after acceptance of a bond guaranteeing payment of the liability

All fees charged by the state or other jurisdiction for both filing and releasing the lien will be added to the balance you owe.

If the time during which the tax can be legally collected has expired, the notice of lien will act as an automatic Certificate of Release unless a lien refiling occurs.

You may sue the Federal government, but not IRS employees, for damages if the IRS knowingly or negligently fails to release a Notice of Federal Tax Lien when a release is warranted. If civil action is successful, you may be compensated for direct losses incurred by the IRS's inaction and the cost of litigation. The award will be reduced by the amount that you could have reasonably mitigated. All administrative appeals must be exhausted before a suit may be instituted. You have two years from the date of the action which gives rise to the claim to file a suit.

Publication 1450, Request for Release of Federal Tax Lien, describes the required contents of your request.

Property subject to a Federal tax lien may be released from the effect of the lien under the following circumstances:

1) Other property subject to the lien is worth at least twice the amount of the tax and additions to tax you owe as well as other prior debts owed on the property (e.g., mortgages).

2) The IRS receives the value of the Government's lien interest in the property and the taxpayer is giving up ownership (e.g., sale of a residence).

3) The IRS determines that the Government's interest in the property is valueless and the taxpayer is giving up ownership (e.g., sale of a residence).

4) The property is being sold and there is a dispute as to who is entitled to the sale proceeds, and the sale proceeds are placed in escrow while the dispute is being resolved.

The IRS may also subordinate its lien to a junior lienor if we receive the dollar value of the interest in the property being acquired by the junior lienor (e.g., a second mortgage). We may also subordinate our lien if we believe that doing so would speed collection of the tax (e.g., a loan to harvest crop).

Subrogation. This is the substitution of one person in the place of another with respect to a lawful claim of right.

There are two kinds of subrogation, conventional and legal. Conventional subrogation arises by contract, and legal subrogation arises by operation of law.

An example is where a taxpayer's property is encumbered by a prior mortgage, a subordinate Federal Tax Lien, and another encumbrance in third position, and the person holding the third ranking claim pays off the prior mortgage on the property. That party would then be subrogated to the rights of the prior mortgagee and be entitled to the same right of priority, (but only with respect to the claim they satisfied, not their original third ranking claim).

For assistance in requesting a discharge or subordination of Federal Tax Lien, see Publication 783, Instructions on How to Apply for Certificate of Discharge of Property from Federal Tax Lien, or Publication 784, How to Prepare Application for Certificate of Subordination of Federal Tax Lien. You should submit a written application in duplicate to the District Director in whose district the property is located.

You should contact the IRS Office where the property is located for information concerning discharge, subordination, or subrogation of Federal Tax Lien and instructions on how to post a bond.

Administrative Appeal of The Erroneous Filing of a Notice of Lien. You may appeal the filing of a notice of federal tax lien if you believe the filing was erroneous. A filing is erroneous when one of the following conditions applies:

1) the liability was satisfied before the notice of lien was filed;

2) you were in bankruptcy and subject to the automatic stay when the lien was filed;

3) an examination assessment was improperly made; or

4) the statute of limitations for collection expired prior to the filing of the notice of lien.

You may not use the administrative appeal provisions to challenge the underlying liability which generated the filing of the notice of lien. If we determine a notice of federal tax lien was erroneously filed, it will generally be released within 14 days after the determination that the lien was erroneously filed. A certificate of release of an erroneously filed notice of lien contains a statement that the notice of lien was in fact erroneously filed.

Levy. A levy is the taking of property to satisfy a tax liability. Levies can be made on property in the hands of third parties (employers, banks, etc.), or in your possession (automobile, real property, etc.).

Once served, a levy on salary or wages continues in effect until it is released, or your tax liability is satisfied or becomes unenforceable due to lapse of time.

Generally, court authorization is not required before levy action is taken unless Collection personnel must enter into private premises to accomplish their levy action (actual seizure of property). Generally, there are three legal requirements before levy action can be taken:

1) the tax must be owed,

2) a notice and demand for payment must have been sent to your last known address; and

3) if payment is not made, a Final Notice (Notice of Intent to Levy) must be given to you at least 30 days in advance. Such notice may be given to you in person, left at your dwelling or usual place of business, or sent by certified or registered mail to your last known address.

If collection is endangered, we may take immediate collection action.

Jeopardy levies may occur when we waive the 10–day Notice and Demand period and/or Final Notice (Notice of Intent to Levy) 30–period, because delay would endanger collection of the tax. You may seek administrative and/or judicial review when a decision is made that collection is endangered. After administrative review, you may, if the underlying liability is an issue in a Tax Court case, secure its review, or the review of the United States District Court. All other cases will be heard in United States District Court.

If your bank account is levied, your bank is required to hold funds you have on deposit, up to the amount you owe for 21 days. The bank is required to send the money, plus interest in certain cases, to the Service.

We must release a levy if:

1) you pay the tax, penalty, and interest for which the levy was made;

2) the statute of limitations for collection has expired prior to service of the levy;

3) the IRS determines the release will help collect the tax;

4) you have an approved, current installment agreement for the tax on the levy, unless you and the IRS have an agreement that a current levy should continue or future levies should be made;

5) the IRS determines the levy is creating an economic hardship, or

6) the fair market value of the property exceeds the levy and its release would not hinder the collection of tax.

If your bank account is levied, you should contact the specific name and/or telephone number listed on the Notice of Levy to discuss your account. You may also refer to the information under **Taxpayer Assistance** and **Problem Resolution Program (PRP)**, if necessary.

Certain types of property are exempt from levy by Federal law. They are:

1) wearing apparel and school books. (However, expensive items of wearing apparel, such as furs, are luxuries and are not exempt from levy.);

2) fuel, provisions, furniture, and personal effects, not to exceed $1,550 in value (for head of household) for 1989 and $1,650 for 1990 and later;

3) books and tools used in your trade, business, or profession, not to exceed $1,050 in value for 1989 and $1,100 for 1990 and later;

4) unemployment benefits;

5) undelivered mail;

6) certain annuity and pension benefits;

7) certain service–connected disability payments;

8) workmen's compensation;

9) salary, wages or other income subject to a prior judgment for court–ordered child support payments;

10) certain public assistance payments;

11) assistance under the job training partnership act;

12) principal residence, unless prior written approval of the district director or assistant district director is secured, or jeopardy exists;

13) deposits to the special Treasury fund made by members of the armed forces and Public Health Service employees on permanent duty assigned outside the United States or its possessions; and

14) a minimum weekly exemption for wages, salary, and other income based on the standard deduction plus the number of allowable personal exemptions divided by 52. In the case of no response, the exempt amount will be computed as if you were married filing separately with one exemption.

If you receive a levy on salary or wages, contact the specific name and/or telephone number listed on the Notice of Levy for assistance.

If you disagree with the value placed on the property by the employee making the levy, you can request a valuation by three disinterested individuals.

Seizures and Sales. Any type of real or personal property you own or in which you have an interest (including residential and business property) may be seized and sold to satisfy your tax bill.

A seizure may not be made on any of your property if the estimated cost of the seizure and sale exceed the fair market value of the property to be seized, at the time of the seizure.

No seizure or levy may be made on the date you appear in response to an administrative summons, which is issued to collect unpaid tax, unless jeopardy exists.

You have the right to an administrative review of our seizure action when we have taken personal property that you own which is necessary to the maintenance of your business.

If your property is seized or levied, you should contact the IRS employee who made the seizure or levy for assistance.

After seizure we will give notice to you and the public about the proposed sale. Unless the property is perishable and must be sold immediately, we will wait at least 10 days before conducting the sale. Prior to sale, we will compute a minimum price that we will accept for the property, and advise you of the amount. If you are in disagreement, you may request a Service valuation engineer or a private appraiser to assist the Internal Revenue Service employee in recomputing the minimum price.

Before the date of sale. we may release the property to you if you pay the amount equal to the amount of the Government's interest in the property, enter into an escrow arrangement, furnish acceptable bond or make an acceptable agreement for payment of the tax.

You also have the right to redeem your property at any time prior to the sale. Redemption consists of paying the tax due, including interest and penalties, together with the expenses of seizure.

You may request that the seized property be sold within 60 days. You should contact the IRS employee who made the seizure to assist you with your request. The request will be honored unless it is in the government's best interest to retain the property. You will be advised if your request is not honored.

After the sale, proceeds are applied first to the expenses of the levy and sale. The remaining amount is then applied against the tax bill. If the sale proceeds are less than the tax bill and the expenses of levy and sale, you will still be liable

IRS FORMS

APPENDIX B

Form **656**
(Rev. Sept. 1993)

Department of the Treasury—Internal Revenue Service
Offer in Compromise

▶ **See Instructions Page 5**

(1) Name and Address of Taxpayers

For Official Use Only	
Offer is *(Check applicable box)*	Serial Number
☐ Cash *(Paid in full)*	
☐ Deferred payment	*(Cashier's stamp)*

(2) Social Security Number | (3) Employer Identification Number

Alpha CSED Ind. _____

To: **Commissioner of Internal Revenue Service**

Amount Paid
$

(4) **I/we** (includes all types of taxpayers) **submit this offer to compromise the tax liabilities plus any interest, penalties, additions to tax, and additional amounts required by law (tax liability)** for the tax type and period checked below: (Please mark "X" for the correct description and fill-in the correct tax period(s), adding additional periods if needed.)

☐ Income tax for the year(s) 19_____ , 19_____ , 19_____ , and 19_____

☐ Trust fund recovery penalty (formerly called the 100-percent penalty) as a responsible person of _____
_____(enter business name) for failure to pay withholding
and Federal Insurance Contributions Act taxes (Social Security taxes) for the period(s) ended _____ /_____ /_____ , _____
/_____ /_____ , _____ /_____ /._____ , _____ /_____ /_____ (for example - 06/30/92)

☐ Withholding and Federal Insurance Contributions Act taxes (Social Security taxes) for the period(s) ended _____ /_____
/_____ , _____ /_____ /_____ , _____ /_____ /_____ , _____ /_____ /_____ (for example - 06/30/92)

☐ Federal Unemployment Tax Act taxes for the year(s) 19_____ , 19_____ , 19_____ , and 19_____

☐ Other (Be specific.) _____

(5) **I/we offer to pay $** _____ .

If you aren't making full payment with your offer, describe below when you will make full payment (for example – within ten (10) days from the date the offer is accepted): See the instructions for Item 5.

_____

_____

_____

As required by section 6621 of the Internal Revenue Code, the Internal Revenue Service (IRS) will add interest to the offered amount from the date IRS accepts the offer until the date you completely pay the amount offered. IRS compounds interest daily, as required by section 6622 of the Internal Revenue Code.

(6) **I/we submit this offer for the reason(s) checked below:**

☐ Doubt as to collectibility ("I can't pay.") You must include a completed financial statement (Form 433-A and/or Form 433-B).

☐ Doubt as to liability ("I don't believe I owe this tax.") You must include a detailed explanation of the reason(s) why you believe you don't owe the tax.

IMPORTANT: SEE REVERSE FOR TERMS AND CONDITIONS

I accept waiver of the statutory period of limitations for the Internal Revenue Service.	Under penalties of perjury, I declare that I have examined this offer, including accompanying schedules and statements, and to the best of my knowledge and belief, it is true, correct and complete.	
Signature of authorized Internal Revenue Service Official	(8a) Signature of Taxpayer-proponent	Date
Title Date	(8b) Signature of Taxpayer-proponent	Date

Dispose of prior issues.

Part 1 IRS Copy   Cat. No. 16728N   Form **656** (Rev. 9-93)

(7) By submitting this offer, **I/we understand and agree to the following terms and conditions:**

(a) I/we voluntarily submit all payments made on this offer.

(b) IRS will apply payments made under the terms of this offer in the best interests of the government.

(c) If IRS rejects the offer or I/we withdraw the offer, IRS will return any amount paid with the offer. If I/we agree in writing, IRS will apply the amount paid with the offer to the amount owed. If I/we agree to apply the payment, the date the offer is rejected or withdrawn will be considered the date of payment. I/we understand that IRS will not pay interest on any amount I/we submit with the offer.

(d) I/we will comply with all provisions of the Internal Revenue Code relating to filing my/our returns and paying my/our required taxes for five (5) years from the date IRS accepts the offer.

(e) I/we waive and agree to the suspension of any statutory periods of limitation (time limits provided for by law) for IRS assessment and collection of the tax liability for the tax periods checked in item (4).

(f) IRS will keep all payments and credits made, received, or applied to the amount being compromised before this offer was submitted. IRS will also keep any payments made under the terms of an installment agreement while this offer is pending.

(g) IRS will keep any refund, including interest, due to me/us because of overpayment of any tax or other liability, for tax periods extending through the calendar year that IRS accepts the offer. This condition doesn't apply if the offer is based only on doubt as to liability.

(h) I/we will return to IRS any refund identified in (g) received after submitting this offer. This condition doesn't apply if the offer is based only on doubt as to liability.

(i) The total amount IRS can collect under this offer can't be more than the full amount of the tax liability.

(j) I//we understand that I/we remain responsible for the full amount of the tax liability unless and until IRS accepts the offer in writing and I/we have met all the terms and conditions of the offer. IRS won't remove the original amount of the tax liability from its records until I/we have met all the terms and conditions of the offer.

(k) I/we understand that the tax I/we offer to compromise is and will remain a tax liability until I/we meet all the terms and conditions of this offer. If I/we file bankruptcy before the terms and conditions of this offer are completed, any claim the IRS files in the bankruptcy proceeding will be a tax claim.

(l) Once IRS accepts the offer in writing, I/we have no right to contest, in court or otherwise, the amount of the tax liability.

(m)The offer is pending starting with the date an authorized IRS official signs this form and accepts my/our waiver of the statutory periods of limitation. The offer remains pending until an authorized IRS official accepts, rejects, or withdraws the offer in writing. If I/we appeal the IRS decision on the offer, IRS will continue to treat the offer as pending until the Appeals Office accepts or rejects the offer in writing. If I/we don't file a protest within 30 days of the date IRS notifies me/us of the right to protest the decision, I/we waive the right to a hearing before the Appeals Office about this offer in compromise.

(n) The waiver and suspension of any statutory periods of limitation for assessment and collection of the amount of the tax liability described in item (4), continues to apply:

(i)   while the offer is pending (see (m) above),

(ii)   during the time I/we haven't paid all of the amount offered,

(iii) during the time I/we haven't completed all terms and conditions of the offer, and

(iv)   for one additional year beyond the time periods identified in (i), (ii), and (iii) above.

(o) If I/we fail to meet any of the terms and conditions of the offer, the offer is in default, and IRS may:

(i)   immediately file suit to collect the entire unpaid balance of the offer;

(ii)   immediately file suit to collect an amount equal to the original amount of the tax liability as liquidated damages, minus any payments already received under the terms of this offer;

(iii) disregard the amount of the offer and apply all amounts already paid under the offer against the original amount of tax liability;

(iv)   file suit or levy to collect the original amount of the tax liability, without further notice of any kind.

IRS will continue to add interest, as required by section 6621 of the Internal Revenue Code, on the amount IRS determines is due after default. IRS will add interest from the date the offer is defaulted until I/we completely satisfy the amount owed. IRS compounds interest daily, as required by section 6622 of the Internal Revenue Code.

INSTRUCTIONS

Background

Section 7122 of the Internal Revenue Code allows delegated Internal Revenue Service (IRS) officials to compromise a tax liability before we refer it to the Department of Justice. The term "tax liability" is the total amount a taxpayer owes, including taxes, penalties, interest, additions to tax, and additional amounts required by law.

Reasons for Compromise

We (IRS) can compromise the amount owed for the following reasons:

(1) Doubt as to collectibility, i.e., doubt that we can collect the full amount owed ("I can't pay") and/or

(2) Doubt as to liability, i.e., doubt as to whether you owe the amount (I don't believe I owe this tax").

We can't legally accept a compromise based on doubt as to collectibility when there is no doubt that we can collect the full amount owed. We also can't legally accept a compromise based on doubt as to liability when the amount owed has already been decided in court.

If you submit an offer based on doubt as to liability, you must include a written statement describing in detail why you don't believe you owe the liability.

IRS Policy

We will accept an offer in compromise when it is unlikely that we can collect the full amount owed and the amount you offered reasonably reflects collection potential. An offer in compromise is an alternative to declaring a case currently not collectible or to a long-term installment agreement. Our goal is to collect what we can at the earliest possible time with the least cost to the government.

In delinquent tax cases where an offer in compromise appears to be a workable solution, an IRS employee will discuss the compromise alternative with you and help prepare the required forms if necessary. You are responsible for making the first specific proposal for compromise.

Our offer in compromise process will be successful only if you make an adequate compromise proposal consistent with your ability to pay and we make prompt and reasonable decisions. Taxpayers are expected to provide reasonable documentation to verify their ability to pay. The goal is a compromise which is in the best interest of both the taxpayer and IRS. Acceptance of an adequate offer also creates a fresh start for the taxpayer regarding future filing and payment requirements.

How to Figure An Acceptable Offer

An acceptable offer must include all amounts available from the following sources: (You may use the spaces provided to figure the minimum amount you must offer.)

(1) The **liquidating value of your assets** (value if you are forced to sell) minus debts against specific assets that have priority over IRS.

Liquidating value of assets $ _____

  Minus: Debts with priority $ _____

Value of available assets $ _____

NOTE: The following examples are debts which you should NOT subtract because IRS has priority over them:

— amounts you owe on credit cards;

— loans you secured without pledging assets as security;

— any amount you borrowed after we recorded a Notice of Federal Tax Lien.

(2) The **amount we could collect from your present and future income**. Generally, the collectible amount is your income minus necessary living expenses. We usually consider what we can collect over five years. Figure the amount as follows: Average monthly income minus necessary expenses x 60 months = value of income

              $ _____

(3) The **amount collectible from third parties**. We may be able to collect part or all of the amount you owe from third parties through the trust fund recovery penalty or transferee liabilities (assets you transferred below market value or transferred assets you still use). Show any amount that we might collect from such sources. $ _____

(4) **Assets or income that are available to you but may not be available to IRS** for direct collection action, e.g., property outside the United States. Show any amount you have access to. $ _____

(5) **Minimum offer** (total items (1) through (4)) $ _____

If your offer is less than the minimum offer amount from item (5), we can't process your offer. If the minimum offer total is more than the amount owed, IRS can't process your offer. You must pay the full amount owed. We will return this form to you.

Offer Investigation

IRS will investigate your offer to determine if the offered amount is the maximum you can pay. This means that we may ask for information to verify your financial statement (Form 433-A or 433-B). We may ask you to increase the amount of your offer or to change the terms of payment, or we may find that we can't accept your offer.

Questions IRS Will Consider

The IRS goal is a compromise that is in the best interest of both the government and the taxpayer. It is your responsibility to show us why it would be in the government's best interest to accept your proposal. When we consider your offer we must ask the following questions:

(1) Could we collect the entire amount owed through liquidation of your assets or through an installment agreement based on your present and future income? If the answer is "yes," we can't accept your offer.

(2) Could we collect more from your assets and future income than you offered? If the answer is "yes", you must offer a larger amount or we will reject your offer.

(3) Would we be better off waiting until a future date because the evidence shows that collection in the future would result in more money than you now offer? If the answer is "yes", you must offer a larger amount or we will reject your offer.

(4) Would the taxpaying public believe that acceptance of your offer was a reasonable action? If the answer is "no", we will reject your offer.

The fact that you currently have no assets or income doesn't mean that IRS should simply accept anything that you offer because that is all we can collect now. IRS won't decide that "something is better than nothing". For example, it is not usually in our best interest to accept $25 on a $1,000 liability or $1,000 on a $100,000 liability. It is usually better for us to reject a nominal amount and wait to see what collection potential arises during the remainder of our ten year collection period.

As we state in our policy, we will accept your offer only if you submit a legitimate proposal that is in the government's best interest.

Possible Additional Requirements

Generally IRS believes that you benefit if we accept your offer because you can then manage your finances without the burden of a tax liability. Therefore, we may require you to submit one of the following agreements before we accept your offer:

(1) A written agreement that requires you to pay a percentage of future earnings.

(2) A written agreement to give up certain present or potential tax benefits.

Tax Compliance

We won't accept your offer if you haven't filed all required returns. In addition, we will expect you to have paid all estimated tax payments and Federal tax deposits due as of the date you file the offer. Please note that the terms of the offer also require your future compliance (i.e., filing and paying) for five years after acceptance.

Suspending Collection

Submitting an offer doesn't automatically suspend our collection activity. If there is any indication that you filed the offer only to delay collection of the tax or that delay would interfere with our ability to collect the tax, we will continue collection efforts. **If you agreed to make installment payments before you submitted your offer, you should continue making those payments.**

How to Complete Form 656

(Item 1) Enter your full name and address. If the tax liability is owed jointly by a husband and wife and both wish to make an offer, show both names. If you owe one amount by yourself (such as employment taxes), and at the same time owe another amount jointly (such as income taxes), but only one person is submitting an offer, complete only one Form 656. If you owe one amount yourself and another amount jointly, and both joint parties submit an offer, you must complete two Forms 656, one for the separate amount and one for the joint amount.

(Item 2) Please enter a social security number for each taxpayer.

(Item 3) If you operate a business, please enter your employer identification number.

(Item 4) Please mark "X" for all liabilities you offer to compromise, listing the specific periods involved. If the type of liability is not preprinted, please specify the type of tax and periods of liability.

(Item 5) Please enter the total amount you offer. Don't include any amount you have already paid or that IRS has already collected. If you send the whole amount with your offer, make no further entry in item 5. If you aren't sending the whole amount with your offer, please describe the details of your offer, including:

(1) Any amount you deposited with this offer.

(2) Any amount you deposited for a prior offer and now want applied to this offer.

(3) The amount of any subsequent payment(s) you will make and the date you will make them.

You should pay the full amount of the offer in the shortest possible time. Under no circumstances should payment extend beyond two years. However, if we find that you can pay in a shorter time, we will require you to pay the full amount offered in less than two years, or we will reject your offer. If you pay earlier, it will reduce the amount of interest due, since IRS charges interest from the date of acceptance until the date you pay the full amount offered.

Item 5 Examples:

(1) $30,000: $5,000 deposited with the offer and $25,000 to be paid within ninety (90) days from the date of acceptance.

(2) $103,000: To be paid within ninety (90) days from the date of acceptance.

(3) $50,000: $10,000 deposited with the offer, $20,000 to be paid within thirty (30) days from the date of acceptance, and $20,000 to be paid within sixty (60) days from the date of acceptance.

If you send a payment with your offer or at any later date, IRS will deposit it in a special fund while we consider your offer. IRS won't pay interest whether your payment is ultimately applied to an accepted offer, applied to the amount owed (if you agree), or returned to you. When IRS cashes your check, that doesn't mean your offer is accepted.

(Item 6) Please check one or both reasons.

(Item 7) It is important that you understand that when you make this offer, you are agreeing that:

(a) Any statutory period for assessment and collection of the amount owed is suspended while the offer is pending, during the time you haven't fulfilled any term or condition of the offer, and for one year after the offer is no longer pending and after the date you fulfill all terms and conditions of the offer.

(b) You won't contest, in court or otherwise, the amount owed if we accept your offer.

(c) You give up any overpayments (i.e., refunds) for all tax periods prior to and including the year IRS accepts your offer.

(d) IRS can reinstate the entire amount owed if you don't comply with all the terms and conditions of the offer, including the requirement to file returns and pay tax for five years.

(Item 8) All persons submitting the offer should sign and date Form 656.

Where to File Your Offer

You should file your offer in compromise in duplicate in the IRS district office in your area. If you have been working with a specific IRS employee on your case, you should file the offer with that employee.

Financial Statement

If you submit your offer on the basis of doubt as to collectibility, you must also submit Form 433-A, Collection Information Statement for Individuals, or Form 433-B Collection Information Statement fo Businesses. If you are an individual an you operate a business, you must subm both forms.

You must complete all blocks on thes forms. Write N/A (not applicable) in an blocks that don't affect you. Pleas pa particular attention to line 26, Other Asset on Form 433-A and line 24, Other Asset on Form 433-B. You should list pensio plans, profit sharing plans, and Individua Retirement Accounts on those lines. Whe you send Form 433-A and/or Form 433-E you should include documentation to verif values of assets, encumbrances, an income and expense information. Whe you determine the "Current Market Value of assets on Forms 433-A and 433-B, us the "quick sale" or "liquidating value."

Returning Your Offer

We will return your offer to you fo clarification if we can't process it because contains any of the following problems:

(1) the taxpayer isn't adequatel identified,

(2) the liabilities to compromise aren identified,

(3) no amount is offered,

(4) appropriate signatures aren't pre sent,

(5) financial statements aren't sub mitted,

(6) the amount offered doesn't equal th minimum offer amount required (Se **How to Figure An Acceptabl Offer** above). We figure that amoun directly from the information yo submit on Forms 433-A and 433-B.

If We Reject Your Offer

If you submit an offer based on doubt tha we can collect the full amount owed an we find that you can pay more than yo offered, we will reject your offer. We wi also reject an offer based on doubt that yo owe the liability if we still believe that yo do owe it. In either case, you may have th right to protest our decision. However, yo don't have the right to protest our decisio if you haven't filed all required returns or you don't provide reasonabl documentation to verify the amount yo can pay.

If you submit a protest, an appeals offic will consider your case. We include specif instructions about filing a protest if w decide to reject your offer.

Public Disclosure

Please note that the law requires that a accepted offers in compromise be avai able for review by the general publi Therefore, it is possible that the details o your personal financial affairs may becom publicly known.

Form **433-A**
(Rev. October 1992)

Department of the Treasury — Internal Revenue Service

Collection Information Statement for Individuals

NOTE: **Complete all blocks, except shaded areas. Write "N/A"** (not applicable) **in those blocks that do not apply.**

1. Taxpayer(s) name(s) and address	2. Home phone number ( )	3. Marital status
County _____	4.a. Taxpayer's social security number	b. Spouse's social security number

Section I.   Employment Information

5. Taxpayer's employer or business (name and address)	a. How long employed	b. Business phone number ( )	c. Occupation
	d. Number of exemptions claimed on Form W-4	e. Paydays	f. (Check appropriate box) ☐ Wage earner ☐ Partner ☐ Sole proprietor

6. Spouse's employer or business (name and address)	a. How long employed	b. Business phone number ( )	c. Occupation
	d. Number of exemptions claimed on Form W-4	e. Paydays	f. (Check appropriate box) ☐ Wage earner ☐ Partner ☐ Sole proprietor

Section II.   Personal Information

7. Name, address and telephone number of next of kin or other reference	8. Other names or aliases	9. Previous address(es)

10. Age and relationship of dependents living in your household (exclude yourself and spouse)

11. Date of Birth ▶	a. Taxpayer	b. Spouse	12. Latest filed income tax return (tax year)	a. Number of exemptions claimed	b. Adjusted Gross Income

Section III.   General Financial Information

13. Bank accounts (Include Savings & Loans, Credit Unions, IRA and Retirement Plans, Certificates of Deposit, etc.)

Name of Institution	Address	Type of Account	Account No.	Balance
		Total (Enter in Item 21)		

Form **433-A**   (Rev. 10-92)

14. Bank charge cards, Credit Unions, Savings and Loans, Lines of credit

Type of Account or Card	Name and Address of Financial Institution	Monthly Payment	Credit Limit	Amount Owed	Credit Available
Totals *(Enter in Item 27)* ▶					

15. Safe deposit boxes rented or accessed *(List all locations, box numbers, and contents.)*

16. Real Property *(Brief description and type of ownership)*	Physical Address
a.	
	County _____
b.	
	County _____
c.	
	County _____

17. Life Insurance *(Name of Company)*	Policy Number	Type	Face Amount	Available Loan Value
Total *(Enter in Item 23)* ▶				

18. Securities *(stocks, bonds, mutual funds, money market funds, government securities, etc.)*:

Kind	Quantity or Denomination	Current Value	Where Located	Owner of Record

19. Other information relating to your financial condition. If you check the yes box, please give dates and explain on page 4, Additional Information or Comments:

a. Court proceedings	☐ Yes ☐ No	b. Bankruptcies	☐ Yes ☐ No
c. Repossessions	☐ Yes ☐ No	d. Recent transfer of assets for less than full value	☐ Yes ☐ No
e. Anticipated increase in income	☐ Yes ☐ No	f. Participant or beneficiary to trust, estate, profit sharing, etc.	☐ Yes ☐ No

Section IV.   Asset and Liability Analysis

Description	Current Market Value	Liabilities Balance Due	Equity in Asset	Amount of Monthly Payment	Name and Address of Lien/Note Holder/Obligee	Date Pledged	Date of Final Payment
20. Cash							
21. Bank accounts *(from Item 13)*							
22. Securities *(from Item 18)*							
23. Cash or loan value of Insur.							
24. Vehicles *(Model, year, license, tag #)*							
a.							
b.							
c.							
25. Real property *(From Section III, item 16)* a.							
b.							
c.							
26. Other assets							
a.							
b.							
c.							
d.							
e.							
27. Bank revolving credit *(from Item 14)*							
28. Other Liabilities *(Including judgments, notes, and other charge accounts)* a.							
b.							
c.							
d.							
e.							
f.							
g.							
29. Federal taxes owed							
30. **Totals**			$	$			

Internal Revenue Service Use Only Below This Line

Financial Verification/Analysis

Item	Date Information or Encumbrance Verified	Date Property Inspected	Estimated Forced Sale Equity
Personal Residence			
Other Real Property			
Vehicles			
Other Personal Property			
State Employment *(Husband and Wife)*			
Income Tax Return			
Wage Statements *(Husband and Wife)*			
Sources of Income/Credit *(D&B Report)*			
Expenses			
Other Assets/Liabilities			

Section V.   Monthly Income and Expense Analysis

Income			Necessary Living Expenses	
Source	**Gross**	**Net**		
31. Wages/Salaries *(Taxpayer)*	$	$	42. Rent *(Do not show mortgage listed in item 25)*	$
32. Wages/Salaries *(Spouse)*			43. Groceries (no. of people _____)	
33. Interest - Dividends			44. Allowable installment payments *(IRS use only)*	
34. Net business income *(from Form 433-B)*			45. Utilities (Gas $_____ Water $_____	
35. Rental income			Electric $_____ Phone $_____)	
36. Pension *(Taxpayer)*			46. Transportation	
37. Pension *(Spouse)*			47. Insurance (Life $_____ Health $_____	
38. Child Support			Home $_____ Car $_____)	
39. Alimony			48. Medical *(Expenses not covered in item 47)*	
40. Other			49. Estimated tax payments	
			50. Court ordered payments	
			51. Other expenses *(specify)*	
41. Total Income	$	$	52. Total Expenses *(IRS use only)*	$
			53. Net difference *(income less necessary living expenses)* *(IRS use only)*	$

Certification   **Under penalties of perjury, I declare that to the best of my knowledge and belief this statement of assets, liabilities, and other information is true, correct, and complete.**

54. Your signature	55. Spouse's signature *(if joint return was filed)*	56. Date

Additional information or comments:

Internal Revenue Service Use Only Below This Line

Explain any difference between Item 53 and the installment agreement payment amount:

Name of originator and IDRS assignment number:	Date

Form **433-A**   page 4   (Rev. 10-92)

★U.S.GPO:1992-0-343-049/71911

Form **433-B**
(Rev. June 1991)

Department of the Treasury — Internal Revenue Service

Collection Information Statement for Businesses

(If you need additional space, please attach a separate sheet)

NOTE: Complete all blocks, except shaded areas. Write "N/A" *(not applicable)* in those blocks that do not apply.

1. Name and address of business	2. Business phone number ( )

County_____

3. *(Check appropriate box)*

☐ Sole proprietor ☐ Partnership ☐ Corporation ☐ Other *(specify)* _____

4. Name and title of person being interviewed	5. Employer Identification Number	6. Type of business

7. Information about owner, partners, officers, major shareholder, etc.

Name and Title	Effective Date	Home Address	Phone Number	Social Security Number	Total Shares or Interest

Section I.   General Financial Information

8. Latest filed income tax return ▶	Form	Tax Year ended	Net income before taxes

9. Bank accounts *(List all types of accounts including payroll and general, savings, certificates of deposit, etc.)*

Name of Institution	Address	Type of Account	Account Number	Balance
		Total *(Enter in Item 17)* ▶		

10. Bank credit available *(Lines of credit, etc.)*

Name of Institution	Address	Credit Limit	Amount Owed	Credit Available	Monthly Payments
Totals *(Enter in Items 24 or 25 as appropriate)*		▶			

11. Location, box number, and contents of all safe deposit boxes rented or accessed

Form **433-B** (Rev. 6-91)

Section I - *continued*   General Financial Information

12. Real property

Brief Description and Type of Ownership	Physical Address
a.	County _____
b.	County _____
c.	County _____
d.	County _____

13. Life insurance policies owned with business as beneficiary

Name Insured	Company	Policy Number	Type	Face Amount	Available Loan Value
	Total *(Enter in Item 19)*		▶		

14a. Additional information regarding financial condition *(Court proceedings, bankruptcies filed or anticipated, transfers of assets for less than full value, changes in market conditions, etc.; include information regarding company participation in trusts, estates, profit-sharing plans, etc.)*

| b. If you know of any person or organization that borrowed or otherwise provided funds to pay net payrolls: | a. Who borrowed funds? |
| | b. Who supplied funds? |

15. Accounts/Notes receivable *(Include current contract jobs, loans to stockholders, officers, partners, etc.)*

Name	Address	Amount Due	Date Due	Status
		$		
	Total (Enter in Item 18) ▶	$		

Form 433-B (Rev. 6-91)

Section II.　　　　　　Asset and Liability Analysis

Description (a)		Cur. Mkt. Value (b)	Liabilities Bal. Due (c)	Equity in Asset (d)	Amt. of Mo. Pymt. (e)	Name and Address of Lien/Note Holder/Obligee (f)	Date Pledged (g)	Date of Final Pymt. (h)
16. Cash on hand								
17. Bank accounts								
18. Accounts/Notes receivable								
19. Life insurance loan value								
20. Real property *(from Item 12)*	a.							
	b.							
	c.							
	d.							
21. Vehicles *(Model, year, and license)*	a.							
	b.							
	c.							
22. Machinery and equipment *(Specify)*	a.							
	b.							
	c.							
23. Merchandise inventory *(Specify)*	a.							
	b.							
24. Other assets *(Specify)*	a.							
	b.							
25. Other liabilities *(Including notes and judgments)*	a.							
	b.							
	c.							
	d.							
	e.							
	f.							
	g.							
	h.							
26. Federal taxes owed								
27. **Total**								

　　　　　　Form **433-B** (Rev. 6-91)

Section III.   Income and Expense Analysis

The following information applies to income and expenses during the period _____to_____		Accounting method used	
Income		**Expenses**	
28. Gross receipts from sales, services, etc.	$	34. Materials purchased	$
29. Gross rental income		35. Net wages and salaries Number of Employees _____	
30. Interest		36. Rent	
31. Dividends		37. Allowable installment payments *(IRS use only)*	
32. Other income *(Specify)*		38. Supplies	
		39. Utilities/Telephone	
		40. Gasoline/Oil	
		41. Repairs and maintenance	
		42. Insurance	
		43. Current taxes	
		44. Other *(Specify)*	
33. **Total Income** ▶	$	45. **Total Expenses** *(IRS use only)* ▶	$
		46. **Net difference** *(IRS use only)* ▶	$

Certification   Under penalties of perjury, I declare that to the best of my knowledge and belief this statement of assets, liabilities, and other information is true, correct, and complete.

47. Signature	48. Date

Internal Revenue Service Use Only Below This Line

Financial Verification/Analysis

Item	Date Information or Encumbrance Verified	Date Property Inspected	Estimated Forced Sale Equity
Sources of Income/Credit (D&B Report)			
Expenses			
Real Property			
Vehicles			
Machinery and Equipment			
Merchandise			
Accounts/Notes Receivable			
Corporate Information, if Applicable			
U.C.C. : Senior/Junior Lienholder			
Other Assets/Liabilities:			

Explain any difference between Item 46 (or P&L) and the installment agreement payment amount:

Name of Originator and IDRS assignment number	Date

Form **2261** (Rev. June 1991)	DEPARTMENT OF THE TREASURY – INTERNAL REVENUE SERVICE **Collateral Agreement** Future Income — Individual

Names and Address of Taxpayers	Social Security and Employer Identification Numbers

To: Commissioner of Internal Revenue

The taxpayers identified above have submitted an offer dated _____ in the amount of $_____ to

compromise unpaid _____ tax liability, plus statutory additions, for the taxable periods _____

The purpose of this collateral agreement (hereinafter referred to as this agreement) is to provide additional consideration for acceptance of the offer in compromise described above. It is understood and agreed:

1. That in addition to the payment of the above amount of $ _____ , the taxpayers will pay out of annual income for the years _____ to _____ , inclusive

    (a) Nothing on the first $ _____ of annual income.

    (b) _____ percent of annual income more than $_____ and not more than $_____ .

    (c) _____ percent of annual income more than $_____ and not more than $_____ .

    (d) _____ percent of annual income more than $_____.

2. That the term annual income, as used in this agreement, means adjusted gross income as defined in section 62 of the Internal Revenue Code (except losses from sales or exchanges of property shall not be allowed), plus all nontaxable income and profits or gains from any source whatsoever (including the fair market value of gifts, bequests, devises, and inheritances), minus (a) the Federal income tax paid for the year for which annual income is being computed, and (b) any payment made under the terms of the offer in compromise (Form 656), as shown in item 2, for the year in which such payment is made. Annual income shall not be reduced by any overpayments waived in item 3, Form 656. The annual income shall not be reduced by net operating losses incurred before or after the period covered by this agreement. However, a net operating loss for any year during such period may be deducted from annual income for the following year only. It is also agreed that annual income shall include all income and gains or profits of the taxpayers, regardless of whether these amounts are community income under State law.

3. That in the event close corporations are directly or indirectly controlled or owned by the taxpayers during the existence of this agreement, the computation of annual income shall include their proportionate share of the total corporate annual income in excess of $10,000. The term corporate annual income, as used in this agreement, means the taxable income of the corporation before net operating loss deduction and special deductions (except, in computing such income, the losses from sales or exchanges of property shall not be allowed), plus all nontaxable income, minus (a) dividends paid, and (b) the Federal income tax paid for the year for which annual income is being computed. For this purpose, the corporate annual income shall not be reduced by any net operating loss incurred before or after the periods covered by this agreement, but a net operating loss for any year during such period may be deducted from the corporate annual income for the following year only.

4. That the annual payments provided for in this agreement (including interest at the rate established under section 6621 of the Internal Revenue Code (compounded under Code section 6622(a)) on delinquent payments computed from the due date of such payment) shall be paid to the Internal Revenue Service, without notice, on or before the 15th day of the 4th month following the close of the calendar or fiscal year, such payments to be accompanied by a sworn statement and a copy of the taxpayers' Federal income tax return. The statement shall refer to this agreement and show the computation of annual income in accordance with items 1, 2, and 3 of this agreement. If the annual income for any year covered by this agreement is insufficient to require a payment under its terms, the taxpayers shall still furnish the Internal Revenue Service a sworn statement of such income and a copy of their Federal income tax return. All books, records, and accounts shall be open at all reasonable times for inspection by the Internal Revenue Service to verify the annual income shown in the statement. Also, the taxpayers hereby expressly consent to the disclosure to each other of the amount of their respective annual income and of all books, records, and accounts necessary to the computation of their annual income for the purpose of administering this agreement. The payments (if any), the sworn statement, and a copy of the Federal income tax return shall be transmitted to:
    Address:

5. That the aggregate amount paid under the terms of the offer in compromise and the additional amounts paid under the terms of this agreement shall not exceed an amount equivalent to the liability covered by the offer plus statutory additions that would have become due in the absence of the compromise.

6. That payments made under the terms of this agreement shall be applied first to tax and penalty, in that order, due for the earliest taxable period, then to tax and penalty, in that order, for each succeeding taxable period with no amount to be allocated to interest until the liabilities for taxes and penalties for all taxable periods sought to be compromised have been satisfied.

7. That upon notice to the taxpayers of the acceptance of the offer in compromise of the liability identified in this agreement, the taxpayers shall have no right, in the event of default in payment of any installment of principal or interest due under the terms of the offer and this agreement or in the event any other provision of this agreement is not carried out in accordance with its terms, to contest in court or otherwise the amount of the liability sought to be compromised; and that in the event of such default or noncompliance or in the event the taxpayers become the subject of any proceeding (except a proceeding under the Bankruptcy Act) whereby their affairs are placed under the control and jurisdiction of a court or other party, the United States, at the option of the Commissioner of Internal Revenue or a delegated official, may (a) proceed immediately by suit to collect the entire unpaid balance of the offer and this agreement, or (b) proceed immediately by suit to collect as liquidated damages an amount equal to the tax liability sought to be compromised, minus any payments already received under the terms of the offer and this agreement, with interest at the rate established under section 6621 of the Internal Revenue Code (compounded under Code section 6622(a)) from the date of default, or (c) disregard the amount of such offer and this agreement, apply all amounts previously paid thereunder against the amount of the liability sought to be compromised and, without further notice of any kind, assess and collect by levy or suit (the restrictions against assessment and collection being waived) the balance of such liability. In the event the taxpayers become the subject of any proceeding under the Bankruptcy Act, the offer in compromise and this agreement may be terminated. Upon such termination, the tax liability sought to be compromised, minus any payments already received under the terms of the offer and this agreement, shall become legally enforceable.

8. That the taxpayers waive the benefit of any statute of limitations applicable to the assessment and collection of the liability sought to be compromised and agree to the suspension of the running of the statutory period of limitations on assessment and collection for the period during which the offer in compromise and this agreement are pending, or the period during which any installment under the offer and this agreement remains unpaid, or any provision of this agreement is not carried out in accordance with its terms, and for 1 year thereafter.

9. That when all sums, including interest, due under the terms of the offer in compromise and this agreement, except those sums which may become due and payable under the provisions of item 1 of this agreement, have been paid in full, then and in that event only, all Federal tax liens at that time securing the tax liabilities which are the subject of the offer shall be immediately released. However, if, at the time consideration is being given to the release of the Federal tax liens, there are any sums due and payable under the terms of item 1, they must also be paid before the release of such liens.

This agreement shall be of no force or effect unless the offer in compromise is accepted.

Taxpayer's Signature	Date
Taxpayer's Signature	Date

I accept the waiver of statutory period of limitations for the Internal Revenue Service.

Signature and Title	Date

Form 2261-B (Rev. May 1988)	DEPARTMENT OF THE TREASURY — INTERNAL REVENUE SERVICE **Collateral Agreement** Adjusted Basis of Specific Assets

Names and Address of Taxpayers	Social Security and Employer Identification Numbers

To: Commissioner of Internal Revenue

The taxpayers identified above have submitted an offer dated _____ in the amount of $ _____

to compromise unpaid _____ tax liability, plus statutory additions, for the

taxable periods _____.

The purpose of this collateral agreement (hereinafter referred to as this agreement) is to provide additional consideration for acceptance of the offer in compromise described above. It is understood and agreed:

1. That for the purpose of computing income taxes of the taxpayers for all taxable years beginning after _____ , the basis for certain assets under the existing law for computing depreciation and the gain or loss upon sale, exchange, or other disposition shall be as follows:

   Name of asset   *Basis*
   _____   _____

2. That in no event shall the basis shown in item 1, above, be in excess of the basis that would otherwise be allowable for tax purposes except for this agreement.

3. That the aggregate amount paid under the terms of the offer in compromise and the additional amounts of taxes paid as the result of the reduction of the basis of the assets described above shall not exceed an amount equivalent to the liability covered by the offer plus statutory additions that would have become due in the absence of the compromise.

4. That upon notice to the taxpayers of the acceptance of the offer in compromise of the liability identified in this agreement, the taxpayers shall have no right, in the event of default in payment of any installment of principal or interest due under the terms of the offer and this agreement or in the event any other provision of this agreement is not carried out in accordance with its terms, to contest in court or otherwise the amount of the liability sought to be compromised; and that in the event of such default or noncompliance or in the event the taxpayers become the subject of any proceeding (except a proceeding under the Bankruptcy Act) whereby their affairs are placed under the control and jurisdiction of a court or other party, the United States, at the option of the Commissioner of Internal Revenue or a delegated official, may (a) proceed immediately by suit to collect the entire unpaid balance of the offer and this agreement, or (b) proceed immediately by suit to collect as liquidated damages an amount equal to the tax liability sought to be compromised, minus any payments already received under the terms of the offer and this agreement, with interest at the rate established under section 6621 of the Internal Revenue Code from the date of default, or (c) disregard the amount of such offer and this agreement, apply all amounts previously paid thereunder against the amount of the liability sought to be compromised and, without further notice of any kind, assess and collect by levy or suit (the restrictions against assessment and collection being waived) the balance of such liability. In the event the taxpayers become the subject of any proceeding under the Bankruptcy Act, the offer in compromise and this agreement may be terminated. Upon such termination, the tax liability sought to be compromised, minus any payments already received under the terms of the offer and this agreement, shall become legally enforceable.

5. That the taxpayers waive the benefit of any statute of limitations applicable to the assessment and collection of the liability sought to be compromised and agree to the suspension of the running of the statutory period of limitations on assessment and collection for the period during which the offer in compromise and this agreement are pending, or the period during which any installment under the offer and this agreement remains unpaid, or any provision of this agreement is not carried out in accordance with its terms, and for 1 year thereafter.

6. That when all sums, including interest, due under the terms of the offer in compromise and this agreement, except those sums which may become due and payable under the provisions of item 1 of this agreement, have been paid in full, then and in that event only, all Federal tax liens at that time securing the tax liabilities which are the subject of the offer shall be immediately released. However, if, at the time consideration is being given to the release of the Federal tax liens, there are any sums due and payable under the terms of item 1, they must also be paid before the release of such liens.

This agreement shall be of no force or effect unless the offer in compromise is accepted.

Taxpayer's Signature	Date
Taxpayer's Signature	Date

I accept the waiver of statutory period of limitations for the Internal Revenue Service.

Signature and Title	Date

*U.S.GPO:1988-202-004/81621

Form 2261-B (Rev. 5-88)

Form **2261-C**	DEPARTMENT OF THE TREASURY — INTERNAL REVENUE SERVICE
(Rev. May 1988)	**Collateral Agreement** Waiver of Net Operating Losses, Capital Losses, and Unused Investment Credits

Names and Address of Taxpayers	Social Security and Employer Identification Numbers

To: Commissioner of Internal Revenue

The taxpayers identified above have submitted an offer dated _____ in the amount of $ _____ to compromise unpaid _____ tax liability, plus statutory additions, for the taxable periods _____ .

The purpose of this collateral agreement (hereinafter referred to as this agreement) is to provide additional consideration for acceptance of the offer in compromise described above. It is understood and agreed that for the purpose of computing the taxpayers' Federal income tax for all taxable years beginning after _____ :

1. That any net operating losses sustained for the years _____ to _____ , inclusive, shall not be claimed as net operating loss deductions under the provisions of section 172 of the Internal Revenue Code.

2. That any net capital losses sustained for the years before _____ shall not be claimed as carryovers or carrybacks under the provisions of section 1212 of the Internal Revenue Code.

3. That any unused investment credits for the years _____ to _____ , inclusive, shall not be claimed as investment credit carrybacks or carryovers under the provisions of Internal Revenue Code section 39 or 46, as applicable.

4. That the aggregate amount paid under the terms of the offer in compromise and the additional amounts of taxes paid as the result of the waiver of the losses and credits involved in this agreement shall not exceed an amount equivalent to the liability covered by the offer plus statutory additions that would become due in the absence of the compromise.

5. That upon notice to the taxpayers of the acceptance of the offer in compromise of the liability identified in this agreement, the taxpayers shall have no right, in the event of default in payment of any installment of principal or interest due under the terms of the offer and this agreement or in the event any other provision of this agreement is not carried out in accordance with its terms, to contest in court or otherwise the amount of the liability sought to be compromised; and that in the event of such default or noncompliance or in the event the taxpayers become the subject of any proceeding (except a proceeding under the Bankruptcy Act) whereby their affairs are placed under the control and jurisdiction of a court or other party, the United States, at the option of the Commissioner of Internal Revenue or a delegated official, may (a) proceed immediately by suit to collect the entire unpaid balance of the offer and this agreement, or (b) proceed immediately by suit to collect as liquidated damages an amount equal to the tax liability sought to be compromised, minus any payments already received under the terms of the offer and this agreement, with interest at the rate established under section 6621 of the Internal Revenue Code from the date of default, or (c) disregard the amount of such offer and this agreement, apply all amounts previously paid thereunder against the amount of the liability sought to be compromised and, without further notice of any kind, assess and collect by levy or suit (the restrictions against assessment and collection being waived) the balance of such liability. In the event the taxpayers become the subject of any proceeding under the Bankruptcy Act, the offer in compromise and this agreement may be terminated. Upon such termination, the tax liability sought to be compromised, minus any payments already received under the terms of the offer and this agreement, shall become legally enforceable.

6. That the taxpayers waive the benefit of any statute of limitations applicable to the assessment and collection of the liability sought to be compromised and agree to the suspension of the running of the statutory period of limitations on assessment and collection for the period during which the offer in compromise and this agreement are pending, or the period during which any installment under the offer and this agreement remains unpaid, or any provision of this agreement is not carried out in accordance with its terms, and for 1 year thereafter.

7. That when all sums, including interest, due under the terms of the offer in compromise and this agreement, except those sums which may become due and payable under the provisions of items 1, 2, and 3 of this agreement, have been paid in full, then and in that event only, all Federal tax liens at that time securing the tax liabilities which are the subject of the offer shall be immediately released. However, if, at the time consideration is being given to the release of the Federal tax liens, there are any sums due and payable under the terms of items 1, 2, and 3, they must also be paid before the release of such liens.

This agreement shall be of no force or effect unless the offer in compromise is accepted.

Taxpayers's Signature	Date

Taxpayer's Signature	Date

I accept the waiver of statutory period of limitations for the Internal Revenue Service.

Signature and Title	Date

U.S. GPO: 1993-343-049/72048
Form **2261-C** (Rev. 5-88)

Form **911**
(Rev. April 1991)

Department of the Treasury — Internal Revenue Service

Application for Taxpayer Assistance Order *(ATAO)* to Relieve Hardship

Note: Filing this application may result in extending the statutory period of limitations. *(See instructions.)*

Section I.   Taxpayer Information

1. Name*(s)* as shown on tax return	2. SSN/EIN	3. Spouse's SSN
	4. Tax form	5. Tax period ended

6. Current address *(Number and street, apt. no., rural route)*	7. City, town, or post office, state, and ZIP code	

8. Person to contact	9. Telephone number ( )	10. Best time to call

11. Description of problem *(If more space is needed, attach additional sheets.)*

12. Description of significant hardship and relief requested *(If more space is needed, attach additional sheets.)*

13. Signature of taxpayer or Corporate Officer *(See instructions.)*	14. Date	15. Signature of spouse shown in block 1	16. Date

Section II.   Representative Information *(If applicable)*

17. Name of authorized representative	18. Firm name
19. Street address or P.O. Box	20. City, town or post office, state, and ZIP code

21. Telephone number ( )	22. Best time to call	23. Centralized Authorization File *(CAF)* number	
24. Signature			25. Date

Section III.   *(For Internal Revenue Service only)*

26. Name of initiating employee	27. ☐ IRS identified ☐ Taxpayer request	28. Telephone	29. Function	30. Office	31. Date

Cat. No. 16965S   Form **911** (Rev. 4-91)

Instructions

Purpose of form.—You should use Form 911, Application for Taxpayer Assistance Order *(ATAO)* to Relieve Hardship, to apply for a review by the Taxpayer Ombudsman, or his designee, of actions being taken by the Internal Revenue Service. Such application may be made in cases where you are undergoing or about to undergo a significant hardship because of the manner in which the Internal Revenue laws are being administered. This application can not be used to contest the merits of any tax liability. If you disagree with the amount of tax assessed, please see Publication 1, Your Rights As A Taxpayer. While we are reviewing your application, we will take no further enforcement action. We will contact you after our review to advise you of our decision. The Internal Revenue Code requires us to suspend applicable statutory periods of limitation until a decision is made on your request.

Where to file.—This application should be addressed to the Internal Revenue Service, Problem Resolution Office in the district where you live. Call the local Taxpayer Assistance number listed in your telephone directory or 1-800-829-1040 for the address of the Problem Resolution Office in your district. **If you live overseas,** mail your request to the Assistant Commissioner *(International)*, Internal Revenue Service, Problem Resolution Office, P.O. Box 144817, L'Enfant Plaza Station, Washington, DC 20026-4817.

CAUTION: Requests submitted to the incorrect office may result in delays. We will acknowledge your request within one week of receiving it. If you do not hear from us within 10 days *(15 days for overseas addresses)* of submitting your application, please contact the Problem Resolution Office in the IRS office to which you sent your application.

Section I. Taxpayer Information

1. **Name***(s)* **as shown on tax return.** Enter your name as it appeared on the tax return for each period you are requesting assistance. If your name has changed since the return was submitted, you should still enter the name as it appeared on your return. If you filed a joint return, enter both names.

2. **SSN/EIN.** Enter your social security number *(SSN)* or the employer identification number *(EIN)* of the business, corporation, trust, etc., for the name you showed in block 1. If you are married, and the request is for assistance on a problem involving a joint return, enter the social security number in block 2 for the first name listed in block 1.

3. **Spouse's SSN.** If the problem involves a joint return, enter the social security number for the second name listed in block 1.

4. **Tax form.** Enter the tax form number of the tax form you filed for which you are requesting assistance. For example, if you are requesting assistance for a problem involving an individual income tax return, enter "1040." If your problem involves more than one tax form, include the information in block 11.

5. **Tax period ended.** If you are requesting assistance on an annually filed return, enter the calendar year or the ending date of the fiscal year for that return. If the problem concerns a return filed quarterly, enter the ending date of the quarter involved. If the problem involves more than one tax period, include the information in block 11.

6. and 7. **Self-explanatory.**

8. **Person to contact.** Enter the name of the person to contact about the problem. In the case of businesses, corporations, trusts, estates, etc., enter the name of a responsible official.

9. **Telephone number.** Enter the telephone number, including area code, of the person to contact.

10. **Self-explanatory.**

11. **Description of problem.** Describe the action*(s)* being taken *(or not being taken)* by the Internal Revenue Service that are causing you significant hardship. If you know it, include the name of the person, office, telephone number, and/or address of the last contact you had with IRS. Please include a copy of the most recent correspondence, if any, you have had with IRS regarding this problem.

12. **Description of significant hardship and relief requested.** Describe the significant hardship which is being caused by the Internal Revenue Service's action *(or lack of action)* as outlined in Section I, block 11. Please tell us what kind of relief you are requesting.

13 and 15. **Signature***(s)*. In order to suspend applicable statutory periods of limitations, you must sign this form in Section I, block 13 and block 15, if applicable; or your authorized representative, acting in your behalf, must sign in Section II, block 24. If your name has changed from the name that appears in Section I, block 1, sign using your current legal name. If the request is for assistance on a problem involving a joint return, both you and the spouse shown in block 1 must sign this form in order for the statutory period of limitations to be suspended.. If one of the taxpayers is no longer living, the taxpayer's spouse or personal representative must sign the form and write "deceased" after the deceased taxpayer's name. If the taxpayer is your dependent child who can not sign this application because of age or other reasons, you may sign your child's name in the space provided followed by the words "By *(your signature)*, parent *(or guardian)* for minor child." If the application is being made for other than an individual taxpayer, a person having authority to sign the return should sign the application. Enter the date the application is signed.

Section II. Representative Information

If you are the taxpayer and you wish to have a representative act in your behalf, your representative must have a power of attorney of tax information authorization on file for the tax form*(s)* and period*(s)* involved. Complete Section II, blocks 17 through 23. *(See Form 2848, Power of Attorney and Declaration of Representative and Instructions for more information.)*

If you are an authorized representative and are submitting this request on behalf of the taxpayer identified in Section I, complete blocks 17 through 23. Sign and date this request in block 24 and block 25 and attach a copy of Form 2848, or the power of attorney.

23. **Centralized Authorization File** *(CAF)* **number.** Enter the representative's CAF number. The CAF number is the unique number that Internal Revenue Service assigns to a representative after a valid Form 2848 is filed with an IRS office.

(For IRS Use only)

ATAO code	Date of determination	Statute suspended
		☐ No ☐ Yes: _____ days
How received	PRO signature	

Form **911** (Rev. 4-91)

Form **1127**
(Rev. 5-92)

Department of the Treasury
Internal Revenue Service

APPLICATION FOR EXTENSION OF TIME FOR PAYMENT OF TAX

(Please read conditions on back before completing this form)

Please Type or Print	Taxpayer's Name (include Spouse if this is for a joint return)	Social Security Number or Employer Identification Number
	Present Address	Spouse's Social Security Number if this is for a Joint Return
	City, Town or Post Office, State, and Zip Code	

District Director of Internal Revenue at _____

(Enter City and State where IRS Office is located)

I request an extension from _____ , 19 _____ , to _____ , 19 _____ ,

(Enter Due Date of Return)

to pay tax of $ _____ for the year ended _____ , 19_____ .

This extension is necessary because *(If more space is needed, please attach a separate sheet):* _____

_____

_____

_____

I can not borrow to pay the tax because: _____

_____

_____

To show the need for the extension, I am attaching: (1) a statement of my assets and liabilities at the end of last month (showing book and market values of assets and whether securities are listed or unlisted); and (2) an itemized list of money I received and spent for 3 months before the date the tax is due.

I propose to secure this liability as follows:

_____

_____

Under penalties of perjury, I declare that I have examined this application, including any accompanying schedules and statements, and to the best of my knowledge and belief it is true, correct, and complete.

_____   _____
SIGNATURE (BOTH SIGNATURES IF THIS IS FOR A JOINT RETURN)   *(DATE)*

The District Director will let you know whether the extension is approved or denied and will tell you the form of bond, if necessary. However, the Director cannot consider an application if it is filed after the due date of the return. A list of approved surety companies will be sent to you upon request.

(The following will be filled in by the IRS.)

This application is   ☐ approved   for the following reasons:
                ☐ denied

_____

_____

Interest _____   Date of assessment _____   Identifying no. _____

Penalty _____   _____   _____
                                 (SIGNATURE)   *(DATE)*

CONDITIONS UNDER WHICH EXTENSIONS FOR PAYMENTS MAY BE GRANTED UNDER SECTION 6161 OF THE INTERNAL REVENUE CODE

The District Director may approve an extension for payment of your tax if you show that it will cause you undue hardship to pay it on the date it is due. Your application must be filed with the District Director on or before the date payment is due.

If you are asking to pay the amount you owe in installments, rather than to delay making any payments, do not complete this form. Instead, contact your local IRS office, or call 1-800-829-1040. However, if you owe a deficiency (an amount owed after your return is examined), you can discuss an installment agreement with the person who examines your return when you agree to the deficiency.

1. **Undue hardship.**—This means more than inconvenience. You must show that you will have substantial financial loss if you pay your tax on the date it is due. (This loss could be caused by selling property at a sacrifice price.) You must show that you do not have enough cash, above necessary working capital, to pay the tax. In determining cash available, include anything you can convert into cash, and use current market prices. Also, show that you can not borrow to pay the tax, except under terms that will cause you severe loss and hardship.

2. **Limits.**—As a general rule, an extension to pay income or gift tax on a return is limited to 6 months from the date payment is due. An extension may be granted for more than 6 months if you are abroad.

An extension to pay a deficiency (an amount you owe after an examination of your return) in income or gift tax is limited to 18 months from the date payment is due and, in exceptional cases, up to another 12 months.

No extension is granted to pay a deficiency caused by negligence, intentional disregard of rules and regulations, or fraud with intent to evade tax.

3. **Interest.**—Interest is charged at the underpayment rate in Code section 6621(a)(2).

4. **Security.**—Security satisfactory to the District Director is required to get an extension. This assures that the risk to the Government is no greater at the end of the extension than at the beginning. The kind of security, such as bond, notice of lien, mortgage, pledge, deed of trust of specific property or general assets, personal surety, or other, will depend on the circumstances in each case. Ordinarily, when you receive approval of your application, deposit with the District Director any collateral that was agreed upon for security. No collateral is required if you have no assets.

5. **Due date of payment for which extension is granted.**—Before the extension runs out, pay the tax for which the extension is granted (without notice and demand from the District Director).

6. **Filing requirements.**—If you need an extension to pay tax, submit an application with supporting documents on or before the date the tax is due. File the application with the District Director (Attn: Chief, Special Procedures function) where you maintain your legal residence or principal place of business. If, however, the tax will be paid to the Assistant Commissioner (International), file the application with that office. If you need an extension to pay estate tax, file Form 4768, Application for Extension of Time to File U.S. Estate Tax Return and/or Pay Estate Tax.

Form 1127 (Rev. 5-92)

*U.S. GPO: 1992-312-711/61562

| Form **9465** (Rev. December 1992) | Department of the Treasury – Internal Revenue Service **Installment Agreement Request** | OMB Clearance No. 1545-1350 Expires 12/31/93 |

General Information

If you can't pay the amount you owe in full at this time, please request an installment agreement by completing this form. Specify the amount of the monthly payment you propose to make in the block marked "Proposed monthly payment amount."

We encourage you to make your payments as large as possible to lower penalty and interest charges. Under law, these charges continue to increase until you pay the balance in full.

Please attach this form to the front of your tax return or to the notice we sent you, and mail it to the appropriate IRS office.

Make your check or money order payable to the Internal Revenue Service, and mark the payment with your name, address, taxpayer identification number, form number and tax period. If you have any questions about this procedure, please call our toll-free number **1-800-829-1040.**

Within 30 days, we will let you know if your request for an installment agreement is approved or denied, or if we need more information.

Taxpayer name(s) as shown on the tax return	Taxpayer identification number *(SSN for primary & secondary filers)* or EIN		
Address	City	State	ZIP Code
Business telephone number *(include area code and extension number, if any)*	Most convenient time for us to call you	Home telephone number *(include area code)*	Most convenient time for us to call you
Form number and tax period	Amount paid with return	Amount owed on return	Proposed monthly payment amount

| | | | Amount I am able to pay each month | Date each month I am able to make the payment *(Must be the 1st through the 28th day)* |

Your signature	Date
Spouse's signature *(joint returns only)*	Date

Privacy Act and Paperwork Reduction Act Notice

We ask for the information on this form under authority of Internal Revenue Code sections 6001, 6011, 6012(a), 6109, and 6159 and their regulations. We use this information to process your request for an installment agreement. The principal reason we need your name and social security number is to secure proper identification. We require this information to gain access to the tax information in our files and properly respond to your request. If you do not disclose the information, the IRS may not be able to process your request.

The time needed to complete and file this form will vary depending on individual circumstances. The estimated average time is 10 minutes.

If you have comments concerning the accuracy of this time estimate or suggestions for making this form more simple, we would be happy to hear from you. You can write to both the **Internal Revenue Service**, Washington, DC 20224, Attention: IRS Reports Clearance Officer, T:FP, and the **Office of Management and Budget** Paperwork Reduction Project (1545-1350), Washington, DC 20503. **DO NOT** send this form to either of these offices. Instead, refer to the instructions above.

---

*U.S. GPO: 1993-343-049/71975 Catalog No. 14842Y Form **9465** (Rev. 12/92)

Form **843**
(Rev. August 1990)
Department of the Treasury
Internal Revenue Service

Claim for Refund and Request for Abatement

▶ **See separate Instructions.**

OMB No. 1545-0024
Expires: 6-30-93

If your claim is for an overpayment of income taxes, do NOT use Form 843. (See Instructions.)
Use Form 843 ONLY if your claim involves one of the taxes shown on line 8a or a refund or abatement of interest or penalties on lines 8b(i)–(iii).

Please type or print

Name of claimant	Telephone number (optional) ( )

Address (number, street, and apt. or suite no. or rural route)(List P.O. box if mail is not delivered to street address.)

City, town, or post office, state, and ZIP code

Fill in applicable items—Use attachments if necessary

1 Your social security number	2 Spouse's social security number	3 Employer identification number

4 Name and address shown on return if different from above

5 Period—prepare a separate Form 843 for each tax period From _____ , 19___ , to _____ , 19___	6 Amount to be refunded or abated $

7 Dates of payment

8a Type of tax or penalty

☐ Employment ☐ Estate ☐ Excise ☐ Gift ☐ Penalty IRC section ▶

b Request for abatement, credit, or refund of:

(i) ☐ Interest under Rev. Proc. 87-42.
(ii) ☐ Interest under Rev. Proc. 87-43.
(iii) ☐ A penalty or addition to tax as a result of erroneous advice from IRS.

9 Kind of return filed (see instructions)

☐ 706 ☐ 709 ☐ 720 IRS No. (s) ▶ _____ ☐ 940 ☐ 941 ☐ 990-PF ☐ 2290 ☐ 4720
☐ Other (specify) ▶

10 Explain why you believe this claim should be allowed and show computation of tax refund or abatement of interest or penalty.

Under penalties of perjury, I declare that I have examined this claim, including accompanying schedules and statements, and to the best of my knowledge and belief it is true, correct, and complete.

Signature (Title, if applicable. Claims by corporations must be signed by an officer.)	Date	Director's Stamp (Date received)
Signature	Date	

For Paperwork Reduction Act Notice, see separate Instructions.

☆ U.S. GPO: 1992-312-699/60112

Form **843** (Rev. 8-90)

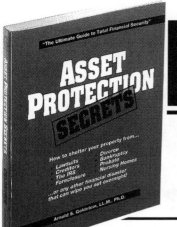

IS YOUR BUSINESS IN TROUBLE?

Here at last is the step-by-step guide to revitalizing any problem business from the turnaround pro Dr. Arnold S. Goldstein. Now, he reveals all his trade secrets on how you too can:

- Sidestep the ten deadly business killers.
- Make your creditors disappear without going bankrupt.
- Turn your business into a creditor-proof fortress.
- Find fast cash for your cash-starved business.
- Forecast whether or not your business is heading for bankruptcy.
- Avoid Chapter 11 — and survive it when you can't.
- Transform losses into huge profits.
- Cash-in by selling your troubled business.
- Settle with creditors (even the IRS) for pennies on the dollar.
- Protect yourself from business debts.
  ...And much more!

Arnold S. Goldstein, Ph.D.

THE BUSINESS DOCTOR

HOW TO TURN YOUR HEADACHE BUSINESS INTO A DEBT-FREE MONEY MACHINE!

Lessons from the "Turnaround Pro" who has saved more than 1,000 near-bankrupt companies!

Here's what they say...

"Dr. Arnold S. Goldstein has established a brilliant reputation in the turnaround field. His strategies should be read by everyone with a faltering business."

Scott Dantuma, President
Corporate Financial Recovery, Inc.

"If you own, manage or have anything to do with a business in trouble (or just want to turn your business into a bigger moneymaker), you absolutely must read this book!"

John Kingsbury, Ph.D.
Nova/Southeastern University

$19.95 plus $4.50 s&h. 6 x 9 soft cover. 320 pages ISBN #1-880539-25-X

Dr. Arnold S. Goldstein, an insolvency lawyer and turnaround specialist, has helped rescue more than 1,000 failing business. His creative turnaround techniques have been featured in numerous publications and taught by Dr. Goldstein at several law and business schools. He also has written more than 60 books on law and finance. Now president of Garrett Group, a national turnaround-consulting firm, his other titles include *Asset Protection Secrets, How to Settle with the IRS...for Pennies on the Dollar,* and *Offshore Havens.*

Yes! Please rush me **THE BUSINESS DOCTOR** at $19.95 plus $4.50 s&h ($24.45 total for each book). *Florida residents add 6% sales tax.

Name: _____

Address: _____

City: _____ State _____ Zip: _____

_____ **Check Enclosed**   _____ **Please charge my credit card**
_____ **VISA**   _____ **MASTER CARD**

Acct. No: _____ Exp. Date: _____

Mail to: **Garrett Publishing, Inc.**   Phone: (305) 480-8543
384 S. Military Trail   Fax: (305) 698-0057
Deerfield Beach, Fl. 33442   24-hour ordering, call 800-333-2069